D1516685

THE NEW TURKEY

THE NEW TURKEY

The Quiet Revolution on the Edge of Europe

CHRIS MORRIS

Granta Books
London

Granta Publications, 2/3 Hanover Yard, Noel Road,
London N1 8BE

First published in Great Britain by Granta Books 2005

A CIP catalogue record for this book is available
from the British Library.

1 3 5 7 9 10 8 6 4 2

ISBN 1 86207 790 8

Typeset by M Rules

Printed and bound in Great Britain by
William Clowes Ltd, Beccles, Suffolk

CONTENTS

ACKNOWLEDGEMENTS

After eight years of countless conversations about Turkey it would be rather pointless to try to thank everyone who crossed my path. From the remotest villages to the centres of political power, however, many people gave generously of their time and their opinions. I didn't agree with all of them and I'm sure many of them won't agree with me. But their input into writing this book is gratefully acknowledged.

I must thank everyone who worked with me in Turkey – especially Mahmut, who accompanied me on many trips around the country, and helped me in many ways. Thanks are also due to Tülin, Ertan, Funja and Ömer in Ankara, and everyone at BBA in Istanbul. Thanks too to Firdevs, who read a draft of this manuscript and made helpful and encouraging comments.

My friends and colleagues at BBC News have been – almost without exception – a pleasure to work with, and my editors have given me the opportunity to explore Turkey and its relationship with Europe over a number of years. Thanks to all of them, and to everyone at Granta Books who helped bring *The New Turkey* to publication.

Finally, and most importantly, I would like to thank my family for their love and support. They had to put up with my long absences and – while I was writing this book – even more idiosyncratic working hours than normal.

Chris Morris
Brussels, April 2005

A NOTE ON PRONUNCIATION

Modern Turkish uses a modified version of the Latin alphabet. Most words can be pronounced phonetically, but there are a few letters which will be strange to readers who are not familiar with the Turkish language:

c is pronounced like an English j, as in jelly.

ç is like ch, as in charity.

Similarly *ş* is like sh, as in shed.

i with a dot is pronounced as you would expect in English, as in sin. The capital letter should strictly speaking also carry a dot, so Istanbul should read İstanbul. I have avoided using the capital İ in this book because to my mind it looks rather off-putting in an English text.

ı without a dot has no direct equivalent in English, but is close to the vowel sound in the second syllable of totem.

ö and *ü* are the same as in German, sounding a bit like oe or ue in English, so Atatürk, is pronounced Atatuerk.

Other vowels are fairly standard – *a* as in cart, *e* as in men, *o* as in shot and *u* as in swoon.

ğ is silent but lengthens the vowel which precedes it – so Erdoğan is pronounced Air-doe-an.

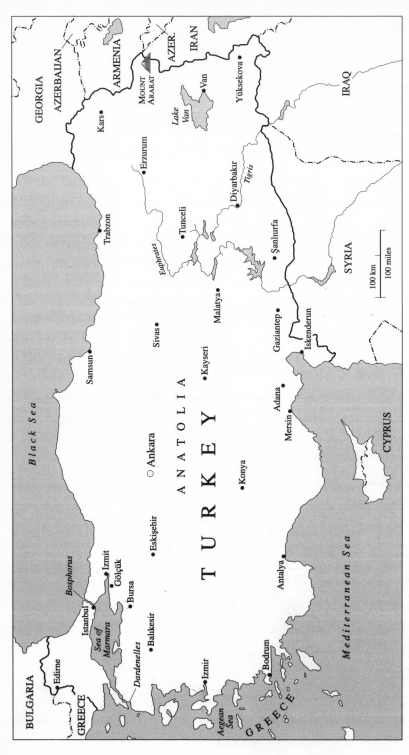

Turkey and its immediate neighbours

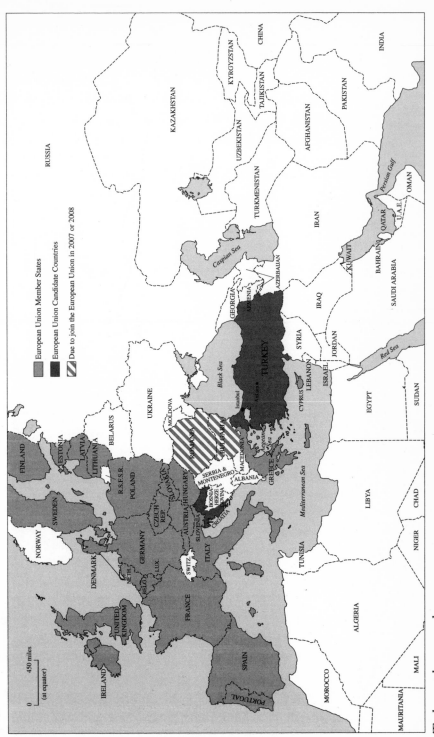

Turkey and surrounds

For Kalpana, Jeffrey and Dylan

INTRODUCTION

Recep Tayyip Erdoğan looked exhausted, and with good reason. He had hardly slept the night before. He had spent hours in tense consultations with his colleagues and bruising negotiations with political leaders from across Europe. The mood of the summit had been grumpy and fractious. Erdoğan had come close to walking out at one stage, before he bumped into Tony Blair in the corridor, who persuaded him to stay. Even at the very end, after a deal had been done, Erdoğan was involved in an angry exchange with the Greek Cypriot president, Tassos Papadopoulos. This was negotiation Turkish style, and some Europeans didn't like what they saw. 'Turkish politicians still have things to learn,' muttered one foreign minister, 'we are not carpet traders here in Europe.'

But beyond the sour grapes was a sense of history in the making. It was 17 December 2004 and Turkey's prime minister, a former Islamist firebrand who had spent time in jail, was the centre of attention. The son of a sea captain from a tough Istanbul neighbourhood, Erdoğan had just achieved something none of his predecessors had come close to managing. After more than forty years of uneasy courtship, the European Union had finally given Turkey a date to start talks on future membership. It was, he said, one of the most important days in modern Turkish history. It was hard to disagree.

Two years earlier, when Erdoğan led his party, the AKP, to an over-whelming election victory, he had identified the challenge posed by Europe, and the changes it required from his country, as his benchmark. All his formidable political energies had been concentrated on pushing through reform and persuading European politicians that they could no longer turn Turkey down. Now, as he looked out over a room packed

with journalists in a five-star hotel in Brussels, his thoughts turned
to home.

'In the last two years,' he said, 'we have made deep-rooted changes to
our society that many countries wouldn't be able to accomplish in ten or
twenty years. We have achieved an extraordinary transformation as a
nation.'

He was right. Turkey has changed in remarkable ways. A torrent of
sweeping democratic, legal and economic reforms has been rushed
through the political system. The power of the military has been cur-
tailed; individual freedoms have been extended; Kurds have begun to
receive rights long denied; and a start has been made to repair the
damage caused by years of economic mismanagement and corruption.
It's not perfect by any means, there is much more to be done, but Turkey
has made a great leap forward.

Huge social changes caused by migration, economic liberalization and
a more general opening to the wider world have been shaking the system
for the last twenty-five years. Tayyip Erdoğan didn't invent reform, but
he has enabled it to happen. Now, after the 'lost decade' of the 1990s,
when the country was beset with weak coalition governments, a brutal
civil war and ideological battles at the heart of the state, a new Turkey
has emerged. The old ways haven't gone for good, and there are still
powerful people who want to turn back the clock. But they seem to be
fighting a losing battle.

Pressure for change has come from within, from ordinary people
fed up with the failures of the status quo; it's also been motivated
by the dominant issue of Turkish political life – that long pursuit
of membership of the European Union. The idea of Europe doesn't
appeal to everyone, but it has been the glue which has kept the
reformers together. The liberal middle classes already see themselves
as European; most of the business community think closer ties with the
EU will bring stability and increased trade and investment; Islamists
hope reform will be accompanied by a more relaxed attitude to religion;
and the Kurds and other minorities see it as a guarantee of greater
cultural freedom.

All of them are part of the noisy debate about what it means to be
Turkish in the twenty-first century. And yet beyond the alluring images
of the travel brochures, which have tempted millions of tourists to visit

the beaches and ancient ruins, Turkey remains a mystery to most outsiders. It's a complex country, hard to understand: secular and Muslim,
Western and Eastern, all at the same time. It's modern and traditional,
democratic and still authoritarian, a place in a constant state of flux,
which seems to have awoken from a deep slumber to find that the rest
of the world has moved on and there is some serious catching up to do.

When Tayyip Erdoğan got back from the summit in Brussels to the
Turkish capital, Ankara, groups of his supporters lined the road from the
airport to cheer him home. Opponents of the European process were
already sharpening their knives, but in the city centre thousands of
people waving Turkish and European flags turned out in the biting cold
to greet the prime minister with firecrackers, balloons and Turkish
music.

'Turkey will become different in every way,' Erdoğan promised, as he
addressed the crowd from an open-topped double-decker bus. 'We will
not rest on our laurels, because our aim every day now is to move forwards, forwards, forwards!'

A few days later Erdoğan flew off in the opposite direction to
Damascus, to sign a free trade agreement with Syria, one of Turkey's
eastern neighbours and for years a bitter foe. Countries in the Middle
East have been watching Turkey's internal reforms and its European
progress as closely as anyone, aware that these are startling changes
which could one day bring the EU to their own borders. Turkey: a
bridge between two worlds? It is an oft-repeated cliché, but today it just
might be coming true.

* * *

Skimming across the Bosphorus in a private water-taxi, you can be forgiven for thinking that life is pretty good. There is serious money in one
of the world's most spectacular cities, and the rich elite in Istanbul
live in the lap of luxury. They have beautiful villas with views across the
water; holiday homes down on the coast; yachts, fast cars and ample
opportunities for education and travel abroad. They shop in swanky
boutiques which wouldn't look out of place in Paris or Milan, and they
party in clubs and restaurants where a good meal for two can cost as
much as some Turks earn in a month.

'People need a place to come and relax,' Şefik Öztek says, 'away from the stress of everyday life. That's what we try to provide.'

He pauses and waves as a large motor cruiser manœuvres its way towards the jetty.

Şefik is the owner of Laila, one of Istanbul's most famous open-air nightclubs, with a prime position next to the Bosphorus. In the summer season, the dance floor is packed every Friday and Saturday night with designer-clad revellers, and the paparazzi hang out near the entrance waiting for the stars to arrive.

'Can you get a view like this anywhere else?' Şefik demands, pointing across the water towards the lights on the Asian shore, and the old Ottoman Palace next to the Bosphorus Bridge. 'We work hard.' He smiles. 'But we're lucky to be here.'

Abdurrahman Kapçek also spends his time by the water, but he lives in a different world. Nearly a thousand miles east of Istanbul, in the shadow of an old Urartian castle, he has a small house built of mud and concrete next to the vast flat expanse of Lake Van. Heavy snow has fallen on the mountains in the distance, and thick ice glistens on the edge of the lake. Abdurrahman lives with his wife Hüsna and six children. He's not entirely sure how old he is. He used to have a second wife, and at least ten other children have already left home. The wooden roof of his house is in need of repair, and there is no sewage connection. Every year his bills for electricity, food and water are getting more and more expensive.

'You can see how we're living here in the snow,' he says, stroking his thick grey moustache. 'We have nothing valuable and no one is helping us. I wish they would.'

He gets a small pension from the work he used to do on a government farm, and he has a few apple trees which sometimes produce enough spare fruit to sell in the market. Europe feels like it's a long way from here, and talk of joining the EU seems out of place.

'People say it would be good,' Abdurrahman says. 'That's what they say on the television. I don't know much about it, but I hope they're right.'

The shores of the Bosphorus and the shores of Lake Van: two extremes, perhaps, but representative of two very different Turkeys. Several million people live in first-world Turkey, but millions more live in the third world, the poorest among them scratching a living in feudal poverty. There's modern Turkey, the Turkey of social mobility, of holiday resorts and nightclubs, of concerts and galleries, booming businesses and rapid economic growth. But there's also tribal Turkey, where equality between the sexes is a myth, where women are killed by members of their own family for looking at a man in the wrong way, where poverty and illiteracy are entrenched problems.

It is easy to find the super-wealthy in Istanbul, and the rural poor living in primitive conditions at the other end of the country. Both are part of Turkey's story, part of its desperately uneven development. But in between the two there is the vast mass of the population who mix modernity with their old traditions, and carve out their own space as their country changes rapidly. For decades this was an inward-looking 'self-sufficient' society; now more and more Turks have direct contact with the outside world. A widespread assumption that the centralized state knew best, and that it would provide from the cradle to the grave, has been challenged by the proliferation of civil society groups who are making their voices heard on environmental issues, human rights, arts and politics. There is a growing middle class of consumers who tighten their belts dramatically when the crises come, but who have the wherewithal to survive and who aspire to better days ahead. Better education, more job opportunities, more personal freedoms – these are the rights they demand.

The biggest change of all has been a change in mentality. The way the country is run is being revolutionized. Plenty of people have risen in the past from humble origins to the highest offices of state – Süleyman Demirel, for example, the shepherd boy from Isparta who became prime minister (many times) and finally president and Turgut Özal who masterminded the last great surge of reform two decades before Tayyip Erdoğan got to the top. But Demirel and others became part of the old system, rather than seeking to change it too much; and Özal died before his time. For decades an elite of 'white' Turks in politics, business and especially the military were indisputably in charge. And throughout most of the 1980s and 90s, as global forces began to change the lives of ordinary people beyond recognition, the 'system' remained resolutely the same.

But no longer. Tayyip Erdoğan has shaken things up, and he's proud to be from the wrong side of the tracks. He never fails to make this point in the tub-thumping stump speeches he gives as he tours Anatolia. 'Your brother Tayyip,' he tells the approving crowds, 'is a "black" Turk.' Like all the best politicians, he runs a constant campaign, addressing political rallies, opening factories and urging change. His opponents still harbour serious suspicions about Erdoğan and his Islamist past (and even some of his admirers worry about his authoritarian political style), but the people are judging him on his results. He's certainly the most important politician to emerge in Turkey for twenty years, perhaps the most important since the man who shaped the modern republic, the man whose image is still ever-present: the founding father, Kemal Atatürk.

* * *

'I was trying to speak to my father but he couldn't stop laughing.'

Mahmut had just got off the phone in our office in Istanbul.

'What was so funny?'

'He was riding back from the orchard with a box of apricots, sitting on Tansu the donkey (named, less than affectionately, after the former prime minister, Tansu Çiller), when his mobile phone rang in his pocket. It was me, but he couldn't really talk. He just kept laughing. "If only they could see me now," he said. "Apricots, a donkey and a mobile phone." I suppose that's what they call progress.'

Turks love to talk, theirs is an expressive language, and it's no surprise that the mobile revolution has penetrated deep into the villages. But for a long time it was forbidden to talk about some subjects, at least in public. Everyone had to be careful what they said. When I first arrived in Turkey in 1997, intrigued by the complex history and modern dynamism I saw all around me, the one thing which caught my eye more than any other was the almost casual way in which extraordinary punishments were handed out to people who simply spoke up for what they believed.

At the time only China rivalled Turkey for the number of writers and journalists thrown into jail for what they had said or written. In such a proud country it was a damaging stain. Some writers practised self-censorship; others became acquainted with the prison system. There were two subjects which most often incurred official wrath: the debilitating war against the Kurdish militants of the PKK in the south-east – a conflict which drained so much of Turkey's time and energy – and the politicization of Islam in a country governed by strict secular rules.

Fortunately, things have begun to change for the better. A few subjects are still beyond the pale: criticizing Atatürk, for example, or declaring that the killing of hundreds of thousands of Armenians under the Ottoman Empire in 1915 was in fact genocide. But most of the big issues facing modern Turkey are debated vigorously. In a vibrant media and on the Internet, a huge variety of opinions can be heard on cultural, religious and political issues. The secular/religious divide, the Kurdish question, high-level corruption and even criticism of the military are all given a thorough airing. Zealous prosecutors are still active, but laws have been liberalized; people are beginning to realize what rights they have, and they are determined to stand up for them.

In all walks of life, in fact, the scale of change in Turkey has been revolutionary; prompted by Europe, the state is being dismantled and rebuilt in a new image: still Turkish, but with Western notions of individual freedoms more deeply embedded. As with any revolution, though, there is still the possibility that things could slip backwards, or veer off in unexpected directions. The change in mentality doesn't always seep down through the system, and in the hurly-burly of Turkish society there is a mass of contradictions. Many Turks say they want to join the European Union but they know next to nothing about it. They live in a strict secular state with a deeply religious population. There is, officially, 'zero tolerance' for torture but it still takes place. And alongside reformers are reactionaries who fear change, and argue that liberalization and the European process will be the end of Turkey as they know it.

'We are sowing the seeds of hate in this country,' says Mehmet Sandir of the far-right Nationalist Action Party, 'and creating divisions where none exist.'

* * *

And all this in a country compared by its most famous poet Nazım Hikmet, to the head of a galloping mare 'jutting into the Mediterranean'; a country set squarely between Europe and Asia, between the Balkans and the Middle East. Turkey is a borderland, the place where the

European Union will have to decide where its outer limits lie. Most of the Turkish elite and, according to current opinion polls, the vast majority of the Turkish people, want to join the EU; and they deserve an answer. They can't be kept in the second-class waiting room for ever. The way the new Turkey develops over the next decade, and the way EU leaders respond, will help draw the map of Europe for the twenty-first century.

Consider for a moment how different Turkey is from any of the new EU members of recent years. The ten countries which joined the union in 2004, most of them former Communist countries from Eastern Europe, have a combined population of about seventy-five million. Turkey on its own has a rapidly growing population of more than seventy million. Within a few years of joining, it would be the most populous nation in the EU. That would give it a dominant role at regular EU summits, and in the policy-making Council of Ministers. Turkey would also wield significant influence in the European Parliament. The balance of power in the EU would swing decisively south and east, away from its original core members.

And is it really Europe? Travel down the long straight roads through Anatolia to the Turkish border with Iraq, where long lines of trucks wait patiently to bring their cargoes of cheap diesel across the border from Iraqi Kurdistan, and London or Brussels suddenly seems a world away. Or take just a few minutes to step away from the picture-postcard image of Istanbul which the authorities want to promote – into the back streets of Fatih, one of the city's most conservative, religious neighbourhoods – and the traditional ideas of Europe fade rather fast. This is a vast melting pot of a country, an overwhelmingly Muslim nation which until the fall of the Ottoman Empire at the end of the First World War was home to the Islamic caliphate.

In other words, there is no doubt that Turkish membership of the EU would change the union dramatically – institutionally, politically and culturally. In some European political circles there is deep-seated hostility to the idea, most significantly – but not exclusively – on the political right in France and Germany. It is, they argue, too big, too poor and too Muslim. The former French president, Valéry Giscard d'Estaing, who chaired the EU's constitutional convention, was one of the first to nail his colours to the mast. Turkish membership, he believes, would spell 'the end of the European Union'. Turkey has 'a different culture, a different approach and a different way of life . . . its capital is not in Europe; ninety-five per cent of its population live outside Europe; it is not a European country.'

There are, however, powerful voices who disagree. They want Turkey in Europe, and they believe that if its democratic transformation continues, then it deserves to be there. As a member of NATO it helped contain and defeat Soviet Communism, and it could play a role in protecting European borders with volatile regions in the Middle East and the Caucasus; it has a young, dynamic population and could become a regional economic power of the future. There are plenty of ifs and buts, and no guarantees. Nevertheless, the leading European politicians of the first years of this century – Gerhard Schröder, Tony Blair and Jacques Chirac – all publicly support Turkey's efforts to join the EU. Whether it eventually happens or not, they argue, the process of reform it has unleashed is something which must be supported. If the end result is a country which is Muslim in belief and practice but secular and democratic in every other respect, then European values will have won.

* * *

I remember once canvassing opinion on the European Union in the vegetable market in Beşiktaş on the European shores of the Bosphorus. It had been snowing earlier in the day, but the weather had grown warmer and it was now pouring with rain.

'Oh yes, we love Europe, we want to be part of Europe,' said one trader with real enthusiasm, taking his cue from the prevailing political mood. 'But if they don't want us,' he grunted, as water dripped off the canopy onto his hat and he sold another bag of tomatoes, 'then they can go to hell.'

Over the next few years political debate in Turkey will be dominated by its relationship with the EU. From the business districts of Istanbul to the smallest villages in the interior, details large and small of the negotiations on membership will be the great political issues of their time. The negotiations will begin (last-minute mishaps notwithstanding) on 3 October 2005, and there will be problems, challenges and opportunities in every direction. Europe still has to decide whether it really wants

Turkey and – just as important – Turkey has to decide whether it wants to be so unambiguously European.

There are bound to be crises in the future. Optimism will evaporate and the talk, suddenly, will be of doom and gloom. The infamously jumpy Istanbul Stock Exchange will fluctuate wildly and a quick survey of the headlines will suggest that 'The End' is probably 'Nigh'. Turkey's relationship with the West, and with Europe in particular, tends to work like that. It is a roller-coaster . . . an emotional white-knuckle ride. It's fascinating, and often entertaining, but it's not always the best way to make vital decisions.

The fate of Turkey's remarkable process of reform, though, is bound up with its European ambitions. It wouldn't have come so far so fast without them. That's one of the reasons why the first chapter of this book about the new Turkey goes back through hundreds of years of history to look at where the Turks came from, their imperial past, and their long and complex relationship with Europe. Turkey is only just rediscovering some of its roots, but many modern-day attitudes and misunderstandings stem from historical memories and half-remembered prejudice.

1

THEY'VE GOT A BIT OF A HISTORY

When J. A. R. Marriott published *The Eastern Question: An Historical Study in European Diplomacy* in 1917, he set out his terms of reference in a manner which would make even Valéry Giscard d'Estaing blush. He wrote:

> The primary and most essential factor in the problem . . . is the presence, embedded in the living flesh of Europe, of an alien substance. That substance is the Ottoman Turk. Akin to the European family neither in creed, in race, in language, in social customs, nor in political aptitudes and traditions, the Ottomans have for more than five hundred years presented to the other European powers a problem, now tragic, now comic, now bordering almost on burlesque, but always baffling and paradoxical.

No wonder the Turks think they get a bad press. It's been like that for centuries.

* * *

For several months, local residents in the old city of Istanbul thought the small construction site which had sprung up in the grounds of a five-star hotel was something to do with repairing the sewage system. The hotel had previously been part of a prison and from the surface the hole in the ground certainly didn't look like anything out of the ordinary. But as we clambered down a series of ladders, and made our way along bits of rickety wooden scaffolding in an excavated passage, a rather more dramatic scene emerged. Archaeologists had discovered part of the lost Grand Palace of Byzantium – a modern byword for treachery and intrigue.

On the walls at the end of a narrow corridor we were confronted by a series of magnificent frescoes, hidden for more than a thousand years: floral patterns in vivid greens, reds and yellows. Historians believe the palace complex once covered a huge triangular area next to the shores of the Sea of Marmara. It contained churches, gardens and ceremonial rooms, all now buried beneath a bustling twenty-first century metropolis.

'This site is typical of Istanbul, and typical of Turkey,' said the archaeologist leading the excavation project, Alpay Pasinli, as we picked our way through the debris. 'There are so many layers, and so many discoveries still to be made. Each new layer of the city sits on top of all the old ones.'

He turned back towards the frescoes. 'Sometimes,' he said, 'the most surprising things are just beneath your feet.'

Trying to understand contemporary Turkey is impossible if you don't know something of its historical roots. A country which is now ninety-nine per cent Muslim contains some of Christianity's earliest sites, such as the underground rock churches of Cappadocia, and the ancient Syriac monasteries of Tur Abdin, where monks still speak Aramaic, the language of Christ. The modern Turkish state, which tried to craft a single ethnic identity for three-quarters of a century, is the main heir of one of the greatest multi-ethnic empires the world has ever seen. When we talk about the new Turkey we need to know about all the old Turkeys as well. History didn't begin when Kemal Atatürk proclaimed the Turkish republic in 1923.

* * *

Anyone in search of a vantage point to watch the world go by on the Bosphorus should head for the castle known as Rumeli Hisarı on the European shore. Sitting majestically between the two suspension bridges which span the strait, it offers a perfect view of the oil tankers and cargo ships which ply their trade between the Black Sea and the eastern

Mediterranean. The crenellated castle walls climb steeply from the shore to dominate the surrounding area, lifting the visitor above the noise and pollution of the modern city.

Rumeli Hisarı was built by the young Sultan Mehmet II – soon to be dubbed Fatih, the Conqueror – in 1452. A stunning example of Ottoman military architecture, it was intended to send a simple message to the embattled defenders of Constantinople about who controlled the supply lines down the Bosphorus; the first ship which tried to slip past the castle without paying tribute was sunk by cannon fire, its crew decapitated and its Venetian captain impaled by the water's edge.

Within a year Constantinople itself had fallen. Mehmet devised and controlled a seven-week siege which finally broke the dogged defence of the city. Ranged against him, under the leadership of the last Byzantine emperor, Constantine, was an unlikely collection of Greeks, Genoese, Venetians and Catalans. They were hugely outnumbered. Even before the siege began, the emperor had made desperate calls for more help from Europe, but it never came. Despite a good deal of talk, Latin Christianity did little to help the Orthodox in their hour of need.

Mehmet's own army was far from mono-ethnic. Turks were in the clear majority, but there were Kurds, Arabs, Persians and plenty of Christian European irregulars: Hungarians and Italians, Greeks and Germans. Even in its early days, the Ottoman Empire was not based around the idea of Islam alone. It was about accumulating power, about state-building, about identifying a winner and sticking with it. To any self-respecting mercenary in the fifteenth century one thing was clear: the Ottomans were on the up.

They already had a well-established toehold in Europe – in Thrace and Bulgaria. Sofia was in Ottoman hands, while their defeat of the Serbs on the Blackbird Field in Kosovo in 1389 was a battle which still inspired thoughts of revenge in Slobodan Milošović six hundred years later. The first Ottoman troops had already gazed out across the Adriatic, and there had been a successful campaign against the Venetians around Salonica in the battle for trade routes and influence. But for Mehmet, Constantinople was the big prize.

In May 1453 he rode through the ruins of the defeated city on a white charger and headed for the incomparable Haghia Sophia – the greatest cathedral of Eastern Christianity. He ordered that it be protected from the wanton violence of the looters and converted immediately into a mosque. The capital of the Byzantine Empire, the Rome of the East, was in the hands of a new dynasty. For nearly five hundred years, the city retained its official name, but it soon became known to the ordinary citizen as Istanbul.

Who were these new rulers, the Ottomans, and where had they come from? Nomadic Turcomen tribes began sweeping out of Central Asia on horseback in the eighth century AD – a massive movement of peoples which turned into a relentless tide. Some were fleeing westward from the advance of the Mongols behind them; others were restless opportunists looking for rich pickings among the settled communities which lay in their path. In the Middle East the Turks soon collided with and converted to Islam, while retaining many of the shamanistic practices they brought with them from the great plains of the east.

As some tribes paused and settled, others moved on in search of more and more land. About a thousand years ago they galloped for the first time into Asia Minor, the Anatolian peninsula, and the eastern realms of the Byzantine Empire. In these rich agricultural lands battle followed battle, and fortunes ebbed and flowed. But amid the confusion of uncertain times the Turks moved slowly westwards. A decisive defeat was inflicted on the Emperor Romanus Diogenes at the Battle of Manzikert near Lake Van in 1071, opening the floodgates for the Turkish takeover of Byzantium.

The transition from one empire to another wasn't just about Muslims against Christians and Turks against Greeks. The Venetians and the Genoese – masters of Mediterranean trade – were among those who attacked the weakened Byzantines, while Constantinople itself was occupied and sacked by the knights of the Fourth Crusade in the name of both profit and pope. Similarly the House of Osman – the future rulers of the Ottoman Empire – fought many times against other Turkish warlords and local dynasties as they slowly established a position of ascendancy.

There were real setbacks for the Turks, including a bloody nose administered by the limping Tartar warrior, Tamburlaine, and his horde of Mongols. For a brief period in the early fourteenth century, the putative empire was in disarray and came close to collapse. But the Mongols disappeared, and Byzantium was in no position to put up much of a fight.

The Turkish advance had reached the western edge of Anatolia – to the Aegean Sea, the Dardanelles and the Bosphorus – and in 1354 it was the Ottomans who were the first Turks to cross permanently into Europe at Gallipoli. The world which had nourished ancient Greece and Rome, the philosophical roots of modern Europe, was falling into the hands of new rulers. Within a hundred years the Ottomans had conquered Constantinople and announced the arrival of one of the world's great empires.

* * *

It was to become Islam's most decisive advance in Europe, but it was hardly the first. Only a hundred years after the death of the prophet Muhammad in AD 632, Berber Arab armies were at the walls of Tours on the Loire in central France and in the fields of Burgundy, pushing northward from their stronghold at Narbonne, in Provence. For several centuries much of the Iberian peninsula was under Muslim control, ruled from the great political and intellectual capital of Córdoba. In the Mediterranean, a cultured Islamic society flourished in Sicily from 902 to 1072 and beyond. And further north, in the thirteenth century, the Golden Horde of Genghis Khan and his successors swept through modern-day Russia to reach parts of Lithuania and Baltic Poland.

All of these great movements into Europe have been pushed back again over time, but in one form or another, Islam has never left. As Norman Davies wrote in *Europe: A History*:

> The interaction of Christians and Muslims has provided one of the most enduring features of Europe's political and cultural life. From the eighth century onwards there has never been a day when the *adhan*, the call of the *muezzin*, could not be heard morning and evening, summoning the faithful to prayer . . .

When the Turks and the Berbers and all the rest first appeared in Europe, they brought many things with them. A thousand years ago, most Europeans were still struggling to emerge from centuries of stagnation and decline following the fall of Rome, and the Islamic world became Europe's link with more advanced civilizations to the east.

Knowledge of medicine and mathematics, astronomy and the arts, hygiene and new agricultural techniques all flooded in with the invading armies of soldiers, sailors and merchants.

Even in the early years of Islam, though, the rivalry between the Christian West and the Muslim East was unmistakable, on the battlefield and beyond. As well as a link, the Ottoman world became a barrier cutting Europe off from the Asian hinterland and the vast trading opportunities it represented. This was an obstacle not entirely overcome for many centuries, until first the Portuguese and then other intrepid Europeans began their great seaborne expeditions around the coast of Africa and across to the New World in the Americas.

All in all, then, Islam was quite a challenge. An aggressive upstart religion, which burst forth from Arabia at uncontrollable speed, it forced Europeans to get organized, to try to respond in kind. The crusades were the first flawed and ultimately failed attempt to hit back, and they embedded images of the Cross versus the Crescent in the popular mind. When they began, the goal of the crusades was to retake Jerusalem and the Holy Land with as much plunder as possible along the way. But over the centuries, things grew more realistic – rape and pillage was still the objective of many, but the later crusades also became the first battles in a long defensive campaign to keep Islam and the Turks at bay.

*　*　*

Modern Turkey loves a good military parade – it's a chance to show off one of the largest armies in the world. But amid the tanks, the artillery pieces and the F-16s screaming through the skies above, I always tend to look out for the volunteers dressed as Ottoman troops. With flamboyant false moustaches, and a splendid variety of pointy hats, they march slowly past the reviewing stand in proper Ottoman military style – two steps forward, one step back . . . two steps forward, one step back.

Unresolved feelings about the sudden loss of an empire still have modern echoes in Turkey today. For a long time the radical secularist reforms pushed through by Kemal Atatürk in the 1920s and 1930s seemed to be part of a cunning plan to lock the door on the messy Ottoman past, and throw away the key. Atatürk himself preferred to seek inspiration from ancient Turkic roots in Central Asia, and one of the weirder theories attributed to him was that Turkish was the first language and all other languages were descended from it. For several decades in the new republic the Ottomans were associated with failure and fundamentalism.

But there has been a shift in opinion, beginning in earnest in the 1980s, and Ottomania has been reborn. Both nationalists and Islamists like to lay claim to the Ottoman heritage and since Islamist mayors took control of Istanbul, starting with Tayyip Erdoğan, the anniversary of the conquest in 1453 has become a major public celebration. Reassessment of the Ottoman past has gathered pace in the last few years and the best of the empire is now regarded with curiosity and growing pride.

Ottoman art and artefacts are proudly displayed in museums, and lavish exhibitions (such as 'Turks' at the Royal Academy, London, in 2005) are sent abroad to showcase Turkey to the world. Ottoman classical music is more popular than ever, and during the holy month of Ramadan the old tradition of shadow puppets has become a big attraction again. In a converted *fez* factory next to the Golden Horn large crowds gather every night to watch the Ottoman characters Karagöz and Hacivat. The puppets appear as silhouettes behind a screen, acting out fables of comic incompetence and bureaucratic bungling. It all seems terribly familiar to the adults in the audience, who hoot with laughter as children run helter-skelter between the chairs, their faces full of candyfloss.

'I think it's good that the old ways are coming back again,' said Fikret Bayramoğlu, as he sat in the front row with his wife and baby daughter. 'Everyone enjoys it, and these things are part of our past. Why shouldn't we be proud of them?'

Why not indeed? At the height of its powers the Ottoman Empire stretched from the Arabian peninsula to the gates of Vienna, and it was a functioning political entity in the childhood of people still alive today. By any measure, the empire was an extraordinary achievement: a monumental mix of people and places which controlled large parts of south-eastern Europe for hundreds of years.

The fall of Constantinople in 1453 sent shock waves across Europe, and greatly enhanced the prestige of the sultan. Over the next three decades, Fatih Mehmet continued his conquests, overrunning the rest of the Greek-speaking world, moving further into the Balkans and annexing the southern Crimea. It wasn't a picture of unbroken Ottoman success, though – European armies fought back in Belgrade, and in Rhodes, where the Knights of the Order of St John held onto their island fortress. In 1480 Ottoman troops landed on the southern toe of Italy and began advancing to the north, a campaign cut short only by news of the sultan's death the following year. Europe, finally, could breathe a sigh of relief: the Conqueror was no more. There were fireworks and celebrations in Rome and Venice and services of thanksgiving across the continent. But anyone who dared hope that the Ottomans were a one-hit wonder was to be disappointed.

The empire was beginning to flourish and grow in confidence, as the old feudal order in south-eastern Europe started to collapse in front of it. In the Balkans Islam became firmly established as a native European religion at around the same time that the great Islamic civilization of Moorish Spain was being beaten back across the Mediterranean, leaving the incomparable buildings of Córdoba and Granada behind it. The Ottomans were also notable in an age of intolerance for the readiness with which they would accept outsiders into the fold. Brutal in war, they governed their people with a relatively light hand. As long as the unquestioned rule of the sultan, and an official status of inferiority before the law, was accepted, Christian subjects could rise and profit from their allegiance. Greeks and Armenians flourished in Istanbul as traders and merchants, and in 1492 Bayezit II gave refuge to thousands of Jews expelled from Catholic Spain. They, too, were respected for who they were, and settled in cities across the Balkans and beyond.

Of course, Ottoman military campaigns into southern and central Europe routinely emphasized their Islamic character. Even then, *jihad* was a useful, inspiring battle cry. Within the boundaries of the early empire, however, intercommunal relations were usually pretty good. There were many times when Jews and Christians were persecuted and killed, but it rarely happened with official sanction from above. Administrators were ordered to allow these fellow 'People of the Book' to practise their religion freely and play a full role in Ottoman society. At this stage of the empire's development, it was Shia Muslims who suffered more than anyone else at the hands of their Sunni Ottoman rulers.

The sultans quickly re-established Istanbul as one of the world's great cities, a place where Europe and Asia overlapped, after years of decline and neglect under the fading grandeur of Byzantium. Magnificent new mosque complexes were built – the Fatih Camii and the Eyüp Camii among them – which still grace the city today; and it was from the new imperial palace of Topkapı that Sultans and their generals would plan the next campaign of conquest. Huge armies would gather with amazing speed, before setting out with the entire Ottoman government in tow, only to return months and sometimes years later with the spoils of victory.

You can still wander through the courtyards of Topkapı Palace today, and try to imagine what it used to be like, how full of intrigue it once was. There are fabulous views along the Bosphorus, and across the Golden Horn and the Sea of Marmara. No wonder they chose this as the perfect place from which to run the family business. From the imperial kitchens, with their huge brick-domed roofs and mighty chimneys, to the mysterious harem on the other side of the great Courtyard of the Imperial Council, it really feels like the engine room of the empire. For hundreds of years this was one of the world's great seats of power, and the Turks held parts of Europe in the palm of their hand.

But the Ottoman advance was not just a remorseless push westward. In the early sixteenth century, during the short but bloody reign of Selim the Grim, the Ottomans also made decisive gains to the east. Selim started as he meant to go on, by killing eight brothers and cousins who might have become rivals to the imperial throne. He then defeated the Mamluk Sultanate based in Cairo, bringing the Muslim holy cities of Mecca and Medina into the Ottoman fold, and giving the sultan the first real claim to the title of Caliph, the supreme ruler of Islam and successor to the prophet Muhammad. Selim also won a convincing victory against a rival Persian–Turkish dynasty, the Safevids, protecting and extending the eastern borders in Anatolia and slaughtering the ancestors of today's Turkish Alevi community.

Selim's death in 1520 was once again the cue for much rejoicing in Europe, where another campaign of Ottoman advance was much feared. 'Selim the Grim died of an infected boil, and thereby Hungary was spared,' wrote an anonymous chronicler. But not for long. The death of Selim ushered in the Golden Age of the Ottoman Empire – the long reign of Süleyman 'Kanuni' (the lawgiver), better known to the world as Süleyman the Magnificent.

* * *

Within a decade, Süleyman had destroyed the Hungarian defences, executed thousands of prisoners, taken Budapest, and advanced for the first time in Ottoman history to the walls of Vienna. The siege of 1529 was a short-lived and rather lacklustre affair, and Süleyman withdrew his armies to Istanbul before the onset of winter. But he now controlled the whole of south-eastern Europe. Belgrade had already fallen, and Ottoman control over the eastern Mediterranean was strengthened by a brilliant campaign to overcome the doughty defenders of the island of Rhodes.

The rest of Europe looked on and shuddered within. How far could the Ottomans go? Was Vienna safe? Was Paris? The Habsburg ambassador to the Court of Süleyman, Ogier de Busbecq, writing in 1562, diplomatically praised the caution of his own emperor, Ferdinand, in confronting such a foe:

> Soleiman stands before us with all the terror inspired by his own successes and those of his ancestors; he overruns the plain of Hungary with two hundred thousand horsemen; he threatens Austria; he menaces the rest of Germany; he brings in his train all the nations that dwell between here and the Persian frontier . . . Like a thunderbolt he smites, shatters and destroys whatever stands in his way; he is at the head of veteran troops and a highly trained army, which is accustomed to his leadership; he spreads far and wide the terror of his name. He roars like a lion along our frontier, seeking to break through, now here, now there.

This was an empire which was at home on the move, true to its nomadic roots. In the Middle Ages the Turks used and developed military technology better than anyone else; they picked the best and brightest young men from across their domains to train and develop – being a Christian by birth was no impediment; you were packed off to Istanbul and forcibly converted. Even the most humble could rise close to the peak of Ottoman society, and for hundreds of years the sultan's elite troops, the Janissary Corps, were the best soldiers in the business.

Little wonder, then, that Europe's chattering classes were both fascinated with and appalled by this emerging superpower to the east. Ever since the crusades, Islam – specifically Turkish Muslims – had been portrayed as the enemy at the gates. The Turks were the threat against which Christendom should unite. As they moved further west, so the hysteria grew. Alongside grudging admiration for Turkish military prowess, literature in Elizabethan England was littered with warnings: Shakespeare's Othello is urged to defend Cyprus against 'the general enemy Ottoman', and when he comes across a drunken brawl he asks, 'Are we all turned Turks . . . ?' In *Tamburlaine the Great* Christopher Marlowe warns that '. . . Turks and Tartars shake their swords at thee, Meaning to mangle all thy provinces', while lesser-known contemporary works explore similar fears: *The Siege of Rhodes*, *Lust's Dominion*, *A Christian Turned Turk* and the wonderfully named *All's Lost by Lust*.

Reality, though, was a complex business. While the Ottoman advance was a clear threat to Christian Europe, neighbouring states and local politicians caught in their path often manœuvred against each other. Political marriages into the House of Osman – under a fairly sobering amount of military pressure – could be a route to survival and advancement, even if it meant a daughter or a cousin abandoning the Christian faith. Venice had regularly made treaties which must have had the odd pope or two shaking his head in despair, even though they made good commercial sense.

In fact, by the sixteenth century Protestant countries in Europe began to look to the Muslim world for alliances of convenience against the dominant Catholic powers, especially Spain. Even the Catholic King of France was happy to form an alliance with Süleyman if it meant putting more pressure on the Habsburgs. But Protestants were to the fore, uninhibited by papal bans on trade with the infidel. Elizabeth I of England was interested in military and mercantile cooperation with the Muslim world, and so were the Dutch. Martin Luther described Turkish attacks on Europe as punishment from God for the wickedness of the ruling Catholic order, but he also reaped the benefit: the threat posed to the Habsburg Empire by the Ottoman advance gave the Lutherans a huge helping hand as they consolidated their gains in Germany.

Nevertheless, in the public mind in Europe, a conventional stereotype of the 'unspeakable Turk' began to take hold: depraved, cruel, unholy and savage – embodied in the person of the sultan and his mysterious harem, despotic and exotic all rolled into one. Even those who knew the Ottoman world, and clearly admired it in parts, like Ogier de Busbecq, made sure they pandered to such prejudice. 'You can hardly expect . . .' he wrote at the end of one of his famous letters, 'elegance of style from such an utterly barbarous country as Turkey.'

Are such thoughts still embedded somewhere in the European psyche? It's hard not to conclude that they are. In an organization which operates on consensus and compromise, one can easily imagine a hidden agenda at some EU meetings about Turkey. Awkward silences, muffled coughs . . . no one willing to say so openly, but many round the table hoping that if we put the problem off enough times, it will eventually go away.

Perhaps they should take their cue from the Ottomans under Süleyman, who continued to expand their empire, their economic wealth and their symbols of power. As well as being a ruthless military genius, who pushed the Ottoman borders further than ever before, Süleyman also constructed a new legal system, combining Islamic and secular law. Goldsmiths and calligraphers, poets and artists all flourished, and the great architect Sinan built a succession of superb buildings in Istanbul and elsewhere – including the Süleymaniye mosque complex for his master. On the day of its dedication, according to the Turkish chronicler Evliya Çelebi, Sinan said to the sultan: 'I have built for thee, O Emperor, a mosque which will remain on the face of the earth till the Day of Judgement.'

The mosque still stands, but amidst the military might and the imperial splendour, we can find the seeds of the Ottomans' downfall. Weaknesses in the system grew with the empire itself. Decadence and corruption were beginning to set in among the military elite and the Ottoman court. Foreign countries were given formal economic powers in Istanbul for the first time – a foretaste of the infamous 'capitulations' which dominated the final years of imperial rule. And in the decades following the death of Süleyman in 1566 the power of the sultan himself began to wane. The harem became the setting for vicious political infighting as powerful women began to wield substantial influence, and in 1622 Osman II had the unhappy distinction of being the first Ottoman victim of regicide: humiliated, raped and killed by his own mutinous soldiers.

The Ottomans were also in the process of being outflanked by rivals with a bolder global vision. Portugal and Spain (with the occasional Italian like Christopher Columbus sworn into service), followed by the

Dutch, the French and the English, had already begun extensive naval explorations far from the Ottoman sphere of influence. The discovery of the New World across the Atlantic and the riches to be had there meant Turkish control of the trade routes to the east was no longer as important a strategic asset as it used to be. New-found wealth poured into European treasuries, as European adventurers took to the high seas to begin establishing their own colonies in Asia and the Americas. In 1571 the mighty Ottoman navy was crushed in its own backyard – the Mediterranean – by the combined fleets of Spain, Venice and the Vatican at the Battle of Lepanto. The victory was so unexpected, and so symbolically important, that it provoked a flurry of artistic tributes from contemporary poets, painters and writers. The Turks no longer seemed to be invincible.

Finally, the Ottomans were failing to keep pace with the intellectual ferment of the sixteenth century. Süleyman turned to a stricter vision of Islam as his long reign progressed, and Islamic scholars with a rigid interpretation of the faith stunted the growth of new ideas and achievements. Over time the empire lost its edge in military technology, and it ignored or suppressed other new inventions which were changing the face of contemporary Europe. The printing press was first memorably used in Europe by Gutenberg to create his Bible in the mid-fifteenth century, but it was banned from the Ottoman realm for nearly three hundred years.

'I allow you to laugh at me for the sensual declaration that I had rather be a rich Effendi with all his ignorance, than Sir Isaac Newton with all his knowledge,' wrote Lady Mary Wortley Montagu – the wise and witty wife of a British ambassador to Constantinople in the early eighteenth century. Not for the first time Lady Mary's comparison was right on the money. The Ottomans were enjoying the fruits of power but they were missing out on the latest technological and scientific discoveries; the Ottoman Renaissance under Süleyman was nothing in comparison with the Renaissance in Western Europe which paved the way towards a new and more modern world. As rival countries headed into an age of revolutions and profound change, the Ottoman Empire began to sink into a long slow decline.

* * *

There was still time for one last hurrah. The Ottomans weren't finished yet, and for much of the seventeenth century they still posed a real military threat to Central Europe. But Süleyman was followed by a succession of sultans who were variously inept, corrupt, unstable or simply deranged, and there came a turning point, a decisive date in European history. In 1683 the Ottoman army led by Kara Mustafa Pasha was routed at the gates of Vienna, a catastrophic defeat which meant that the Turks, and the flag of the prophet, would never threaten the city again.

Modern Vienna is littered with reminders of these momentous events. Opposite the university stands a statue of Johann Andreas von Liebenberg, the city's mayor during the siege, and right outside the Hofburg Palace Prince Eugene – the man who pushed the Turks back down through the Balkans – sits proudly astride his horse. In the neo-Byzantine Military History Museum there are collections of curved swords and fading turbans, quivers full of Ottoman arrows, and a pasha's tent captured in Belgrade. My favourite spot is the Kahlenberg, though. From the wooded hill which looms over the city you get a bird's-eye view of the battle site. This is where Jan Sobieski, king of Poland, appeared with his troops on 12 September 1683 and charged into the Ottoman forces below, forcing them to scatter in panic. A small church, consecrated on the two hundredth anniversary of the battle, pays him solemn tribute. This was as far as the Ottoman Empire got.

The Turks are back, of course. Nearly a quarter of a million of them live in Austria today, but migration is a sensitive subject and there are still those who seek to stir up old historical memories for their own ends. During the 2004 European Parliamentary election campaign, the right-wing Freedom Party plastered Vienna with posters saying 'Turkey in the EU? Not with me!' One supportive magazine even coined the slogan THE THIRD TURKISH SIEGE, and combined images of the EU and Turkish flags with marauding Ottoman troops from the seventeenth century. The message was hardly subtle, tapping into deep Austrian ambivalence about Turkey joining Europe. But it didn't do much for the Freedom Party, whose election results were a disaster.

* * *

In 1699 the Ottomans were forced to sign the humiliating Treaty of Karlowitz which stripped away half of their European possessions; and the empire failed to strike back. It fell victim instead to stagnation and internal feuding. The economy continued to grow, but not nearly as fast as the rest of Europe, and occasional military victories did nothing to reverse the overall trend of defeat on the battlefield and territorial withdrawal. The Ottomans struggled to compete economically or militarily with countries to the west, and they were forced to turn their attention to the growing power of Russia to the north as well. Meanwhile European colonizers were taking control of the riches of the Asian trade routes.

The influence of the Ottoman world was still trickling down into everyday European life – from drinking coffee to planting tulips; from playing the kettle drum and the triangle to eating rice, dried fruit and all manner of spices. Lady Mary Wortley Montagu admired the smallpox inoculations used by the Turks in Constantinople and was the first person to introduce the practice in England, while in the eighteenth and nineteenth centuries the craze for Oriental fashions reached its height: in clothing, carpets, textiles and design. But the image of the 'terrible Turk' in art and literature was gone, replaced by a rather comic figure with funny slippers, elaborate turbans and too much jewellery.

The Ottoman system had its fans in Europe. 'Turks,' wrote Voltaire, 'have taught Christians how to be moderate in peace and gentle in victory.' But the power of the empire itself was fading. The political and military elites became progressively more corrupt, and the loss of territory meant the loss of tax revenues as well. When Europe was reordered at the Congress of Vienna in 1814 after the defeat of Napoleon, all the continent's rulers took part – but no one bothered to send an invitation to the sultan. The Janissary Corps – once feared and respected across Europe – had degenerated into an unruly militia, terrorizing the homelands and routinely rising up in rebellion against the Ottoman court. By the time the Janissaries were finally disbanded by force in 1826, in spectacularly bloody fashion, they had become a sorry shadow of their former selves.

In other words, the Ottomans were no longer seen as a threat abroad. The empire stumbled on, mainly because the great European powers refused to let it collapse completely, fearful that their rivals would seize the advantage, and grab all the best land. A series of short-term alliances with, among others, the Russians, the French and the British did little to help the Ottoman cause – and in 1830 a landmark event which is still remembered today was brokered by the Western powers: Greece won its long battle for independence.

In the face of all this grim news for a succession of sultans and their grand viziers there were real efforts to reform the system. During the *tanzimat* or reorganization, knowledge of European affairs gradually became more important as the Ottomans tried to emulate some of the successes they faced in the West. European military advisers became part of the scenery, and knowledge of foreign languages was suddenly a valuable tool in the fight to climb the ever-greasy bureaucratic pole. A new Translation Bureau – set up to replace the old 'dragoman' system which had been run exclusively by Ottoman Greeks – was the launch pad for many a political career.

'Westernization' may sound like a familiar rallying cry to observers of modern Turkey, but for centuries the Ottomans had maintained a haughty distance from the political machinations of the rest of Europe. Many diplomatic representatives to the sultan's court had been treated with contempt – some of them forced to sit in the rain for hours before being granted an audience with the back of the sultan's head. By the mid-nineteenth century though, out of necessity a more pragmatic approach was being adopted. The Ottomans wanted formal recognition as a European power. But when it came, it came at a time when the empire was weaker and more vulnerable than ever.

In the 1850s the Ottomans teamed up with the British and the French to see off the encroaching power of Russia in the Crimean War. You can still visit the Florence Nightingale Museum in the Selimiye Military Barracks in Istanbul where the 'Lady of the Lamp' tended to the wounded and helped lay the foundations for modern nursing care. At the end of the war in 1856, as one of the victors, the Ottoman Empire was included for the first time in the Concert of Europe – giving it a role in diplomatic consultations and meetings as part of the European society of states. But there was also a price to pay. Czar Nicholas I had already dubbed the Ottoman Empire 'the Sick Man of Europe' and the Crimean War was expensive. The Ottomans had to borrow an awful lot of money from European financial institutions and, predictably, they couldn't afford to pay it back. By the end of the century a consortium of creditors known as the Ottoman Public Debt Administration had developed a vast bureaucracy running significant parts of the imperial economy and collecting taxes to help repay the debts.

Not surprisingly, it bred resentment, especially as the mounting foreign debt came on top of the long-running system of 'capitulations', which gave foreign nationals exemption from local laws and taxes. The first of the capitulations was granted as long ago as 1352 as a casual favour to the Genoese, but over time they began to take on the form of bilateral treaties. By the nineteenth century the French, the British, the Germans and others were roundly abusing the system. Foreigners had an unfair advantage, and Ottoman sovereignty was routinely violated. Local pride was easily hurt, and the capitulations came to be seen as a symbol of inferiority, with European countries cashing in on the growing weakness of Ottoman rule. It hasn't been forgotten. Criticism of the power of foreign capital, and of economic interference from abroad, lives on in the widespread suspicion among ordinary Turks of the motives of the International Monetary Fund and foreign investors in general, as modern Turkey struggles to climb out of deep economic crisis.

In fact many of the problems facing Turkey today loomed large in the final years of the Ottoman Empire: battles for power between conservatives and pro-Western reformers, problems with ethnic minorities, and efforts to clean up the financial mess caused by years of mismanagement. And overseeing it all was one of the most secretive and paranoid men ever to sit on the Ottoman throne. Sultan Abdul Hamid II, who reigned for more than thirty years until he was deposed in 1909, developed an obsession with spying on everyone around him. He also played up his religious role as caliph – the leader of the Muslim world – to try to prop up his legitimacy in Anatolia and the Middle Eastern provinces.

Perhaps he was hoping for divine intervention, because the Ottomans suffered further territorial losses shortly after Abdul Hamid's reign began. Romania and Serbia gained independence in 1878, parts of north-eastern Anatolia had to be handed to the Russians, and Cyprus was leased to Britain. Millions of Muslims came flooding back into the heartland of the empire from the Balkans, and with them came a change in mood – a transformation from a broadly tolerant multi-ethnic empire into a nineteenth-century nationalistic state. Alongside reforms which were supposed to sweep away the old legal distinctions between Muslims and the Christian minorities, came ethnic tensions and widespread killings. In the 1870s, the killing of Bulgarian civilians by Turkish troops (dubbed the 'Bulgarian Horrors' by William Gladstone) were followed by Armenian massacres in the 1890s, when thousands of people were killed in Istanbul – a portent of the grim events of 1915.

As the twentieth century dawned, the empire was on its last legs. Within years, most of the remaining Balkan provinces won their independence, a huge blow because they were still the most heavily populated part of the Ottoman realm. Even in 1906, when the Ottomans controlled only a fragment of the territory they had once held, a quarter of the empire's citizens lived in the Balkans. The political power of the sultan was gradually being chipped away by nationalists known as the 'Young Turks', and if the House of Osman was to survive, it desperately needed a period of stability. It could have done without a young man named Gavrilo Princip pulling the trigger in Sarajevo and starting the First World War.

* * *

During the long reign of Abdul Hamid, the empire had grown close to the Germans, and in 1914 the Ottomans picked the losing side for the final time. The 'Young Turk' politicians and generals who now ran the empire dreamed of glory, but the war was a disaster. The only significant victory came at enormous human cost, as a previously unknown colonel named Mustafa Kemal commanded the remarkable defence of the Gallipoli peninsula, against attacks by troops from Britain, Australia and New Zealand. But there was also a much darker, more gruesome side to the collapse of the empire, epitomized by the slaughter of hundreds of thousands of Armenians in eastern Anatolia in 1915 (of which more later). Modern Turkey is still struggling to come to terms with what happened in those last imperial years, and furious debates about the legacy of that period continue to colour the perceptions of many outsiders looking in.

By the end of the war in 1918, the Ottomans were in disarray, and the sultan was an irrelevant puppet. The victorious allies occupied Istanbul, the Greeks took Smyrna (now Izmir), the Italians advanced into southern

Anatolia, and the French and British between them gobbled up the Middle Eastern provinces. In 1920, at Sèvres on the outskirts of Paris, representatives of the sultan signed a treaty imposed by the allies which carved up the empire completely. Greek and Italian gains in Anatolia were made permanent, there was the prospect of new independent countries in the east for the Kurds and the Armenians, and the Turks were left with a rump state in the middle, of little value to anyone.

And that was that, or so the allies thought – the Eastern Question resolved once and for all. But rarely has the phrase 'cometh the hour, cometh the man' seemed so appropriate. Turkish nationalist resistance in Anatolia was led by Mustafa Kemal, soon to be known as 'Atatürk' – the 'father of Turks'. He rallied the troops of a broken, dispirited army and, against improbable odds, began to fight back.

The main battle was against the Greeks, who had been pushing ever deeper into Anatolia, and there were some fairly desperate moments for Atatürk and his supporters. The incipient Turkish uprising could have been crushed by Greek military victories. How different the world would be now if it had been. But once the Greeks were forced into a headlong retreat and were thrown (literally) into the sea at Izmir, there was little appetite anywhere else for another major war so soon after the horrors of 1914–18. Anatolia was regained in full, and Istanbul was restored to Turkish control. At Lausanne in 1923, the Turks re-established a firmer foothold in Europe, reclaiming the eastern half of Thrace as well, with new borders adjoining Greece and Bulgaria.

Mutual suspicion, laced liberally with hatred, was as strong as ever, especially with local enemies like the Greeks and the Armenians. Most of the Greeks who remained within the new Republic of Turkey were sent packing and most of the Armenians had already been killed. European perceptions remained ambivalent at best. For Atatürk, though, this was a time to turn his attention to the home front. Having secured his borders, he now needed to create a functioning country within them. He kicked out the sultan, abolished the caliphate, and threw himself into a revolutionary programme of modernization.

The net effect was that modern Turkey was born with a sizeable chip on its shoulder, which it carries to this day. The Ottomans ran a multi-national multi-ethnic Empire – there were Turks, Arabs, Greeks, Kurds, Albanians, Armenians, Bosnians, Bulgarians . . . in fact, more than thirty countries can be counted as successor states, and the rise and fall of the Ottomans was about far more than the success and failure of the Turks in Europe. But the man who rescued the heart of the empire from complete humiliation was a European himself, and he fervently believed that Turkey's best hope of future success lay across its western borders.

'The West has always been prejudiced against the Turks,' Atatürk once said, with his customary directness. 'But we Turks have always consistently moved towards the West . . . in order to be a civilized nation, there is no alternative.'

Eighty years on, in a very different era, the challenges identified by Turkey's latest generation of leaders remain the same: how to modernize the country, and how to claim a place at Europe's top table? And eighty years on, rather more remarkably, Atatürk is still a central figure in modern Turkish life.

2

'DEVLET': ATATÜRK AND HIS LEGACY

I came across Can and his friends outside McDonald's in Taksim Square, right in the bustling heart of Istanbul. They had set up a little table and were selling their magazine with evangelical fervour. Sport? Music? Youth culture? No, it was a paean of praise for Kemal Atatürk.

'Why are you doing this?' I asked, and Can looked genuinely surprised.

'Because Atatürk is the most important person in Turkey,' he said, speaking in the present tense.

'Why?'

'Because if it weren't for him, our country wouldn't exist as it is now.'

Well, true, but the same could perhaps be said of Britain and Winston Churchill, and yet it's hard to imagine a group of teenage Londoners staking out a patch in Piccadilly Circus to sell magazines dedicated to the man who swore to 'fight them on the beaches'.

Now Can and his friends may not be too representative of today's Turkish youth either, but they help to illustrate a point. What is it about Atatürk, nearly seventy years after his death, which inspires such an extraordinary and emotional response?

* * *

In the run-up to the year 2000, *TIME Magazine* launched a campaign to find the most influential and important people of the twentieth century. The magazine's editors asked for votes to be cast on their website, little knowing what a storm of Kemalist enthusiasm they were about to unleash.

In Turkey it became, for a while, a national priority to promote the greatness of Mustafa Kemal Atatürk on the *TIME* website. Both the prime minister and the president appealed to all patriotic citizens to do their bit, and the Turkish media quickly took up the challenge. My bank in Ankara began handing out ready-made forms. All you had to do was fill in the details, and the bank clerk would fax it to *TIME* with a vote for Atatürk. Where else, I remember thinking, could this possibly happen? North Korea?

As the Atatürk bandwagon began to roll, the spoilers intervened. There were dark rumours of Greek Cypriots voting in droves for Winston Churchill – 'anyone but Atatürk!' – and it all became terribly exciting. When voting closed, our hero hadn't quite made it. In the 'Leaders and Revolutionaries' category Atatürk polled an impressive 33.19 per cent, but fell just a few thousand votes short of Churchill; and in the 'Heroes and Icons' category he had to settle for third, just behind Yuri Gagarin and Nelson Mandela. At one early stage in proceedings, even Bob Dylan had found himself a distant second behind the iconic Turk in the 'Artists and Entertainers' vote.

The folk from *TIME*, however, weren't impressed. They chose Albert Einstein as their 'Person of the Century', and Atatürk, a man little known outside his home country, didn't even make their top 100. There was much wailing and gnashing of teeth from Internet Turks everywhere: once again, they concluded, the rest of the world had conspired against them. One of the most successful wartime leaders of the twentieth century, and one of the boldest revolutionaries, had been ignored.

There was, you see, nothing tongue-in-cheek about the 'Vote Atatürk' campaign. It was deadly serious, and it was a vivid demonstration of how deeply Atatürk – man and myth – is embedded in the national psyche. International recognition of Atatürk means international recognition of Turkey, and vice versa. When Turkish TV hosted the 2004 Eurovision Song Contest in Istanbul, it even managed to close this modern festival of kitsch with a quote from the great leader. 'Peace in the country, peace in the world,' said the presenter proudly in English, as Ukrainian dancers cavorted onto the stage behind her.

On the one hand, it's all very appealing. There is a genuine sense of patriotism and national pride in Turkey which most countries in

Western Europe have lost. On the other hand, it's appalling. Too many people in positions of power in modern Turkey remain wedded to a distorted vision of their founding father's legacy. I say 'distorted' because they seem to have become stuck in a time warp, where change often feels like something to be treated with suspicion. Atatürk, though, was a man who changed everything and, even after taking his legendary vanity into account, I think he would be surprised if he knew how his memory is sometimes kept alive today. It is a true cult of personality with an ideology – 'Kemalism' – to match. Most of all, it is a strange foundation for a country which aspires to become a modern European state.

Put that argument to Kemalist Turks, though, and they will more than likely throw it back in your face.

'Look at Britain: ruled by a family whose only qualification is an accident of birth,' a combative defender of the faith once remarked to me. 'We got rid of ours years ago.'

It was an interesting comparison, but Atatürk has risen above the ranks of mere royalty. Nearly seventy years after his death, he is still treated like some kind of demigod. It often feels as if his modern successors in the presidential palace are simply keeping the seat warm.

Take his mausoleum in the capital, Ankara. Anıtkabir is one of my favourite places in the city, with its goose-stepping guards of honour and its wonderful museum full of Atatürk memorabilia. They've kept everything from tiepins to toilet sets, from his carefully preserved rowing machine to his faithful dog, Foks, embalmed behind glass. The huge marble columns and monumental courtyard give Anıtkabir the look and the feel of a temple, and that's precisely what it is: the foundation stone of the secular cult of Kemalism. Every official foreign visitor is expected to begin a visit to Ankara with a pilgrimage to the great man's tomb. They lay a wreath and write something suitable in the visitors' book. Only after that, does the president or prime minister of the day get a look in.

In fact, you can't escape Atatürk anywhere in modern Turkey. His statue stands at the centre of every town and village square. Schoolchildren pledge their allegiance every morning. Nearly every office and shop has a picture of the father of the nation on the walls, or a gold-painted bust prominently displayed on a desk or a shelf. Not to have one is seen as strangely suspect. Many of the grainy photographic images are instantly recognizable . . . Atatürk in formal Western dress, or leaning out of a train to collect a petition; here he is again in military uniform during the war of independence, and later in front of a blackboard, teaching his people how to modernize. These are iconic moments of nation-building for Turkey, and they have seeped unavoidably into the memory of every Turk alive.

Then there are the great festivals of remembrance – 19 May, when he landed in Anatolia to begin the nationalist uprising against occupation; Victory Day in August and Republic Day in October, when the troops and tanks are on parade; and most sombre of all 10 November, the anniversary of Atatürk's death, when the air-raid sirens wail mournfully at the exact moment of his passing, and true believers get out of their cars to stand to attention in the street.

Many Turks conspicuously don't mark the anniversaries with such evangelical fervour, but they can't escape the Atatürk cult even if they want to. On every occasion huge banners are hung from the tallest buildings – massive pictorial representations of Atatürk in his prime, twenty storeys high. His face appears in the corner of television screens, and on every street you can buy his likeness on badges, pens and paper-weights. You get used to it, it becomes part of the scenery, but there really is nothing quite like it anywhere else in the democratic world.

That's how hardline elements of the Kemalist elite keep the flame alive. They believe they are on a mission to protect and extend the legacy of the founding father. It keeps them constantly on guard against threats real and imagined: threats to the 'indivisible unity of the Republic'; threats to the secular system which Atatürk championed; threats at home and abroad. Their shock troops hold positions of power and influence in the judiciary, the bureaucracy and above all the military. They are the guardians of the system, suspicious of the change they see around them. Collectively, they represent 'Devlet' – the State.

'Moderate Islam?' grunted one of their leaders. 'What kind of label is that? You can drink Diet Coke for as long as you like, but you shouldn't forget that it's still Coke.'

These diehard Kemalists continue to wield real power, but they are on the defensive – partly because that is their default position, partly because they know a trend when they see one. Turkey has changed in extraordinary ways in the last few years – massive internal migration, liberalization of the media and economic upheaval have now been followed by dramatic political reform and the arrival of a new generation of leaders with new ideas. It's the biggest revolution in the way this country works since, well, a man called Atatürk.

*   *   *

Run the clock back eighty years and imagine a country where everything is suddenly turned on its head. Never mind the system of government or the role of religion, how about names, clothes, the alphabet? That's how profoundly Mustafa Kemal's revolution in the 1920s changed daily life, and it was an almost unprecedented achievement. Winning the War of Independence, and preserving a country worth having, was merely the beginning. When Kemal looked around at the impoverished wreck he'd inherited, he decided that radical reform was his only option. The fallen empire was archaic and backward; the new republic was to be modern and secular – part, he declared, of 'contemporary civilization'.

It didn't take him long to act. Kemal moved the capital of his new country from the worldly metropolis of Istanbul to Ankara, a sleepy backwater deep in the Anatolian heartland. He ordered the National Assembly to abolish the Ottoman monarchy and he had himself elected the first president of the new Turkish Republic. The Islamic caliphate was dispensed with, and the last caliph, Abdul Mejid, was packed off unceremoniously on a train to Switzerland (where he was nearly refused entry under a law banning polygamy). Political opponents of the Kemalist revolution from communists to rebellious Kurdish tribesmen were ruthlessly crushed. An all-encompassing law 'for the maintenance of order' and a new system of 'independence tribunals' established something close to dictatorship.

With the consolidation of power came the imposition of momentous social change, year after year. It was a crash course of reform which helped make modern Turkey so different from other states which emerged from the ruins of the Ottoman Empire: Saudi Arabia, for example, or Iraq. Even today, Turks and Arabs have a prickly relationship. Well-to-do Turks tend to look down on Arabs for tainting them by association as non-European; while many Arabs still resent their former colonial masters. Thus the Sunni and Shia of Iraq were no keener to have Turkish troops in their country after the US-led invasion in 2003 than the Kurds were.

What else did Kemal do? Religious brotherhoods were declared illegal, and forced underground; Islamic courts were dissolved. Women were given the right to vote, polygamy was banned and Muslim women were allowed to marry non-Muslim men. The Muslim calendar was replaced by the European one; Sunday became the day of rest; and the traditional Arabic script was dismissed as 'incomprehensible'. Instead Kemal gathered a group of specialists together to transliterate the Turkish language into Latin letters, and he went from town to town to introduce the new alphabet in person to his bewildered citizens.

And it wasn't just what he did, but what he wore while he was doing it: linen suits, a shirt and tie, peaked caps, panamas and homburgs. It's hard to overstate the effect it must have had on people in conservative provincial towns when the Hero of the Revolution turned up in a world of robes and turbans dressed like a Western infidel, and listening to Beethoven and Mozart. The fez and any other clothing connected to Islam were banned, at a time when most Turks couldn't even bring themselves to use the word *şapka* or hat.

The Ottoman authorities had already made various attempts to change the sartorial habits of the population, but gradualism wasn't Kemal's style. Civilization and costume were inextricably linked, and he famously told a dazed audience in the northern port of Inebolu in 1925 precisely what was expected of them: 'Boots or shoes on our feet, trousers on our legs, shirt and tie, jacket and waistcoat – and of course, to complete these, a cover with a brim on our heads. I want to make this clear. This head-covering is called "hat".'

A few years later Mustafa Kemal became Kemal Atatürk. Everyone, he decreed, should have a surname in the Western style – books full of suggestions were sent around the country for citizens who found it hard to choose. No one else was allowed to take the president's new name – the ever-modest Father of Turks. Instead the tough guys went for tough names like Kaya (Rock) or Yıldırım (Lightning); others chose to remember their fathers – Ekmekçioğlu (Son of a Bread-seller), Kilimçioğlu (Son of a Carpet-maker) or rather more rarely Salakoğlu (Son of an Idiot); among recent political leaders we've had President Iron Hand, Prime

Minister Who Never Gives Up and Deputy Prime Minister with a Garden.

In the early republican years centuries of tradition were swept away, and the dust never had a chance to settle. It wasn't a democratic revolution, it was Atatürk's personal revolution – often imposed against the will of the uncomprehending majority. It was a remarkable feat and he probably couldn't have done it any other way, but it meant that his successors inherited an incomplete model. Scattered among all the positive aspects of Atatürk's legacy – the secular state and his relentless drive towards modernity – were the autocratic tendencies and democratic flaws which still live on in the system today. The changes he wrought were so far-reaching that it is hardly surprising that they are still the subject of such intense debate.

Kemal Atatürk lived fast, he loved women, and he drank heavily. In 1938, at the age of 58, he died of cirrhosis of the liver, worn out by the extraordinary pace of his life. Scenes of mass mourning followed as Turks turned to face the future without the man who had created a country from scratch. In fifteen years as President of the Republic he had tried to take much of Turkey from medieval feudalism to the modern age. It wasn't a finished product by any means, but many people seemed to think it was. No one could replace Atatürk, and for the rest of the twentieth century the most influential political forces in Turkey, dedicated to protecting his legacy, were the ones in uniform – the armed forces.

* * *

I was once taken by the Turkish army on a three-day guided tour which began in the rebellious mountain province of Tunceli (or Dersim as the Kurds still prefer to call it). The purpose was to show us how normal things were, how comprehensively the PKK Kurdish rebel movement had been defeated, and how delighted everyone was to be Turkish. *'Ne Mutlu Türküm Diyene!'* is the army's favourite quotation from Atatürk: 'What happiness to say I'm a Turk!' It's written in huge stone letters on mountainsides across the Kurdish provinces.

A young army captain was assigned as our minder on the trip, and shadowed us wherever we went. Every time I asked an awkward question he snorted with derision at a foolish foreigner. We were flown from place to place in military helicopters, to be shown new roads and schools, smiling Kurdish folk dancers, and a row of tables in the middle of a field where a mass wedding witnessed by army officers was taking place. None of the Kurdish women cooking food for the wedding celebration could speak more than a very few words of Turkish, but their children were being moulded, the soldiers would have us believe, into identikit Turks of the future.

There was no doubt that development was desperately needed, and the army wanted to show us that their secular modernization was doing an enormous amount of good. But this was social engineering on a grand scale – change imposed from above on the Atatürk model.

'It's our duty,' one senior officer explained, 'our responsibility as the Turkish army. All these people are citizens of the Turkish Republic.'

'I can see how much you're changing things,' I said, 'but what about individual rights, what about their ethnic identity, does that matter?'

'Their future is with us,' the officer replied as he strode away, leaving us with our angry young minder.

'I don't think you understand us at all,' the captain hissed. 'You never ask the questions we want to answer.'

* * *

You can't walk too far in any of Turkey's big cities before you come across a small red sign emblazoned with a stencilled version of a fierce-looking soldier wielding a gun. You don't have to read the small print to know what it means: 'Keep out, this is military territory, and don't forget who's in charge here.' Vast swathes of central Istanbul and Ankara are reserved for the armed forces who dominate these cities like they have dominated their country for decades. Now they face a new challenge. Not a war at home or abroad, but a political conundrum: they have already loosened their grip, but can they (should they) really abandon the central role they have played in national life for so long?

Like any military institution, the Turkish army likes things done its way. Whether it's running an errand or running the country, the army has its views. It has never fully trusted the civilians who seek power, often with good reason: Turkish politics has been littered with corruption and incompetence. So the generals still speak out routinely in a way which would get them the sack in most other European countries: on education, religion, politics and foreign policy. When they talk, the country listens and headlines are made – old habits die hard. The way it works is this: a select band of trusted journalists is summoned to a briefing with the chief of the general staff or his deputy, and they emerge to report their findings live on television. 'The General is displeased,' they tell us breathlessly, 'and the army is worried that too many people with reactionary [i.e. Islamic] backgrounds are getting government jobs.' The oracle has spoken, and the message is carefully digested by one and all.

The military has been the ultimate arbiter on the political scene for years. Generations of officers have been taught that they have a mission, and a sacred duty: to ensure that the vision of Atatürk is fulfilled. That means Turkey has to be accepted as part of the West; as a modern and 'civilized' European state. Secularism and national unity have to be protected at all costs – the enemies are fundamentalism and ethnic separatists who seek to tear the country apart. As soon as the founding father died in 1938, the fight to protect his legacy began.

For most of the Second World War Atatürk's immediate successors maintained awkward neutrality, still in shock at the loss of their leader, but they joined the Western camp before the Iron Curtain fell across Europe. Since the 1950s Turkey has had a key security role as a member of NATO, and for several decades it was a frontline state in the cold war against the Soviet Union. But the litmus test now, at the start of the twenty-first century, is joining the European Union. It has become the biggest incentive for reform that Turkey has ever seen, and it has changed the role of the military as much as anything else.

The generals know they have some useful cards to play in the European debate. If you put the ambiguous relationship with civilian authority to one side, then Turkey's military is one of the main assets it can offer Europe. The EU is struggling to set up a credible security and defence policy because only Britain and France have armed forces with anything approaching a global reach. Turkey could help. It has the largest fleet of F-16s in the world outside the United States, and the second largest army in NATO – more than half a million soldiers bearing arms. Many, admittedly, are poorly trained conscripts, but there is also a battle-hardened core which has fought the PKK in the mountains. Turkey could give EU defence plans real muscle, and provide much-needed 'boots on the ground' for peacekeeping missions around the globe. The Turks wouldn't solve all Europe's defence dilemmas at a stroke. They may be ahead of the game in terms of manpower, but they lack many of the things the EU really needs: high-tech communications and the massive transport planes (known in the trade as 'heavy airlift') which only the Americans can really provide. But think of the alternatives, argue the strategic enthusiasts in Brussels: either have Turkey in the club and guarding the volatile eastern flank, or keep Turkey out and risk having it turn angrily for sympathy towards Russia, Iran and China.

So it stands to reason, you might think, that the generals must be delighted by the current turn of events, as Turkey looks down the road towards EU membership – an ambition shared by senior Turkish officers for many years, the fulfilment of Atatürk's dream. But it's not quite that simple. The men in uniform now have a problem, and the old guard among them are worried. The more they look at the sweeping reforms required by the EU the less they like them. Ethnic rights, democratic rights, more civilian control – could this be a threat to the very essence of Turkey they have sworn to protect? Many of them believe it is, and a Kemalist coalition of military officers, judges and other senior officials is clinging onto the status quo. It creates a constant tension between conservatives and reformers which haunts Turkey still, and will do so for the foreseeable future.

Since the turn of the new century, Turkey has been living through the most radical reforms it has experienced since the time of Atatürk. So much has changed, and the military high command – to its credit – has allowed the changes to happen. Not without a good deal of soul-searching, and plenty of dragging of feet: behind the imposing walls of the General Staff building in Ankara some ferocious debates are still taking place, and there are clear lines which the generals would not allow the country to cross. But in the last few years, in pursuit of EU membership, reforms have been pushed through parliament which would have been unthinkable a decade ago.

Most importantly the National Security Council, where government and military leaders meet regularly to discuss the issues of the day, has been put under civilian control and its power has been proscribed. As recently as the late 1990s, the council was a 'parallel government', the forum from which the military controlled the country. Squabbling politicians would troop in nervously once a month to be confronted by stern-faced generals with thick files of information and policy 'requests' for their consideration. Now the most senior military officials say plainly that parliament is the country's supreme authority, and it is their duty to serve it. That is quite an admission for a Turkish general to make, especially at a time when parliament is run by a party with Islamist roots and the largest popular mandate for many years.

In the spring of 2004, Cyprus became a test case for this new spirit of democratization and civilian authority. The army has nearly forty thousand troops based in the Turkish-controlled north of the island, and it had many reservations about the latest United Nations plan for reunification. Cyprus gives the generals strategic depth – an 'aircraft carrier' in the middle of the Mediterranean to guard the soft underbelly of Anatolia. They know that any eventual deal between the Greek Cypriots in the south and the Turkish Cypriots in the north will include provisions for the withdrawal of all but a handful of Turkish troops, and the National Security Council was extremely sceptical.

The government in Ankara, though, had other ideas, and it threw thirty years of Turkish policy on Cyprus into the waste bin. When Prime Minister Erdoğan, supported by the rest of the international community, urged Turkish Cypriots to vote in favour of the UN plan, defenders of the 'Devlet' objected loudly. But the government stood its ground, and the military high command acquiesced. The Defence Ministry still takes orders from the armed forces on a daily basis, but on this occasion civilian rule prevailed.

It may well prove to have been a turning point in government–military relations in Turkey: elected politicians with strong popular support persuaded the generals to go against their natural instincts. Military leaders had always regarded security issues like Cyprus as part of their personal fiefdom – the politicians were useful only when they needed someone to sign the cheques. For many years after 1950, when Turkey held its first free multi-party elections, the security establishment wondered whether it had simply made a terrible mistake. The voters knew that if the politicians made a real mess of things, the military would intervene. 'For a while I suppose we had power without responsibility,' former Prime Minister Bülent Ecevit once told me, 'and it wasn't good for our system.'

In fact, between 1960 and 1980 the armed forces carried out three

coups. These were not Latin American or African-style coups. None of
them were for personal gain, there were no missing millions stashed
away in Swiss bank accounts, and on each occasion they withdrew to the
barracks after a few years. It was deeply undemocratic and a lot of people
lost their lives: thousands were tortured and imprisoned without trial,
and many political scores were settled. The scars left in the aftermath of
the 1980 coup still haven't healed a quarter of a century later. But at the
time the main motivation was simple – to put the country 'back on the
right path'. The civilians couldn't be trusted, the path was too narrow,
and the army had to show them the way forward.

In 1997, the military intervened once more to help remove Turkey's
first Islamist prime minister, Necmettin Erbakan, from office. Erbakan
had talked of an Islamic NATO, an Islamic currency and the return of
religious rule. The generals took many security decisions without
consulting him at all, and they soon made it clear that Mr Erbakan had
to go. There were no tanks outside the prime ministry this time, no
troops on the streets – instead the military engineered it all with
concerted pressure from behind the scenes, spiced with more of those
famous briefings to convey their message to the country. The pundits
dubbed it a 'postmodern coup' but the result was the same. Elected
politicians were shown the door, and even if most people weren't that
sorry to see them go, the outside world took note of who still had the
final word in Turkish politics.

Could it happen again? Well, in theory it could (although it is hard to
imagine the army destabilizing or even overthrowing a government
which was actually negotiating entry into the European Union). But this
time the military has, on the surface, withdrawn further than ever before
from routine control over the affairs of state. To take just a few examples:
there are no longer military representatives on the supervisory bodies
which oversee higher education and broadcasting; security courts which,
with a military judge on the panel, were set up to deal with 'offences
against the indivisible integrity of the state' have been abolished; and
military spending – worth billions of pounds a year – has been brought
under some kind of civilian control for the first time.

All these reforms are seen by hardliners among the Kemalist faithful
as huge and sometimes dangerous concessions, under pressure from
Europe.

'They don't understand us,' is the constant refrain. 'If you're Sweden or Luxembourg, then threats from ethnic separatism or radical Islam may seem rather distant. Here, they are our reality.'

They have a point, but sometimes they take it too far. In January 2004 army intelligence officers sent a letter to military units and local governors asking them to collect information on groups who engage in 'divisive and destructive activities' in Turkey. Among them, the letter advised, could be religious orders, ethnic minorities, Masonic lodges, Satanists, and (was this worst of all?) 'individuals known to support the United States and the European Union'.

'Perhaps they've become confused and they're spying on themselves,' mused a friend in Istanbul, with memories of military service still fresh in his mind. 'These must be trying times for them.'

Trying times indeed, because many in the military thought they already had the political checks and balances they wanted. The current constitution was written under military instruction in 1982 as 'an armoured wall against those who want to split our country'. Now the reforms demanded by the EU, and strongly supported by a majority of Turks, are picking it apart line by line. On a sliding scale running from 'cautious' through 'uneasy' up to 'apoplectic', senior military officers find it hard to take. Even the most reform-minded chief of the general staff for years, General Hilmi Özkök, told reporters in May 2003 that 'it is not right to do everything in order to join the EU. We must be allowed,' he concluded, 'to join Europe with our honour intact.'

Honour and duty: the watchwords of these self-appointed guardians of the Kemalist tradition. For years, the armed forces have been the most popular and most revered institution in the country. And the most trusted. Even when the generals intervened directly in politics – in 1960, 1971 and 1980 – they did so with the support of much of the population. They still retain respect as the heirs of Atatürk, and of the men who won the War of Independence. But that was all a long time ago, and since the 1980s, in particular, their country has been changing before their eyes.

It started with Turgut Özal, an Anatolian whirlwind of a man, who brought back civilian rule with a bang in 1983. When the generals decided to hold an election to restore parliamentary democracy, they allowed Özal, an economic technocrat, to form what they thought would be a minor opposition party. He won the election easily, routing the party favoured by the military. As prime minister and then president in the 1980s and early 90s, he went on to threaten many entrenched interests.

Born in a village and educated in America, he liberalized the economy and broke many taboos, talking about Kurds and Islam in a way which was shocking then in its frankness. He declared publicly that twelve million Turkish citizens were Kurds (his own grandmother had been one of them); he stood up to the military and once vetoed the appointment of a new chief of the general staff; he became the first Turkish president to make the *haj* to Mecca, but he was also partial to the finest brandy; and he persuaded his people that consumerism was good, and that it was time for them all to express themselves more freely.

By giving Turkey a tantalizing glimpse of the wider world, Özal took the genie out of the bottle. If he hadn't died before his time in 1993, he might have pushed through many of the changes which Tayyip Erdoğan has since accomplished. Özal was followed by a string of weak leaders, which helped the Kemalist establishment to hang onto power for a few more years. But it was clear that the pace of change in society had begun to outrun it. Turkey today is a far more open place than it was twenty years ago, more questions are being asked, and the assumption that the old ways are the only ways no longer holds good.

Even the image of the armed forces as honest and diligent has taken quite a few knocks, despite concerted efforts to keep it unblemished. You can still see proud families gathering near intercity bus stops, a troupe of local musicians in tow, waiting to wave their sons away on military service. In an era of mobile phones and Internet cafés, being cut off is not the absolute concept it used to be. But for many village boys two years of military service is often their first real view of the outside world, a rite of passage which can offer a route out of poverty and a chance to build a new life.

Some of them travel far and wide – Turkish troops have served abroad with great distinction from the Korean War to Kosovo, and lately in post-9/11 Afghanistan. But the greatest traumas come closest to home. The Kurdish insurrection of the 1980s and 1990s was the most brutal of civil wars, and no army can escape unscathed from such an experience. Many ordinary people from the south-eastern provinces where the conflict raged grew to fear and hate the men in uniform. The regular army was never quite as unpopular as the gendarmerie or the despised 'special team' police units, but much blood was spilt all the same, and it hasn't been forgotten.

As the war dragged on, efforts to protect the image of the loyal 'Mehmet' doing his duty intensified. The media ran a campaign called 'Hand in Hand with Mehmetçik' to raise money, support the troops and show them at their best.

'Schoolchildren gave their pocket money and our poorer citizens donated their livestock, an ox or a sheep,' the president of the Turkish Journalists Association announced. 'Mehmetçik is the substance and core of our nation, and by embracing Mehmetçik, the nation also embraced its unity and integrity.'

Most popular of all was a long-running TV programme called *Mehmetçik* (literally 'Little Mehmet'), which featured soldiers doing what soldiers are supposed to do in the movies. I have to admit I was a bit of a fan of its heady combination of fierce patriotism and sentimentality. Conscripts ran through fields and fired their weapons, they looked aggressive on the parade ground, and they shouted 'I love Turkey' at the camera. Family members were brought in for surprise reunions with their sons, there was lots of cheering and crying and martial music. Intrigued by the programme's undoubted success, I went to see Mehmet Özer at TGRT, the television station which produced it. When I asked him to explain its timeless appeal, he shrugged his shoulders, and said it was simple.

'As a nation we love soldiers. It's something we've inherited from our fathers and our grandfathers. When people watch this programme they feel that they're watching themselves . . . we've all been there at one time or another.'

Mehmetçik struck me as harmless fun, but it also served the army's purpose rather well. This was the image that the high command wanted the public to see: Mehmet and his comrades, proud of their army, serving their country and returning safely to their towns and villages. But as restrictions on freedom of expression began to be challenged more and more openly, a less rose-tinted version of military life emerged as well. The most powerful indictment appeared in a book written by the campaigning journalist, Nadire Mater: *Mehmet's Book* contained eye-witness accounts from forty-two soldiers who fought in the south-east against the PKK.

In graphic first-person narratives, these anonymous conscripts talk of the camaraderie and intensity of military life in a war zone. They also describe scenes of brutality and corruption, incompetence and drug-smuggling. No one in Turkey had ever read anything quite like it before:

'Filth, discipline, cursing and beating . . . I can't tell you how much I was beaten.'

'One of our vehicles hit a mine and was damaged, but no one was hurt. An old couple from the village were walking by on their way to the hospital. One of the soldiers got out of his car and shot the man on the spot. He was killed. The old woman was crying . . .'

'The first person I hit was a child. He was throwing stones. Five or six of us hit him. He was about thirteen or fourteen years old.'

'The military is supplied with trucks full of food and it disappears. Corruption is widespread. It's absurd. What are we dying for? The war is fought for money, for filling people's pockets.'

Nadire Mater began compiling her interviews after a neighbour sat down for four hours without prompting and poured out his story. When *Mehmet's Book* was first published it caused a sensation, quickly selling out its first print runs and producing a thriving trade in pirated copies. But it also attracted the attention of the military high command. A senior general made a formal complaint and a few days later a court in Istanbul banned the book and started legal proceedings against her.

'It's not me who has been banned by the court,' she said at the time. 'It's the soldiers who served in the south-east. If they are heroes why are they being prevented from speaking out?'

Nadire Mater was facing up to twelve years in jail for 'insulting the armed forces of the state'. Eventually, under a changing legal climate, freedom of speech prevailed and the case against her and her publisher was dismissed, although other related cases were pursued through the judicial system by zealous prosecutors for several years. The truth of course is that *Mehmet's Book* only scratched the surface. More than two million young men served in the south-east during the worst years of the

Kurdish conflict, and many of them witnessed terrible events. But issues such as post-traumatic stress are rarely discussed. Nothing is allowed to sully the military's heroic role and the depiction of the war as a patriotic struggle against terrorism. Relatives of soldiers who died fighting against the PKK, known as the 'Families of the Martyrs', are often at the forefront of efforts to maintain the pretence that this was a good clean war – who can blame them for needing to believe that their sons died for the best of causes.

Many young Turks, though, have heard all about the more sobering reality of life in uniform. Many of them will now go to great lengths to avoid military service, even though the south-east became far more peaceful following the capture of the PKK leader, Abdullah Öcalan. Students are forever discussing how they can avoid being drafted, whether they can beat the system, and trying to find someone who might have a quiet word about where they might be sent. So it was no surprise that when a new system was introduced in 1999, to allow would-be recruits to buy their way out of all but a few weeks of their military obligation, thousands jumped at the chance. For those who could afford it, fifteen thousand German marks was a price worth paying to avoid a year or more in uniform. They were sent off for a few weeks to run round the parade ground and listen to lectures about how great their country is.

'It was absurd,' one reluctant attendee told me, 'and I hated every minute of it. These people are living on a different planet.'

But even the new system didn't last long. It was, the armed forces explained, only a temporary measure, designed to get rid of an embarrassing backlog of cases. The length of military service has been shortened slightly but it remains compulsory. Without a good medical reason every young Turkish man passes through the military system for a short time, and all attempts by the AKP government to change the rules have failed. Many conscripts clearly believe it's a waste of their time, and they wonder whether the threats they are supposed to be defending their country against have been exaggerated for years. There would be plenty more volunteers willing to pay to avoid life in uniform but why, asks the army, should the privileged be exempt?

Out in the villages, a majority of Turks would still agree. Imam Yaşayan's family, for example, are too poor to ever imagine buying their way out of military service. They live on a remote hillside in the province of Erzurum, where they farm a small plot of land. Imam's son Bilgin was killed by the PKK while he was on military service and a second son committed suicide shortly after his brother's death. Their gravestones now stand in the windswept field behind the house where they grew up.

'I'm a proud father, but I miss them,' Imam said as we stood next to the graves, staring down at the river in the valley below. 'They had a lot to live for here, but it was God's will, and I don't think they died in vain.'

On our way back from the Yaşayans' house, we were detained at a checkpoint in the middle of nowhere for passing through the same place earlier in the day without an officer's permission. We were escorted to the headquarters of the local gendarmerie and ushered in to see the boss, a major as I recall.

'Why did you go through my checkpoint?'

'Er, well, your soldiers lifted the barrier and let us through.'

'You shouldn't have done it. I'm in charge here. I should have been informed.'

He was courteous but relentlessly suspicious. What were we doing on this quiet country road? Whom were we going to see? Why hadn't the security forces been told of our plans?

Since we were a long way from anywhere which could remotely be described as rebel-infested territory, I was tempted to cry 'paranoia', 'none of your business' and lose my temper. Instead I paced grumpily up and down his office, and rather gracelessly refused his offer of a cup of tea. Our story was checked and checked again, radio messages were sent and received, and finally we were free to go. As we rushed outside to embark upon a near-suicidal drive to catch the last plane of the day from a distant airport, the major threw in a parting thought.

'The Turkish armed forces are always doing the right thing, you know. I hope that's what you're going to say.'

* * *

The father of our landlady in Istanbul was a man called Hüseyin. He lived in the bottom half of our old wooden house and he had scant regard for most people in authority.

On warm summer evenings we used to sit on his small terrace and watch the world go by on the Bosphorus. Hüseyin had worked in

Germany for many years, and he'd come home to enjoy his retirement, and enjoy the view.

When he wasn't fixing the boiler in the basement, he always had a few words of advice on how to survive in the big city. No real surprise – it was all about knowing the right person.

'You have to know who does what if you want to get anything done,' he said. 'We've got three million bureaucrats in this country. Three million! Who do you think is really in charge?'

If doubts about the wisdom of reform were confined to parts of the military then perhaps Turkey's great debate could be dismissed as an argument which has already been won. The pressure for change would be too strong for the armed forces alone to resist. But the unapologetically hardline version of Kemalism has its placemen elsewhere: in politics and the judiciary, in the media and the world of business. These are the secular fundamentalists, for whom the end justifies the means. Change is to be treated with suspicion, because change brings hidden dangers. You can read their opinions in the papers, you can listen to their speeches in parliament, and you can study the verdicts passed by a generation of judges who seem to believe their role is to protect the state from its unruly people.

Then there are the bureaucrats, and there really are about three million of them. Politicians can pass as many laws as they please, but it's the bureaucracy that has to implement them. At every level of Turkish society there are state officials who wield enormous power over everyday life – granting permission, refusing permission, taking bribes and, when it suits them, taking their time. So resistance to reform has moved into a new phase. The old establishment knows it can't stop the revolutionary changes taking place in parliament, but it can try to neutralize them in the real world of regional governors, official stamps and endless forms to be signed in triplicate.

Within the system, there are still plenty of people who aren't going to go down without a fight, but this guerrilla campaign of bureaucratic resistance could be their last hurrah. However stubborn they are, members of the old guard are suddenly under real pressure. For most of the 1990s a succession of weak coalition governments meant that opponents of democratization still had the upper hand. Fears of ethnic separatism (i.e. Kurds) and religious extremism (i.e. political Islam) added to the firm belief in parts of the establishment that now was the time to batten down the hatches.

Eagle-eyed prosecutors were encouraged to hunt far and wide for enemies of the state, and there was a mania for closing down political parties, with the usual suspects in the frame. The pro-Islamist parties, Welfare and Virtue, forerunners of the current government, were banned in the 1990s; and the main pro-Kurdish party became accustomed to reinventing itself after a succession of legal onslaughts. Between 1993 and 2003 the People's Labour Party (HEP) and its successor the Democracy Party (DEP) were banned and replaced by the People's Democracy Party (HADEP), which was banned and replaced by the Democratic People's Party (DEHAP), which is in turn under threat of closure itself. An alphabet soup of political labels if ever there was one, but these were all deliberate variations on the same name, in essence the same party, run and supported by the same people.

'You'd never let all these separatists sit in your parliament!' an indignant lady with lifelong Kemalist sympathies told a friend of mine, forgetting for a moment about Scottish Nationalists, Welsh nationalists and Sinn Fein. Defenders of the old system weren't that interested in what the rest of the world was doing. But in the country at large the clamour for change in all walks of life was growing louder and louder, and the impetus for reform coincided with progress in Turkey's longstanding application to join the European Union (a Kemalist goal, don't forget). In 1999 the EU decided for the first time that Turkey should have the official status of 'candidate for membership'. To many Turks it all seemed rather grudging, especially as they had just suffered the indignity of watching countries as influential as Estonia, Malta and Slovakia jump the queue. But it *was* progress, and the government of the day, led by Bülent Ecevit, was under pressure to prove that Turkey meant business.

It started slowly, with Mr Ecevit's awkward coalition of nationalists, conservatives and reformers bickering about what to do next and finally making some initial changes. But under the next government, led by Recep Tayyip Erdoğan – the first single-party government in more than a decade – the trickle has become a flood. Curbing the power of the military was just the start. The civil and criminal codes have been thoroughly overhauled, hundreds of laws have been rewritten and dozens of constitutional amendments have sailed through parliament. The death penalty has been abolished, broadcasting and education in Kurdish has been legalized, it's been made more difficult (but certainly not impossible) to close down political parties, there's much greater protection for individual rights, and many restrictions on free speech have been swept away.

In less than four years, Turkey has been transformed – on paper, at least. Most galling for the old guard is the fact that this new revolution has been led not by traditional secular republican politicians, but by a party with Islamist roots, a party many of them still fear and mistrust. They find it hard to accept that the road to Europe has been paved by the very people they think want to cut them off from 'civilization' for ever. I wonder what some of the judges I've seen in court cases in various parts of Turkey must have thought when they were asked to take part, under the government of the AKP, in the Ministry of Justice's new human rights initiative, backed by the European Union. Thousands of judges and prosecutors have been given training in the basic standards of human rights law – something they would never before have been taught in detail.

Even for the most enthusiastic reformers, the speed and scale of the legal changes is a daunting challenge. I always found attending Turkish courts a bewildering experience at the best of times, but new courts of every kind – for divorce cases, juvenile cases and intellectual property infringements – have sprung up almost overnight. There's a new court of appeal as well, and the most distinguished lawyers have been throwing out their well-thumbed books and restocking their shelves.

Canan Arın answers the door with a telephone in each hand, apparently in the middle of three conversations at once. A lawyer specializing in women's rights, she has never known such a busy time.

'It's exhausting,' she says cheerfully, 'a constant battle. Sit down if you can find a space.'

There are huge piles of paper on her desk, and the phone rings again. Everyone has to learn the new laws from scratch.

'We have to fight to make sure the laws they pass in parliament are good,' she says. 'When it comes to laws affecting women, there's no guarantee of that. Then we have to fight to make sure they're implemented properly, and that people know what rights they have.'

'Can the system cope with so much so quickly?'

'It's going to have to cope. We'll all work a little harder. We've been waiting for these reforms for a long time.'

Many modernizing judges are equally pleased, even if it will take years to get through the backlog of cases, but some of their colleagues must be dismayed by the general tone of the changes taking place. The zealots among them have long assumed that the rights of the state take precedence over the rights of the individual. That is the basic premise of the 1982 constitution, and it is being thoroughly undermined. There are many shades of opinion at senior levels of both the judiciary and the armed forces, and many high-ranking individuals in military and civilian life are torn, not quite knowing which way to turn.

The Turkish president, Ahmet Necdet Sezer, is a former chief justice of the Constitutional Court, and no one would question his Kemalist credentials, nor his defence of secularism. In the summer of 2004 he vetoed an education bill which would have allowed graduates of religious schools better access to university, and a local government bill which he thought would relax bans on wearing the Islamic headscarf in public buildings. Yet at the same time he is seen as a reformer, committed to greater freedom of speech, to anti-corruption investigations, and to Turkey's bid to join the European Union. With his strained public persona, and his deeply ingrained sense of duty, he seems to embody the dilemma of the ruling elite: how much freedom can we really afford?

And so the battle for Turkey's soul goes on, a complex many-layered debate. Just as it would be absurd to argue that all Islamists are fundamentalists, so it would be ridiculous to claim that all Kemalists are opposed to change. Many of them are passionate supporters of reform, who have been working for years to create a more modern and dynamic country. But within their ranks there is an unbending faction which wants to keep Turkey in glorious isolation. They are authoritarian supporters of a strong state, anti-Western and anti-democratic. They quote and follow Kemal Atatürk selectively, and they don't like the direction in which the new Turkey is heading.

During the NATO summit in Istanbul in June 2004, with George W. Bush in town and half the Turkish navy anchored in the Bosphorus, I sat in a garden on the Asian side of the city admiring the view across the water. I'd come to see Cüneyt Ülsever – a perceptive columnist who has the interesting job of putting the alternative view to the readers of *Hürriyet*, one of the newspapers of the establishment.

As we munched cherries and watched the warships in the distance, we talked about the future for the hardline defenders of the faith.

'I call them the status quo,' he said, 'because that's what they want: no change. Think about it – no one likes to give up power, and they have a lot of it . . . political power, economic power; they won't let it go without a big struggle.'

'But can they win? Can they turn the clock back again?'

'I doubt it. The tug of war will continue, but I think the old-style Kemalists are swimming against the tide.'

* * *

A lot of it has got to do with how public perceptions have changed, sometimes dramatically, during the course of the last decade. The myth of 'Baba Devlet' – the Daddy State which knew best and would provide from the cradle to the grave – has taken some hard knocks. Many supporters of the old system grew rich and powerful because of their control over the national economy – an often unholy alliance of bureaucrats and businessmen who carved things up between them while the rest of the country was suffering from soaring inflation, rampant corruption and a string of economic crises. The worst of them, in 2001, caused untold misery for millions of Turks. It was one mistake too many for a system in which politics, business and money had formed a self-perpetuating elite.

There have been other infamous low points – devastating scandals involving shady characters and dubious links with the criminal underworld and the violent extremes of Turkish politics. Most prominent was a famous car crash in the western town of Susurluk in 1996, which sent out shock waves which were felt for years. A senior police chief died in the crash, so did a wanted gangster named Abdullah Çatlı, and his girlfriend, a former beauty queen. They had all been travelling in a black Mercedes which careered into a truck at high speed on a rainy night. The only survivor was Sedat Bucak, a powerful Kurdish clan leader and a member of parliament friendly to the state. He had made millions from running his private army of village guards during the war against the

PKK. Bucak lost his memory completely in the crash, which was extremely convenient. False diplomatic passports, weapons, money and a host of incriminating documents were recovered from the wreckage.

This was what Turks call the 'deep state' unmasked. Compelling evidence emerged of collusion between politicians, the security forces and the criminal underworld – Çatlı had been a state-sponsored assassin heavily involved in the heroin-smuggling trade. Many ordinary citizens were outraged, and for a while it became fashionable in Turkish cities to turn off your lights at nine o'clock every night as part of a mass civil protest against 'deep state' corruption. People would fling open their windows and bang saucepans together as the 'One Minute of Darkness for Enlightenment' campaign launched a growing public demand for explanations.

A few middle-ranking officials were prosecuted, and a senior intelligence official, retired colonel Korkut Eken, was eventually sent to jail for 'forming an illegal gang'. But others higher up the chain of command emerged unscathed. On his release in July 2004 Eken was unrepentant. His first act was to visit Atatürk's mausoleum, where he rededicated himself to fighting for his version of the founding father's legacy.

'I never lost my commitment to eliminate threats directed at the security of the state,' he told a crowd of his supporters who accompanied him in a long convoy of cars. 'I was put in jail because of a campaign of slander waged by traitors trying to pacify us.'

Sedat Bucak was also eventually put on trial, after he lost his parliamentary seat and the guarantee of immunity from prosecution which accompanied it. By the end of 2004 the trial was still dragging on, and Bucak still couldn't remember anything about the accident which uncovered the Susurluk scandal.

Corruption, incompetence, and shady underworld connections: add all of these things together and it was clear that the idea of the state as an all-seeing, all-knowing force for good had lost its credibility. The state wasn't all bad, but the old sense of subservience has now gone for ever. It has been a gradual process, hastened by a growing awareness of the outside world, and an impatient desire to throw off the shackles of centralized control. But I have a very precise personal memory of when I think change became irreversible.

17 August 1999: in the middle of a sweltering summer. At just after three in the morning I was fast asleep in Ankara when my wife got out of bed and woke me up.

'I thought someone was trying to get in through the window,' she said. 'I heard banging . . . there are people out on the street. What's happening?'

I grunted and tried to close my eyes, but a few minutes later the phone rang. 'There's been an earthquake . . .' said a disembodied BBC voice from London, and all thoughts of sleep were gone.

We were lucky to be a long way from the epicentre at the eastern end of the Sea of Marmara, an hour's drive from Istanbul. Thousands of people died instantly in their beds, thousands more lost their lives trapped in the rubble, waiting for help that never came. The earthquake was a devastating example of the destructive power of nature, and any country would have struggled to cope. But when the Turkish state came face to face with a massive humanitarian disaster, it failed time and time again.

Snapshots from the first forty-eight hours have stayed in my mind. An elderly man armed only with a shovel trying to dig through layers of collapsed concrete, looking for his three grandchildren; young soldiers ordered to stand guard at the gate of the shattered naval base in Gölçük, as chaos reigned in the streets around them and people begged for help; the dust-covered face of a boy we could see but couldn't reach, trapped in the ruins of his home. And while the system creaked, and politicians dithered, private rescue teams of mountaineers and cavers turned up to help. Satellite trucks from local TV stations arrived faster than emergency vehicles run by the state – and when offers of foreign aid began pouring in, the Minister of Health said he didn't want any Greek or Armenian blood. Turks watched, horrified but transfixed, as the drama was played out live on their screens.

Five days after the earthquake I was looking rather forlornly for a bit of shade in the middle of Adapazarı, one of the cities worst hit by the disaster. On the other side of the road, I saw a man digging through the rubble with his bare hands. After a couple of moments he pulled something out, through a shower of dust. It was a typewriter. He set it down, cleaned it carefully with the bottom of his shirt, and walked away. It was stiflingly hot. A few minutes later he was back, with a slightly tattered piece of paper. I've no idea where he'd found it, but he sat on a bit of concrete, put the typewriter on a broken chair, and began to type.

I think he was writing a letter. I didn't ask him why, or to whom. There was nowhere he could possibly post it. Strangely enough, it didn't seem to matter. He was simply happy to be doing something. A couple of days before, I'd seen little more than people staring at the tableau of twisted buildings all around them, struck dumb by a feeling of helplessness, by the enormity of what had happened. Now there was a change of mood. The situation was still desperate, the region remained in a dangerous state of flux with almost no infrastructure and not much leadership, but human activity had resumed. Some people cycled down the road at high speed. Others picked up bits of litter, or began to sweep small sections of the pavement. There was so much to do. And they were all suddenly doing something.

It had taken only forty-five seconds to tear their world apart. Forty-five seconds when the earth moved beneath them as they slept. Lives were broken and myths were shattered. The biggest myth of all: that the state was supremely powerful, that it would always provide. When the moment of greatest need arrived, the state could not deliver. Shock was followed by anger, and then – five days later – by action. People were doing it for themselves. They cursed their politicians, their bureaucrats and their system, and then they got on with things. Belatedly the authorities sprang into action: the paralysis of the first few days passed, but the damage had already been done.

For several generations of Turks who had been brought up to believe in their state, and in its central role in their lives, that became the biggest aftershock of all. 'Fiasco' screamed the Turkish media, 'Chaos', 'Shame'. Shadowy building contractors – the men who built castles out of sand – had been allowed to get away with murder. Development was progress, they had said, and Turkey was developing fast. But it was all about profit before safety, and when the walls came tumbling down, the thieves slipped away into the night. One contractor who failed to go to ground quickly enough was nearly lynched by an angry crowd.

Private enterprise had been given free rein, and allowed to abuse the system with petty corruption. Regulations were ignored, corners cut, and people lived in high-rise death traps. One day, warned the experts, an earthquake will come. No one in the system was prepared to listen, and ordinary people paid the price. Well-to-do middle-class Turks were buried in their holiday homes in the seaside town of Yalova. Poor rural migrants from the east of the country disappeared under the concrete in Izmit. Few people across this vast land were unaffected by the tragedy. Almost everyone knew someone who was there, and only the lucky ones survived.

Suddenly they wanted to know who would be held accountable. The scale of the disaster was huge; any country would have been reeling. But delay and incompetence and inaction cost lives. Calls for fundamental political and social reform were in the air – and that became the earthquake's lasting legacy. Even the military, the symbol of a strong centralized state, came under fire. Soldiers were insulted on the streets. 'You could have helped us,' sobbed one woman near Gölçük, 'but you chose not to come. Please tell me why.'

In the midst of confusion and grief, some looked for answers elsewhere. The pious suggested the earthquake was a sign from God – punishing the country for abandoning its beliefs. Islamist politicians hoped to gain protest votes, and their grass-roots networks proved far more efficient in helping the survivors than the cumbersome centralized bureaucracy. The government of the time, led by the veteran Bülent Ecevit, thought it could wait for the storm to pass. It appealed for national unity as it turned to the massive task of reconstruction. But I don't think the old political order ever recovered entirely from the failures of those terrible August days. As rebuilding began, there was a nagging fear at the back of everyone's mind: will the same mistakes be made again, in a country where memories are sometimes short?

I was struck at the time by one particular campaign: Turkish newspapers urged their readers to play a simple role – to donate at least one brick each to reconstruct cities from scratch. It was a good symbol then, and it remains one now. A wall in which every brick is important, just like a state in which every citizen plays a valued role. After the earthquake, survivors wanted to rebuild in a safer and more modern way. Not just their cities, but also their system. They wanted a blueprint for the future. The man with the typewriter in Adapazarı may have been writing the same thing.

* * *

On the eve of the fifth anniversary of the earthquake I sought out Ahmet Mete Işıkara, who must have been as surprised as anyone when he was voted Turkey's sexiest man in the months after disaster struck. A hunched figure with a striking resemblance to Albert Einstein, he was an unlikely candidate for such an accolade, but for years Professor Işıkara had been like a prophet in the wilderness. As the director of the Kandilli Earthquake Research Institute in Istanbul he had been preaching a message which no one chose to hear – an earthquake is coming, and we're not ready. When it actually happened (twice in the space of three months) Turks suddenly hung on his every word. He became a cult figure. Kids knew him as 'depremdede' – Grandpa Earthquake – as he launched a huge public awareness campaign to prepare the country for the next Big One.

Now retired, Professor Işıkara is kept busy with his educational work.

'It's not a question of whether Istanbul will be hit, but when,' he says. 'We know that, and we have to be prepared.'

A start has been made. Survey ships track the mysteries of the North Anatolian fault beneath the Sea of Marmara, and a network of extra seismic monitoring stations records even the tiniest movement. Building regulations have been tightened, and rules are actually being followed. A significant proportion of survivors in 1999 believed God would decide the timing of the next earthquake, and God would decide who lives and who dies. With such fatalism deeply ingrained, the battle to make sure the right long-term decisions are taken – better quality housing in safer geological areas, for example – may be harder than many people expect.

In parts of the city the only really safe solution would be to knock down thousands of buildings and relocate millions of people. Politically, that may be too hard to do, but new earthquake-proof buildings – which could have saved thousands of lives in 1999 – are now being built in Istanbul and elsewhere. It's not perfect, there is still corruption, but it's much better than it used to be. When Professor Işıkara moved into one new building development, sales there suddenly boomed. If it was safe enough for him, they thought . . .

Now, sitting in the relative calm of his daughter's Istanbul café, he looked at his food, set down his fork, and twirled his prayer beads through his fingers one more time.

'I think we'll be much better prepared next time. At least we'll have a plan. There's always a bit of chaos, there's bound to be confusion, but it can be managed. The earthquake in 99 changed so many things: Turkey's a different place today.'

3

ISLAM AND THE POLITICS OF PRAYER

In March 1999 Tayyip Erdoğan arrived in the small western town of Pınarhisar accompanied by thousands of his supporters in a huge convoy of cars. The mood was determined but subdued. This was no celebration. Turkey's most ambitious politician, a devout Muslim, was about to go to prison for inciting religious hatred.

You can still see evidence of his 'crime' in grainy video footage of a speech he gave in the small south-eastern town of Siirt, where he belted out a rousing Islamist poem.

'The mosques are our barracks, the domes our helmets,' he thunders, 'the minarets our bayonets and the faithful our soldiers.'

No one, he declares, can ever intimidate us. 'My reference is Islam. If I am not able to speak of this – what is the point of living?'

It was all too much for Turkey's powerful secular establishment, led by the military. No matter that the offending poem had been written by a well-known nationalist ideologue in the early twentieth century, the charismatic Erdoğan was seen as a threat. He had already been appointed the first pro-Islamist mayor of Istanbul – a rising political star and a man of the people, who had begun modernizing and cleaning up Turkey's biggest city. Now it was time to put him in his place.

So Tayyip Erdoğan was convicted and removed from office; but he wasn't beaten.

'This is not a farewell,' he said on the day his sentence began. 'I hope it is just a pause in a series of songs still to be finished.'

Little more than five years later, witness Erdoğan's transformation:

not only a free man but prime minister, armed with a huge parliamentary majority, and at the end of 2004 winning an elusive date from the European Union for talks on Turkey's membership. The man of faith now says he wants to prove that Islam and democracy can go hand in hand.

'Religion shouldn't interfere with issues of government,' he said carefully, when we met at the prime minister's official residence in Ankara. 'But government shouldn't interfere with issues of religion either. That's the message we're trying to spread.'

* * *

He was a tall pious young man from Kasımpaşa, on the northern shores of the Golden Horn, who mixed his studies at the religious high school with his love of football. They used to call him Imam Beckenbauer. When he was growing up in working-class Istanbul, selling bread in the streets to buy his books, Tayyip Erdoğan stood out as a footballer of rare promise. Taking his nickname from the legendary German Franz Beckenbauer, Erdoğan went on to play for amateur and semi-professional teams for sixteen years. Remember Beckenbauer? My own childhood memories are of an unquestioned leader, the most influential player on the pitch, the man in charge. And that's still Erdoğan today. He may not be the greatest political visionary, and he's not entirely comfortable on the international stage, but he has a dogged determination to succeed.

Plenty of people still remember the fiery young activist who wouldn't shake hands with a woman, and thought Turkey should be looking east rather than west. He was photographed sitting at the feet of the Afghan warlord Gulbeddin Hekmatyar, and when he became mayor of Istanbul he quickly banned alcohol from city-run cafés and restaurants. But after cutting his teeth in radical Islamic politics Erdoğan insists that he has changed. He now comes across as a pragmatist, and a proud nationalist, who wants what's best for himself and his country. His political party, the Justice and Development Party (in Turkish: Adalet ve Kalkınma Partisi or AKP), is a broad and sometimes fractious coalition. It ranges from the modernizing middle ground of Turkish politics to traditional religious conservatives rooted in political Islam. Erdoğan's task is to hold this grand alliance together – and his main rallying cry has been Europe.

He was tired when I met him ('a permanent condition,' said one of his aides, 'it goes with the job'). It was near the end of another gruelling political day, but he wasn't complaining. After all, he said, this was what he dreamt about when he was in jail – his desire to serve his people. Erdoğan told me that prison had another, more important effect – it matured and revitalized him. In his first two years as Turkey's leader he passed more democratic reforms than previous Turkish governments had managed in two decades. And yet, the suspicions still linger.

'Some people,' I suggested, 'still think you're a fundamentalist.'

The prime minister sighed, then smiled, then fixed me with his hard stare.

'We're fed up with accusations like this.' He frowned. 'We're not a party based on religious values. When I'm at home, I'm a Muslim; when I'm in the office, I work for democracy. We've got a job to do here and we shouldn't get distracted.'

But there's a question which continues to haunt him, a question he can't quite brush off. Is he practising political *takkiye* – the idea that a Muslim can hide his real opinion to gain a practical advantage?

His recent record suggests that he's not, despite a few stutters along the way, and most observers of Turkish politics seem prepared to give him the benefit of the doubt.

'It's a legitimate thing to ask, given the militancy of his youth and his post-youth. But I think he's been able to prove that he is a case of change.'

I was drinking tea in Istanbul with Cengiz Çandar, one of Turkey's most perceptive political columnists. As we watched the commuter ferries scurrying to and fro across the water, we discussed the Erdoğan effect.

'He's got backbone,' Çandar said, 'which is rare on the Turkish political scene. And he is willing to learn from his mistakes.'

But his political opponents aren't convinced. They see a not-so-hidden agenda of promoting Islam and its values. Why does he always mention religion in his speeches, they ask? Why does he give senior positions in the state bureaucracy to people who don't support the secular system? And why, from time to time, does he provoke sudden unease by turning to an Islamist agenda – trying to get more religious students into universities or supporting plans to make adultery a criminal offence?

The sense of suspicion has been heightened by the clear divide in the Turkish parliament. When the AKP swept to power in 2002, the only other party to win any seats at all was the staunchly secular Republican People's Party (CHP), founded by Atatürk and still the standard-bearer of Kemalism.

'I just don't think that Mr Erdoğan shares our commitment to European values,' Onur Öymen, a former ambassador to NATO and a leading member of the CHP, told me. 'He can tick the boxes, he understands what it's all about, and that's fine. But I'm not sure that he believes in it.'

Perhaps Tayyip Erdoğan can't win, because he's trying to be all things to all men. Many of his supporters are Islamic conservatives – and he's under as much pressure from them as he is from European politicians or Turkish generals. His decision to back the adultery bill caused consternation in the late summer of 2004, and threatened a crisis in relations with Europe. Erdoğan was in the process of finalizing a major reform and modernization of Turkey's penal code – increasing penalties for torture, and for violence against women. Did he really think he could make adultery illegal at the same time, just to keep everyone happy? If so, he miscalculated.

Turkish feminists howled in protest – they were convinced that the law would be biased against women – and European officials suggested Erdoğan was signing his own political death warrant. So the pragmatist took a step back, and the plans were withdrawn, but his critics were already in full flow. Pragmatic perhaps, they still sniff, but he mixes his politics with piety.

Bedri Baykam is an outspoken sceptic when it comes to analyzing Tayyip Erdoğan's motives.

'Maybe the adultery law opened a few eyes,' he said, leaning across the table towards me. His thick mane of hair bounced vigorously, and the small Atatürk badge on his lapel gleamed under the café lights. Baykam had begun exhibiting vivid drawings and paintings at the age of seven, when the *Daily Mail* called him a 'prodigy with a paintbrush'; now he is one of Turkey's most famous artists. When he's not dreaming up another artistic coup, designed to shock or provoke someone or other, he is an outspoken defender of the secular faith.

'There are all these people in Turkey today,' he said, jabbing his finger in my general direction, 'who portray traditional Kemalists as dinosaurs. They have made Islamists respectable and it's dangerous.'

'You see, the Islamists are very patient,' he went on, warming to his theme. 'If they can't do it this year, they'll try next year; if not next year, then in five years or ten. With Erdoğan, it's a case of there he goes again, he just can't help himself.'

Baykam thumped his fist on the table for emphasis. 'In fact,' he concluded, 'it's just like the headscarf.'

* * *

I met Selma standing in a shower of warm rain outside the gates of her university campus. She was twenty-three years old, a student from the south-eastern city of Diyarbakır, where she had grown up surrounded by the PKK's bitter guerrilla war against the Turkish state. It wasn't a happy place to be. So she worked long and hard to get into university; demand for places is far higher than supply, but education was Selma's ticket out. She won a place at the prestigious Ankara University to study philosophy and when we met she was supposed to be starting the final year of her degree. Sometimes things don't work out in quite the way you expect, but Selma probably never thought she'd spend the first week of term outside the university gates, blowing a whistle and chanting slogans with her friends, as police officers looked on.

This was no ordinary student protest – classes had already started, and a steady stream of students was entering the university grounds. But Selma is different. She wears an Islamic-style headscarf, known in Turkey as a *türban*, pinned down at the chin and around the neck. Your scarf can be as multicoloured and chic as you like, as long as only the face can be seen, and the rest of the head and neck are entirely covered. That's what distinguishes the türban from the traditional loose-fitting scarf worn by many Turkish women; and it is the reason why Selma and thousands like her have been banned from the education system. In Selma's faculty, there had been no problem the previous year, and no indication that the rules were going to change. She was thinking about the future, about further academic research – but she suddenly found herself on the pavement rather than in the library.

On the first day of term the new dean of the faculty – herself a woman – had taken an even harder line. Male students wearing beards were also turned away – facial hair is enough to set alarm bells ringing among the more insistent defenders of the secular system. On day two, in a burst of liberal tolerance, the beards were let in. But Selma and the other covered women were still locked out, and they were refusing to compromise their beliefs.

'They're trying to create a uniform type of person in this country,' she told me, above the din of whistles and chants. 'They want everyone to look the same, and think the same.'

'It's not possible,' she shrugged, 'it won't happen.'

The irony is that those who seek to ban the headscarf make exactly the same point in reverse. They fear that it's a symbol of a radical polit- ical ideology, of an attempt to force all Turkish women to cover their heads. 'It's not possible,' they insist, 'it won't happen.'

'Just like the Nazi black shirts or the brown shirts of Mussolini,' warns Onur Öymen of the CHP darkly. 'Whenever anyone uses a piece of clothing in this way we have to be on our guard.'

And that's why education is one of the battlegrounds on which Turkey's secular elite has chosen to stand and fight. 'Attending univer- sity with a headscarf,' said a stern official letter sent to colleges across the country before the start of one term, 'is regarded as an ideological state- ment which disturbs the peace.'

Those who can afford to do so – or who can find sponsors among sympathizers in the pro-Islamist business community – get round the ban by studying abroad. Dilek Gölet was a medical student at Istanbul University for four years until tough new rules were imposed. Eventually she graduated as a qualified doctor in Hungary in 2003 but she still can't work in her home country. Her English is good, her qualifications are impeccable, and her expertise is needed. In fact she comes across as a model for the outward-looking pro-Western Turkey which the urban elite want to promote . . . in every sense but one.

'I'd have to take an exam to get my degree recognized by the State Medical Board,' she explained. 'And to sit that exam I'd have to take off my headscarf. So I'm still trapped.'

Her friend Ayşe Yelliburun is facing the same dilemma. She insists it was her choice to start wearing her scarf at the age of twelve, even though her mother told her to wait. Later, she says, her father told her she should take off the scarf to avoid any trouble at university.

'I didn't want to do that. Why should I? I don't force anyone else to wear a scarf. They can wear their T-shirts and their blue jeans if they like, and they should leave me to wear what I want.'

Does she expect Tayyip Erdoğan and the AKP to end the stand-off? I ask.

'I've been waiting for a political solution for years,' she replies. 'Only Allah can solve this problem.'

For a long time Turks had dealt with the headscarf issue in the most sensible way – by ignoring it wherever possible. In many Anatolian villages it is pretty rare to see a woman walking in the street without a scarf, but in big cities such as Istanbul or Ankara covered women sit alongside women wearing miniskirts in cafés and on buses and no one pays any attention. In the last few years, though, this most divisive of debates has been thrust onto the national political agenda by Islamists and secularists alike, and no one seems to have any idea how it will be resolved. After the 'soft coup' which removed Necmettin Erbakan from power in 1997, the campaign against Islamic head gear in schools, universities and public offices suddenly moved into a more aggressive phase.

In 1999 a huge row broke out in the Turkish parliament when a newly elected pro-Islamist deputy named Merve Kavakçı (hand-picked by Erbakan) became the first woman ever to wear a headscarf in the parliamentary chamber. I watched from the public gallery as she was applauded by members of her own party, the Virtue Party, but secular deputies were beside themselves with anger. They thumped their desks and screamed 'Out! Out! Out!' before the session had to be adjourned in chaos, without Merve Kavakçı taking her oath of office.

Turkey's president at the time, Süleyman Demirel, went on television to describe her as a 'provocateur' and a 'foreign agent'.

'This is very serious,' he said, 'it's a symbol of bigger things, with its roots in fundamentalism.'

For twenty-five years, the Turkish establishment has been haunted by memories of the Khomeini revolution across the border in Iran, and however over-sensitive it may seem to outsiders, they have laid down the law clearly: some things are politically unacceptable. Merve Kavakçı, a qualified software engineer with a Texas twang from her years studying in the USA, had just blundered deliberately through the red zone.

In the minds of the secular elite it was obvious that something had to be done, and within weeks they had found their solution. Merve Kavakçı, it emerged, was a dual citizen of Turkey and the United States and that disqualified her from being a parliamentary deputy. At the time the Turkish parliament included some fairly dubious characters – including a man charged with two murders, and several others who had well-established links to drug-smuggling and the mafia. They continued to benefit from parliamentary immunity while Merve Kavakçı was thrown out of her job and, eventually, out of the country.

She now makes a living, in part, by writing columns from Washington for one of Turkey's most aggressively Islamic newspapers. Perhaps her name still strikes a chord with the devout, but her intervention in parliament persuaded Turkey's leading prosecutor to launch a sweeping (and in due course successful) court case to close down the Virtue Party. He accused party members of trying to provoke religious conflict and of acting 'like vampires who will only be satisfied with blood'. The headscarf dispute in parliament had been the last straw.

And that's where Tayyip Erdoğan is different. It's hard to imagine a Merve Kavakçı appearing on his watch, if only because he knows it's a tactic which won't work. Unlike his early political mentor, Necmettin Erbakan, he doesn't want to ram political Islam down people's throats. If he senses he has pushed too far, he prefers to ease back rather than face a confrontation. When the Virtue Party was shut down, he and other more moderate members of the party split from Erbakan to form the AKP. So Erdoğan doesn't see himself as Erbakan's natural successor and he says he dislikes terms such as 'political Islam' and even 'moderate Islam' ('Are you telling me,' he once asked, 'that there is such a thing as immoderate Islam?').

Instead he refers back to two previous eras of liberalization – the reforming zeal of Turgut Özal in the 1980s and the religious revival which took place under Adnan Menderes in the 1950s. For the devout, Menderes and the Democrat Party had been a breath of fresh air – the call to prayer in Arabic was reintroduced, thousands of mosques were built and broadcasts from the Koran were allowed on the radio for the first time in modern Turkey. It was all about giving Islam more public space in which to operate, while working within the boundaries of the secular system. Menderes got it wrong in the end, rather dramatically so. There were allegations of creeping authoritarianism and he was overthrown and executed after the 1960 military coup. Erdoğan lives in a different era, but he still has to deal with tensions about the role of religion, and critics who fear that he is a wolf in sheep's clothing will never be entirely convinced.

And what about the headscarf dispute? As restrictions on the scarf have proliferated, so has a variety of ingenious methods to get around them. For years wigs worn on top of the scarf have been popular, but a little sweaty in summer. Devout women buy wigs made of synthetic hair – real hair, they say, would still be a sin – to allow them to study or work while fulfilling their religious beliefs. In one Istanbul wig shop the owner told me that he gets about twenty per cent of his business from women needing to hide their scarves. ('Crazy,' he said, 'but this is Turkey.') There's also a thriving trade in doctored photographs for official documents like diplomas or driving licences. For a price, photo shops will transform that awkward headscarf snap by growing hair and ears on top of it with the aid of computer technology. Everyone knows it's a fake, but honour is somehow satisfied.

It is, as many Turks admit, an increasingly bizarre situation. Every year thousands of young women see their education or their career grind to a halt because of their choice of headgear. Are they really the foot soldiers of a religious revolution, or has the state simply not yet learned to trust its own people? Sooner or later, in this overwhelmingly Muslim country, something will have to give. Banning the headscarf in French schools is one thing, banning it even more comprehensively in a country where well over half of all women cover their heads is quite another. A majority of Turks wants the ban to be lifted, but many millions of them don't. It has become a big dividing line.

And yet in the summer of 2004 the Turkish establishment claimed a significant victory in the headscarf wars, when the European Court of Human Rights rejected a claim from two Turkish students that their exclusion from university violated their freedom of religion. 'The court has not overlooked the fact that there are extremist political movements in Turkey,' the judges said, 'that are trying to impose on all society their religious symbols and their idea of a society based on religious rules.'

The court ruling must have infuriated Tayyip Erdoğan; this wasn't the kind of European freedom he had promised his conservative supporters. Erdoğan would love to lift or at least ease the official ban on the headscarf, not least because it is, for him, an issue close to home. His wife and two daughters all cover their hair with trendy türbans. Both his daughters went to university in the United States because they were unable to study in Turkey, while his wife, Emine, is in an even more difficult position. She is in effect banned from formal state occasions such as military parades and presidential banquets because of her scarf. And when she represents Turkey abroad – at the opening ceremony of the Olympics, for example, or at the White House – secular columnists grind their teeth and squirm in their seats. It's all so backward, they say, so uncivilized . . . what an embarrassment!

In the end it comes down to what secularism in Turkey really means. For the old elite, the essence is to keep religion and religious symbols out of politics and public life, even while state-appointed bureaucrats maintain absolute control over a vast religious hierarchy. Their goal is to ensure that the faithful never step out of line. It's French-style laicism, strictly enforced, and if that means banning the headscarf to make a point, then so be it. But Tayyip Erdoğan has a different interpretation, and this is shared by many Turks. He agrees that religion should not be politicized. But true secularism, he argues, should protect all beliefs and religions, allowing believers and followers the freedom to act as they please. He wants to be more democratic and more Islamic at the same time: the state may be secular but society isn't, and the headscarf should be left alone.

The trouble is that some people in Turkey interpret that as a threat rather than as a benign promise of greater democracy. They fear that fundamentalists will hide behind the mainstream Islamists, and then use their freedom to force their views on others. That's why the army will never let down its guard entirely. When I sought the opinion of a retired general, Armağan Kuloğlu, he was very clear.

'I don't think there's a big threat at the moment,' he said, 'but we always have to remain vigilant. If there was a real threat in the future, and I mean a real one, then the armed forces would . . .' He paused, and then finished his sentence, 'They would make their feelings known.'

He nodded and smiled, and I knew what he meant.

* * *

Driving down one of Istanbul's main thoroughfares through the suburb of Okmeydanı you can't miss the local headquarters of the AK Party (the initials are important – 'ak' in Turkish means 'white' or 'pure'). A huge yellow light bulb, the ubiquitous party symbol, looms out of the smog. Like everything else associated with the AKP it is a clever mix of modernity and tradition, suggesting Islamic notions of enlightenment. Alongside the light bulb a huge picture of Tayyip Erdoğan and a cheering crowd looms over the road. '*Herşey Türkiye için,*' says the slogan. 'Everything for Turkey.'

Inside, all is hectic activity. The smoke-filled cafeteria is packed with local people waiting to see local officials; someone has a complaint about corruption which is being dealt with by a senior party member; and the women's branch (covered and uncovered) is holding a seminar on Cyprus. It's not just the price of bread which gets debated at the grass roots – every policy followed by the government is explained and discussed.

While the latest United Nations peace plan for the island was being dissected at length, I fell into conversation with one of the young activists who'd come to show me around. He had been brought up in Germany before coming back to Turkey to try to make a living.

'Which party did you support before?' I asked him.

'I didn't,' he said. 'I wasn't interested in politics. There was no one there for the people of this country. They were all in it for themselves.'

It is a point worth emphasizing. The AKP has brought new blood into politics, and many of its supporters were attracted by things other than the party's views on religion. Two-thirds of the people who voted for the AKP had never voted for Islamist parties before – and while Erdoğan's own political roots are not hard to fathom, many of his members of parliament used to belong to other parties planted firmly in the political mainstream. When the AKP surveyed potential voters in the run-up to the 2002 general election, to find out what their main priorities were, the headscarf issue was down in eighth place – way below concerns about the economy, and making progress on joining the European Union.

So Erdoğan had done his homework. Armed with in-depth knowledge of what the public wanted, he created his grand alliance of 'conservative

Democrats'. Others have coined the phrase 'Muslim Democrats' to describe the AKP, in a conscious echo of the Christian Democratic parties in Europe. It's not a label which Erdoğan cares for, because he fears his critics at home and abroad will pick up on the 'Muslim' and ignore the 'Democrat'. Many Christian Democrats, after all, are among the most vociferous opponents of Turkey's EU membership bid for precisely that reason. But, whatever the label, the formation of the AKP became a hugely successful effort to claim the centre ground of Turkish politics. And while Islamists remain highly influential within the party hierarchy, they are not alone.

'Many people,' said my young friend from Germany, 'are like me. We were thoroughly fed up with the old politicians, and that's why we kicked them out. It was time for Turkey to start afresh.'

* * *

'The most important thing to remember is this: our party is with the people, not against the people. It's all about practical politics.'

On a patch of waste ground in a dusty side street, Hasan Altın was expounding on the same theme – showing me round the site of a new centre for distributing food to the poor, being built by the municipal government.

'People used to have to queue up for food, and some of them were ashamed,' he said, as workmen scrambled through a jungle of wooden scaffolding behind us. 'Now we're going to make the food here, and then deliver it to their houses. That's what the people want.'

Mr Altın is the AKP mayor of Sincan, a conservative suburb of Ankara which shot to fame in early 1997 in more controversial circumstances. Local Islamists held a 'Jerusalem night' which involved the Iranian ambassador and several others calling, in short, for Islamic revolution. 'Never be afraid to call yourselves fundamentalists!' the ambassador roared. Anti-state slogans were shouted, the army was shocked, and a few days later it sent tanks rumbling through the streets of Sincan on what was described with an official straight face as a routine manoeuvre. Sincan was the final catalyst for the 'soft coup' which forced Necmettin Erbakan from power.

But the AKP, in Sincan and elsewhere, has moved on. It has dropped the radical element of confrontation which characterized political Islam in the 1990s, but maintained the formidable network of local organizations and activists which brought the Islamists their initial electoral success. Years of mass migration and huge economic disparities between rich and poor had left many Turks searching for familiar roots. Kemalism was far too distant: it was the project of the elite, centralized, paternalistic and imposed from the top down. All the established parties seemed to be playing the same old game, whereas the Islamists and their grassroots networks were just the opposite. They practised politics from the bottom up, drawing on the basic conservative instincts of small-town Anatolia. Religion was part of the mix and Islamist parties – the Welfare Party in particular – campaigned from house to house to become the authentic voice of political protest.

I once accompanied a group of Welfare Party activists for several hours as they knocked on doors in a suburb of the city of Konya. They were ferociously well-organized; leading the charge were women who had previously played no political role. They knew everyone's name, they knew their problems and they remembered dates of weddings and funerals. The political talk was of clean streets and good housing. In short, they connected with the voters as no other party had quite done before. 'We understand you,' was the message, 'because we're just like you.' The AKP has built on those foundations, and inherited a winning electoral strategy.

So people didn't suddenly become more religious in the 1990s; but a new kind of politics emerged, in which social conservatives were more confident and more vocal. And if the army was a little unnerved by the rise of political Islam, it shouldn't have been surprised. The military regime which ruled Turkey in the early 1980s was obsessed with the threat from communism. It was a time when Ronald Reagan was talking up the battle of good and evil in the cold war, and Turkish generals decided that the best way to combat the considerable strength of popular Marxism as a vehicle for protest in Turkey was to use religion as a counterweight.

After the military coup in 1980 anyone perceived as a 'leftist' was purged from the state system, left-wing organizations were shut down en masse and the power of the radical left collapsed. Members of the intelligentsia were hounded, and clear limits were placed on individual freedoms.

Instead the secular guardians in the military chose to put the emphasis on traditional values – and that meant mixing Turkish nationalism with religion. They introduced compulsory religious education for all primary and secondary school pupils; they allowed special Koranic schools and many more religious high schools to open; and another mosque-building boom began. But by emasculating the left so completely, the military helped the Islamists to attract the votes of the discontented.

Imagine the surprise of many Turks when the austere leader of the military coup, General Kenan Evren, kicked off his set speech at town meetings around the country with a reading from the Koran. By the time the soldiers decided they had taken their enthusiasm for religion a bit too far, it was too late. As prime minister and president, Turgut Özal tried to bring the devout back into politics. But after his untimely death in 1993, no one of any stature emerged to take on the mantle on behalf of the Anatolian masses. Instead, the Islamists in the Welfare Party were best positioned to take advantage of the more liberalized society which Özal had begun to create.

A decade later Tayyip Erdoğan has cherry-picked the most effective bits of the Welfare model, brought back Özal's instinct for reform, and taken over the centre ground of Turkish politics. The urban poor, rural conservatives and the emerging Islamist middle classes have been joined in his coalition by liberal democrats and other supporters of membership of the European Union. Even big business, part of the old elite, has been won over by evidence of his reforming zeal, and his desire to take Turkey into Europe.

Significant elements in the military and the bureaucracy, as well as millions of ordinary Turks who voted for the CHP and other parties, still find it hard to put up with Erdoğan's deliberately moderate brand of Islamist politics. But the election results have been conclusive, and in the new Turkey the AKP has for now become the natural party of government. New political forces will of course regroup to challenge the ruling party, and it can't afford to be complacent. At the general election in 2002 nearly half the electorate were in effect disenfranchised by the law which stipulates that only parties with more than ten per cent of the national vote get any seats in parliament at all.

The voters are also notoriously volatile and if the AKP were to stumble, or more specifically if the EU process were to go horribly wrong, a much more nationalist and xenophobic alternative could emerge. Witness the success of the Young Party, led by the maverick businessman Cem Uzan, which came from nowhere to win seven per cent of the vote in 2002 with a campaign of populist promises and virulent hostility to outsiders. But with good news from Brussels, and continued economic stability, the AKP could be running Turkey for some years to come. And for as long as he chooses to be so, Tayyip Erdoğan will be the pivotal figure, as prime minister and possibly in the future as president of the republic.

It won't always be easy though – Turkish politics never is. Erdoğan has already upset some of the competing factions within his party and there has been a trickle of defections involving dissatisfied members of parliament. The prime minister has also been taken to task for being increasingly intolerant of criticism. He sued a political cartoonist, for example, for portraying him as a cat entangled in a ball of wool; and when local TV stations carried graphic pictures of Turkish policemen beating women demonstrators in March 2005 (just as a senior delegation from the EU arrived) he accused the media of working against Turkey's national interest. 'The prime minister,' thundered one newspaper, 'has described EU membership as the modernization project for Turkish society. He should start the modernization inside his own head.'

And if it's not Erdoğan himself straying 'off message', there are plenty of other candidates to be found within the ranks of the AKP. When the prime minister's campaign to convince the EU of Turkey's 'western' democratic credentials was at its height, one municipality controlled by his party ordered the police to prevent young couples holding hands or kissing in the park; on another occasion one of his cabinet colleagues called for a ban on an advertisement for anti-cellulite cream, which showed a woman's naked back. It was, the minister explained, exploitative and a 'violation of Turkey's traditions'. European values? Not exactly.

'What Erdoğan has done is bring many different elements in Turkish society together,' Cengiz Çandar observes, 'modern and traditional, rich and poor, and he's managed to balance their demands. But one day he will have to choose where his loyalties really lie, what his priorities are, and who he is willing to upset. That's when things will become difficult.'

In the meantime it's hardly surprising that religious issues have once again come to the fore, as restrictions on freedom of expression have gradually been relaxed. Lest anyone forget, this is a very devout country, a stark contrast in many ways to the increasingly godless societies of Western Europe. On matters of religion and faith, Turkey has more in common with conservative American values than with much of what can be found in the EU. Religion is part of daily life, even among the middle classes. Walk around the smart new suburbs and commuter towns which are springing up around the big cities and you'll find a substantial mosque nearly always has pride of place. As a social and cultural focus for the community it brings to mind the protestant mega-churches of the United States rather than the secular world of old Europe.

Shortly after I first arrived to live in Turkey in 1997 I wrote that trying to understand the real role of religion in the country was like peeling an onion – layer after layer of complexity. I'm still peeling, but I haven't forgotten the advice I was given back then by an unexpectedly friendly mid-level bureaucrat in one of Ankara's many government offices.

'Don't forget that the debate about religion in Turkey is about much more than party politics,' he said. 'It's about what you believe in, and why.'

* * *

A few weeks after modern Turkey's first military coup in 1960 a group of soldiers was given a grim task. In a city under curfew, they broke into a tomb and stole a body. It was placed in a coffin and flown to the other end of the country to be buried by night in an unmarked grave. It was the body of Said Nursi, a Kurdish holy man who had died just before the coup took place. Nursi had spent his life campaigning for Islam and contemplating its place in a modernizing secular society. He led the influential Islamist Nurcu movement – based on his collected writings *The Epistles of Light* – and the generals were nervous about the power he could wield from beyond the grave. They didn't want his tomb to become a place of pilgrimage.

But Said Nursi's disciples stayed one step ahead of the soldiers. They know where his body was buried, in a quiet hillside cemetery in western Turkey, and his movement has flourished. Millions of Turks now follow his teachings. They are part of a complex world of Turkish Islam which lies just beneath the surface of all the familiar political tensions between religious and secular forces. Ancient Muslim brotherhoods based on mystical interpretations of Islam, along with new religious communities which have emerged in the last few years, continue to flourish in semi-legal surroundings. They serve as spiritual and social centres for the many people who retain their traditional links with Islam.

The old religious orders – the *tarikats* – were formally abolished in 1925 at the height of Kemal Atatürk's great revolution, but they never went away. Ancient sects like the Nakşibendi and the Mevlevi (better known to outsiders as the Whirling Dervishes) survived as underground organizations during the early crusading years of the secular state. They gained more confidence during the gradual liberalization of the system under the Democrat Party in the 1950s, and they came into their own again in the 1980s as Islam was re-established permanently in the public domain.

Like their more openly political counterparts, the tarikats have been quick to take advantage of the pace of change in Turkey. When mass migration uprooted millions of people from their traditional communities and threw them into the confusing world of the metropolis, it was the religious orders which helped provide a sense of identity. Today they are among the most active voluntary organizations in the country, offering financial support and a social network for business and personal contacts. Although still technically illegal, they now run well-established foundations and charitable institutions, and play an important role in the lives of many Turks.

So the politicians court the tarikat vote. Parties identified with political Islam are sometimes favoured, but other conservative parties – the True Path Party and Turgut Özal's Motherland Party among them – have also benefited from close links with the religious orders. Even political leaders who have made a career out of defending secularism know they have to make the effort. When the exiled leader of the Nakşibendi tarikat, Professor Mahmud Esad Çoşan, died in a car crash in Australia in February 2001, Bülent Ecevit's cabinet quickly passed a decree allowing his body to be buried in the garden of Süleymaniye mosque in Istanbul. There was a storm of protest, led by members of Ecevit's own party, the (proudly secularist) Democratic Left. Is the mosque, they asked, becoming a tarikat cemetery? The decree was rejected by the president, Ahmet Necdet Sezer, and Ecevit was left to point out that other religious figures had been buried in prominent places without any fuss.

The AKP has inherited a multitude of contacts with tarikats and religious communities, but its most significant link is with the conservative Islamist movement known as Milli Goruş – the National Vision – founded by Necmettin Erbakan. This is an openly political movement, with additional strength among Turks living in other countries in Europe. Many local activists and provincial functionaries in the AKP are affiliated with Milli Goruş, and they expect their views to be reflected in national politics. What those views really are is the subject of some debate. Milli Goruş was originally opposed to developing greater contacts with Europe and the West, and it had its sights set on the Islamic world for future economic and military partnerships. Now reformers in the movement say they've changed, but the message may take quite a while to filter down to the grass roots.

It's not just about politics, though. Fethullah Gülen is perhaps the most prominent Turkish religious leader alive, and he says he has never voted and never been involved formally with any political party. Gülen leads a hugely successful offshoot of the Nurcu movement which has established a substantial network of high-achieving schools in Turkey and abroad, in former Soviet Central Asia, in the Balkans and the Middle East. He owns a media empire, and runs hospitals and a bank. Like Said Nursi he emphasizes the importance of science and technology and says he wants to reconcile tradition and modernity, faith and the secular system.

Gülen's followers will tell you that he celebrates Turkey's Ottoman heritage as well as Atatürk's efforts to drag the country into the modern world. It doesn't sound terribly threatening, but his long-term aims remain a source of controversy within Turkey. He wants to create a 'golden generation' of Muslims who will promote the moral values of Islam in a new way, and influence state policy. His movement has openly recruited in police academies and military schools, advocating a mix of Islam and Turkish nationalism. (They have to be careful: army officers who show too much enthusiasm either for religious communities or for the mosque in general are regularly purged from the ranks.) Gülen wants his followers to be modern and Muslim at the same time (as does Tayyip Erdoğan), but his modus operandi still inspires suspicion in the Kemalist bastions of the military and civilian establishments.

He suffers from serious health problems, and he has been in self-imposed exile in the United States for several years. When I visited the headquarters of his publishing house, the Journalists and Writers Association, in a posh street in the heart of Istanbul, his photographs adorned the walls – Gülen with former president Demirel, and with leaders of countries from across Central Asia; Gülen meeting the pope, and the ecumenical patriarch.

'Jesus Christ was a great man in religion,' I was told, 'and yet look at what he suffered. People who are working for peace and brotherhood aren't always welcomed, so there will always be those who oppose Fethullah Gülen.'

His real problems began with a vitriolic court case launched in 2000. Although the case eventually collapsed, the original indictment accused him of plotting to set up an 'Islamic dictatorship' and described him as 'the strongest and most effective Islamic fundamentalist in Turkey' who 'camouflages his methods with a democratic and moderate image'. The charges followed a judicial investigation of secretly recorded tapes in which Gülen allegedly urged his supporters in the state bureaucracy to lie low and wait for his orders to undermine the system from within. On the tapes, released by a retired general, Gülen appeared to warn a group of his followers that 'if they come out early, the world will squash their heads. They would make Muslims once again relive incidents such as those that occurred in Algeria.'

Gülen always denied the charges filed against him, and said the tapes were a forgery. He speaks only rarely to the media these days, but in a lengthy series of interviews published in March 2004 in *Zaman* (not too many hard questions – he's the newspaper's owner) he sets out his thinking at some length. 'There are no drawbacks,' he argues, 'to blending Islamic traditions and customs with democracy.' He portrays himself as a voice of tolerance and regeneration, he advocates piety, he cultivates ties with other religions, and he is widely admired and trusted by many ordinary Turkish citizens.

But he doesn't speak for everyone. Never mind those in the secular elite who instinctively distrust him, Fethullah Gülen also stands on one side of another of Turkey's great fault lines – the sectarian divide between the Sunni Muslim majority and the Alevis. A liberal sect with Shia Muslim roots and unorthodox beliefs, the Alevis have developed a unique identity in Anatolia, and suffered centuries of persecution in response.

I wasn't quite sure what to expect when I arrived on a windswept evening at the *cemevi* in Küçükçekmece on the outskirts of Istanbul. I'd come to attend a Muslim religious ceremony, but it was nothing like the traditional image I had in my mind of rows of men praying in the mosque. A cemevi is an Alevi prayer house, and they do things very differently there. About two hundred men and women were sitting on cushions on the floor in a large plain room, listening to their community leader – the *dede* – speaking from a raised platform at the front.

There are millions of Alevis in Turkey today, of Turkish, Kurdish and Arabic descent, and political Islam makes them nervous. They fear any form of Sunni Muslim revivalism, whether in politics or society. They have always had an uneasy relationship with central authority as well, but from their distant villages and their new urban communities the Alevis have long been staunch supporters of Atatürk's secular vision. It's been the best guarantee of protection they have ever had.

Lamps were lit and a man playing a *saz* (a traditional Turkish stringed instrument similar to a lute or an Indian sitar) began singing vigorously. People held their right hands to their hearts as the dede began to lead them in prayer and song. Suddenly the main ritual began – the *Semah*. A group of men and women with green ribbons tied around their waists started to dance together, round and round in circles, as the music grew louder. There was more prayer, more singing and dancing – part of an elaborate ceremony which remained hidden for years. Today it is as much to do with cultural tradition as with religious belief.

When it was over, two members of the congregation were summoned to the front to be asked why they had been smiling inappropriately during the Semah. One of the two men confessed rather guiltily that it was because he remembered a previous dance when someone had nearly fallen over. The dede frowned briefly, reminded everyone that this was a serious occasion, and passed sentence – bring some fruit next week to share with your friends.

As people began to leave, the dede wandered over for a chat.

'We need recognition of this building,' he said, gesturing at pictures of Ali, the son-in-law of the prophet Muhammad, which adorned the walls. 'It is technically illegal for us to pray here.'

Alevis are growing in confidence as a community, and opening more cemevis, and they are gradually demanding equal treatment. Either the government should spend no money on religion, they argue, or we should get as much help as the mosques do.

'We'd like our children to be taught about Alevism at school,' the dede said. 'Otherwise our religion will be assimilated, and our culture will disappear.'

The rain was beginning to fall outside, and people were buttoning up their coats against the cold.

'One other thing,' he said, as we turned to go. 'Please tell your friends in Europe that we don't want to be called a minority. We just want to be ourselves. There are twenty million of us, we've been here for a long time, and there's no point in creating problems where they don't exist.'

It is a sensitive subject, because there have been some dark moments in the recent past. Just a few miles away, in the rundown suburb of Gaziosmanpaşa, Istanbul saw some of its worst riots in years after an unknown gunman opened fire on an Alevi café in 1995, killing three people. The furious protests which followed quickly turned violent, as extreme left-wing groups fought running battles with the police for several days. At least sixteen people died before the anger subsided. Two years earlier an even more frightening incident had taken place in the central Anatolian town of Sivas. Thirty-seven people were killed when Sunni fundamentalists set fire to a hotel where Alevi intellectuals were holding a conference. Much of the left–right violence of the late 1970s was also heavily influenced by the Alevi–Sunni divide, and there were several massacres of Alevis which haven't been forgotten.

The strength of these sectarian ties, which for years were never publicly discussed, is often more significant than any ethnic loyalties. Some Sunni Kurds who are strongly Islamist, for example, have more in common with Sunni Turks than with Alevi Kurds. It is a useful reminder of the complexities of Turkish political and social life: very few people fit neatly into a single box.

'Think about it like this,' said one of my Turkish friends with a wicked smile. 'Some Islamists are nationalists, and some nationalists are staunch secularists; some secularists are liberal democrats, but many liberals (confused yet?) now support a former Islamist radical as their best hope for greater democracy.'

* * *

Every week an authorized sermon goes out from Ankara by email and fax to tens of thousands of mosques across the country. It comes from the Directorate General for Religious Affairs, or Diyanet, which has tried to keep (Sunni) Islam in Turkey under strict control since the formation of the republic. The Diyanet has a huge budget and a paternalistic mentality: it employs more than seventy thousand clerics, it runs religious schools and foundations, and it tries to keep a close watch on the whole system. It preaches moderation, and the virtues of the secular system; but it can no longer pretend that it prevents others working in their own manner, independent of the long arm of the state.

Some people operate through Islamist politics; others prefer to use social networks, business associations, education or new media outlets. There is an extraordinary variety of voices which leaves one lasting impression – trying to pigeonhole Islam in Turkey, as the state has done for three-quarters of a century, is utterly pointless.

Whichever way you turn something quite different is happening: the biggest mosque in Ankara sits on top of an underground car park and a busy department store; illegal courses to teach young children the Koran are proliferating across the country; an Imam in Kayseri paints nudes in his spare time; at unofficial mosques in Istanbul radical preachers are learning Kurdish so they can convert newly arrived migrants to their cause; and when the religious authorities suggest that it is not appropriate to celebrate the New Year too excessively, the secular youth parties on regardless.

Islamists can have a good time too. In the last few years, a new generation of beach resorts, spas and five-star hotels has begun to cater specifically to the more conservative holidaymaker. No alcohol, the call to prayer five times a day, segregated beaches and full-body swimsuits for pious women: it might not sound like everyone's idea of fun, but there is a growing demand from wealthy religious Turks who want to combine their beliefs with Western-style consumerism. When the Caprice Hotel on the Aegean coast became the first place of its kind to open in 1996 it was criticized as inappropriate by some Islamist commentators, but the owners argued that there was nothing wrong with worldly pleasures enjoyed in the right way.

Rich Muslims enjoying consumer culture? The secularists are nearly as upset as the Islamists, because all these new trends pose a challenge to the basic principles of their ideology – that they, and only they, truly represent what it means to be modern in Turkey. And while most Turks get on with life, the search for the pernicious influence of Islam pops up in the most unlikely of places. When Turkey's football team reached the semi-finals of the World Cup in 2002 a huge row broke out when one newspaper alleged that the players had fallen under the spell of a tarikat led by star striker Hakan Şükür. They only pass to players who pray, the reporter suggested, before angry readers denounced him as a heretic.

No wonder the people running the country fail so often to live up to expectations – they face the constant challenge of competing forces pulling Turkey in different directions. Tayyip Erdoğan's solution is to press ahead with trying to join the European Union. It is, he believes, the best guarantee of freedom for everyone, and the best way to bridge the secular–religious divide. There will always be doubters at both ends of the spectrum. But most secularists would be happy if Europe were to become the guarantee that radical Islam could never gain a firm foothold in Turkey; and most believers would be happy if Europe were to become the guarantee of more democratic freedom to practise their faith in the way they choose. If Erdoğan can keep most of the people happy most of the time, he has a real chance of success.

His admirers abroad – Tony Blair and George Bush among them – also have more than a passing interest in whether Erdoğan can actually make the new Turkey work. They have been searching frantically for leaders in the Muslim world who have both popular legitimacy and a belief that their future lies in democratic pluralism. That's why the internal Turkish debate about politics and religion has much broader implications as well. If a country which borders Iran, Iraq and Syria can prove that Islam and greater democracy flourish together, then that matters – the fundamentalists lose. If Turkey can make real progress in membership talks with the European Union, however lengthy a process it turns out to be, then that sends another powerful signal – that there doesn't have to be a clash of civilizations. There is a lot riding on how the Erdoğan experiment turns out, and from time to time the scale of the challenge becomes brutally clear.

* * *

It was a typically busy Beyoğlu morning. The cafés and shops were open, and the residents of Istanbul were going about their business in one of the city's most vibrant and cosmopolitan neighbourhoods. The fish market was bustling into life, and the British Consul-General Roger Short had just got back to his office after having his shoes shined across the road. Suddenly, at just after 11 a.m., a green catering van packed with five hundred and fifty pounds of explosives accelerated up a narrow side street, slammed into the wrought-iron gates of the Consulate-General, and blew up.

A few minutes earlier on a busy road just a few miles away, another suicide bomber driving a pickup truck had hit another British target – the eighteen-storey headquarters of the HSBC bank in the heart of Istanbul's modern business district. In the immediate aftermath of these deadly bombings, there was chaos. Body parts lay scattered in the streets and cars were engulfed in flames. Glass shards and debris were hurled into the air across a wide area. 20 November 2003 was the day the 'war on terror' came home to roost in Istanbul; it was, said the predictable newspaper headlines, 'Our 9/11'.

Five days earlier two more truck bombs had exploded outside two Istanbul synagogues – striking a grievous blow against one of the city's oldest minority communities. Altogether sixty-one people died and six hundred were wounded in the attacks. The most prominent victim was Roger Short, the senior British official in the city, whose body was recovered in the ruins of a shop across the road from his office. But most of the dead were Turks, including two police officers stationed at the Consulate gate, who had opened fire on the van seconds before it exploded.

The bombings bore the hallmarks of groups linked to al-Qaeda – simultaneous suicide attacks against symbols of Western influence. An indictment in the trial of sixty-nine suspects arrested over the next few weeks alleged that Osama bin Laden had suggested targets in Turkey and al-Qaeda had helped finance an operation carried out by local Islamic militants. The four suicide bombers, it emerged, were all Turkish Kurds from the tough south-eastern town of Bingöl. They had links with the extremist group, Turkish Hizbollah (no relation to the Lebanese group of the same name), and all four of them are believed to have been trained or to have fought abroad in the name of Islam. Several thousand Turks may have done the same thing in the last few years – training in Pakistan, Iran and the Gulf, fighting in Afghanistan, Chechnya and Bosnia. They were never really considered a major threat until the bombers struck in Istanbul.

But the warning signs have been there for a long time. Groups like Hizbollah and IBDA-C – the Great Eastern Raiders Islamic Front – have been active for years, even though their support has never moved beyond a hard core of fanatics. During the 1990s there was a series of fundamentalist assassinations of prominent Turkish secularists – academics and writers such as Uğur Mumcu, one of Turkey's best-known journalists, and a former culture minister, Ahmet Taner Kışlalı. Persistent leaks to the media put the blame on Iran, but there was a nagging suspicion which wouldn't go away: that the people responsible had once been trained by rogue elements within the Turkish state to do their dirty work. As ever, it was all terribly murky.

There were certainly proven links between state security forces and the Islamic extremists who had fought against the Marxist rebellion of the PKK in the south-east. In the late 1980s members of Hizbollah were armed, trained and funded by the state, as the counter-insurgency campaign against the PKK got into full swing. For a decade they served a bloody purpose, responsible for countless 'unsolved' murders, while officials looked the other way. But by the year 2000 leading members of Hizbollah had become a law unto themselves – no longer killing enemies of the state, but targeting opponents of Islamic revolution. So the authorities decided to wipe them out.

The turning point began with a routine police operation in the Istanbul suburb of Beykoz, near the banks of the Bosphorus. Officers who were trying to trace the credit cards of several missing businessmen suddenly came under sustained fire. For several hours a dramatic shoot-out was shown live on TV, and when it came to an end the anti-terrorist police realized that they had killed Hizbollah's top man, Hüseyin Velioğlu. Two of his lieutenants were captured in a house which also contained stacks of documents and gruesome video tapes recording unspeakable acts of torture and murder.

Over the next few weeks the bodies of Hizbollah's tortured victims were found buried in various locations across the country: among them a well-known Islamist feminist, named Konca Kuriş, who had suggested on television that women should be allowed to pray alongside men during Muslim funerals. The video tapes showed that she had been tortured for more than thirty hours before she was strangled by her captors. Hizbollah was a truly malignant force, which was thrown into disarray by the police operations against it but not completely destroyed. The survivors regrouped and became more radical still, gaining even more menacing patrons in Afghanistan and elsewhere.

So the threat from extremist violence carried out in the name of Islam is real. And since November 2003 those charged with the responsibility of protecting Turkey have had to think on a different scale. For groups linked, however loosely, to the brand name of al-Qaeda, Turkey presents an obvious target – a place where east and west coexist; a secular state founded on the ruins of the Islamic caliphate. But the most important point is this: the vast majority of the Turkish people are not interested in radical Islamic agendas, still less in wanton acts of terror. In some opinion polls about twenty per cent of the population say they would like to live under strict shariah law, but they are often referring to an ethical system rather than a new legal regime. I think the chances of violent Islamic revolution or civil war taking place in Turkey are close to zero. It is not Algeria, or Afghanistan.

Nevertheless many secular commentators used the Istanbul bombings to focus criticism on Tayyip Erdoğan and members of his government. Their political history in the Islamist movement, the critics maintained, made it less likely that they would take decisive steps against violent Islamic radicals. Many junior members of Hizbollah, they pointed out, had been released from prison under a government-sponsored amnesty in the months leading up to the Istanbul bomb blasts. The prime minister was quick to hit back – the people responsible for the attacks, he said, 'will account for it in both worlds. They will be damned until eternity.'

A few months later the authorities announced that they had foiled a big plot to launch further suicide bombs during a NATO summit in Istanbul. Many Turks still wonder where and when the next attack will happen. Violent groups of home-grown activists have received added inspiration from international networks, and events across the border in Iraq have also served to radicalize a minority. But the threat from Islamic extremism in Turkey can be exaggerated. During the past thirty years much greater challenges to the state have come from the reawakening of radical Kurdish nationalism, and from violent clashes between the extreme left and the extreme right which took thousands of lives in the late 1970s and led to the military coup in 1980. Islam in Turkey is changing all the time, but there's precious little evidence to suggest that it's suddenly going to take a violent or fundamentalist turn.

One thing is clear. After more than eighty years of Atatürk's secular system, Turkish Islam has been neither marginalized nor cast aside. It is too deeply rooted, and it has always maintained substantial influence. But that does not mean Turks have to choose between religion and the secular state, they are not mutually exclusive. The real choice is between the old centralized system of state control over so many aspects of life and a new Turkey of more genuine democracy and personal choice. Tayyip Erdoğan may not be everyone's favourite, but – with a few stumbles along the way – he has been pushing his country down the path of greater democratic freedoms, the path which leads towards the EU. The notion that the state has more rights than the people is gradually being revised. But the biggest democratic challenge still lies in Turkey's poorest and most troubled region, in eastern Anatolia, in the Kurdish heartland.

4

THE KURDISH QUESTION

Everyone bound to the Turkish state through the bond of citizenship is a Turk.
>
> Article 66, Constitution of the Republic of Turkey

I arrived at Halil Cindik's house as he was having a chat with his friend Küçük. You know the sort of thing, just a couple of neighbours chewing the fat across the garden fence . . . except in this case, they were somewhat further apart, several hundred metres apart in fact, across a rather wide valley. They're used to it, of course, having grown up in a land of vibrant green mountains and steep wooded slopes in the province of Giresun, near the southern shores of the Black Sea. They live in the village of Kuşköy, where houses perch precariously on the sides of the valley above little more than thin air.

The telephone only arrived in the mountains a few years ago, so for generations if you did want to talk to your neighbours there was little choice. Kuşköy means literally the 'bird village' and if you can't whistle, well you're probably from somewhere else. I stood and watched as Halil ran through his full repertoire – twenty-nine separate whistled noises which make up a whole language. It's used by about a thousand people in and around Kuşköy, and when your best friend is just across the valley – but it takes an hour of rock scrambling to get there – it's a pretty useful talent to have.

I was encouraged to learn a few whistle-words myself and I'd love to say I became an expert, but sadly all I could manage was a rather unpleasant raspberry sound. Intensive training from my hosts on how precisely to angle my tongue and rest my forefinger on my front teeth produced only further embarrassment. In the end, I had to settle for yet another cup of tea.

No one really knows exactly when this strange linguistic phenomenon started, only why. But the writer Xenophon described people shouting across valleys in the same region more than two thousand years ago. Long-distance whistling was probably a natural progression, and in Kuşköy it's been passed down from generation to generation – all the local kids pick it up in the end. There are a handful of other villages around the world where the same tradition thrives in remote regions of Mexico, Greece and Spain. But Kuşköy believes it boasts the largest concentration of whistlers on the planet. It is quietly determined that its language will not be allowed to wither and die as people move away from the village, and the modern technology of mobile phones intrudes into the mountains.

'Hasn't anyone ever tried to stop you?' I asked, as Halil paused for breath. He looked a little confused, so I pressed on.

'Well, the whistling – it's not an official language is it? People can be a bit sensitive about that sort of thing.'

Halil was so bemused that he ignored me entirely and launched into another ear-splitting exchange with Küçük.

Perhaps I wasn't being entirely serious, and yet here it was – a minority language in the heart of the Turkish republic, which no one viewed as remotely suspicious or subversive. Granted there's never been a Birdsong Liberation Front to alarm officialdom in Ankara, and Kuşköy has never laid claim to a separate ethnic identity. But if the whistlers of the Black Sea can be left to get on with life, I reasoned, why not the Kurds, or in their own ways the Greeks, the Armenians or the Laz, who live in Turkey's far north-eastern corner and speak a language akin to Georgian.

'Whistling is part of our tradition, part of who we are,' said Halil, as we gazed down the valley. 'We just want to be ourselves, and if this is the best way we can communicate, then why not?'

It was a simple but eminently sensible philosophy, in one of the most ethnically diverse countries on earth. Kuşköy left me thinking that Turkey's ruling classes could learn some useful lessons from this small farming community in the mountains. They talk a lot about their cultural mosaic; now's the time to let all the pieces shine, to accept once and for all that ethnicity and nationality aren't quite the same thing.

* * *

9 June 2004 was a memorable day for the estimated twelve million people in Turkey who call themselves Kurds. Four Kurdish politicians, led by the Nobel Peace Prize nominee, Leyla Zana, were released from prison after a long international struggle to secure their freedom. A few hours earlier, state television had broken with decades of official denial and broadcast a programme in the main Kurdish dialect, Kurmanji, for the first time.

The noise outside Ankara's Ulucanlar prison was deafening. Impromptu Kurdish dances were performed on the street and bouquets of flowers were hurled through the air. Hundreds of Kurds began to ululate as Leyla Zana and her three fellow former members of parliament walked free after ten years in captivity.

'This country has entered a new era, it has turned a new page,' Leyla Zana said. 'I hope everyone can now set our disputes aside, and we can solve our problems hand in hand.'

She and her colleagues had been imprisoned on charges of supporting Kurdish terrorism – among the crimes for which Leyla Zana was convicted were speaking in Kurdish while taking her parliamentary oath of office in 1991 (when she pledged to work for peace between Turks and Kurds), and wearing a headband in parliament in the traditional Kurdish colours of red, yellow and green.

Leyla Zana became a cause célèbre while she was in prison. She was nominated for the Nobel Peace Prize and awarded the European Parliament's Sakharov Prize for Human Rights, which she eventually collected in Brussels after she was set free. The EU regarded her as a prisoner of conscience and made it clear that her release was a precondition if Turkey wanted to start negotiations on membership. For decades the Turkish state had denied that the Kurds even existed, and had banned the use of their language. A brutal ethnic conflict had been fought for fifteen years. The symbolism of freedom for Leyla Zana and her colleagues was difficult to miss.

'Turkey's eighty-year ban on the Kurds is over today,' said Sırrı Sakık, a political activist waiting at the prison gates, who was originally jailed alongside her. 'It shows Turkey recognizes the Kurdish reality.'

By coincidence that wave of recognition reached the state television channel, TRT, on the same day. Laws allowing broadcasts in minority languages had first been approved two years previously but, as ever, implementation proved extremely difficult, and plenty of people were willing to drag their feet. Everyone knew the change in the law was all about the Kurds but, just to prove a point, the first minority broadcast on TRT was in Bosnian (and the Bosnians promptly said they didn't want anything to do with it). Then came the Arabic offering, and Turkey's Arabs said the dialect used was unintelligible. But a few days later, at 10.30 a.m. on 9 June, came the one that mattered. Kurds across the country settled down to watch a thirty-minute programme in Kurmanji. *Our Cultural Riches* was a rather strange mix of slightly old news, folk songs and a short documentary on wildlife. But the content was unimportant; a cultural Rubicon had been crossed, and before the week was out a similar programme was shown in the other main Kurdish dialect, Zaza – the language of the long-suffering inhabitants of Tunceli.

'We have been presented with a single flower,' an elderly Kurdish man said after watching the Kurmanji broadcast. 'We like the way it smells, and we hope we will eventually be given a garden.'

There is indeed hope, but there are still no guarantees. The government had to fight hard to persuade conservatives in the bureaucracy, the military and even in its own party on two counts: that cautious broadcasts like this would not threaten the unity of the country; and, separately, that Leyla Zana and her colleagues should be released. Many weren't convinced, and within weeks the four Kurds had once again incurred the displeasure of the security establishment. The police filed charges against them for speaking Kurdish at political rallies, something which is still illegal, and for breaking traffic regulations and laws on freedom of assembly. Funnily enough, the police acted a day after the deputy chief of the general staff, General Ilker Başbuğ issued a warning of his own. 'At the political rallies they held they spoke in a language other than the official language of the nation,' he intoned. 'They even had the temerity to propose that the terrorist PKK extend its ceasefire for another six months. They have taken advantage of hesitation within the bureaucracy.'

They were condemned, in other words, for calling for peace and for asking the PKK to rethink its decision to return to armed struggle. After a five-year unilateral ceasefire the Kurdish rebel movement had declared on 1 June that the fight against the state would resume. It may be a shadow of its former self, but the PKK still has several thousand young men and women under arms in northern Iraq, and several hundred in Turkey itself. Over the next two months more than sixty people were killed in renewed violence in the south-east, casting a shadow over what could have become a summer of opportunity for Turkey's Kurds.

* * *

Batman was one of my least favourite places in the south-east (the only thing I really liked about it was the name of its football team, Batman Petrol). It's a dusty oil town, which was kept tightly under control by mean-looking security men for years. The atmosphere always seemed oppressive, in many ways typical of the south-east: high unemployment and simmering resentment, part police state but now part democracy too.

The last time I visited Batman I walked around the old centre of town with the Kurdish mayor, Abdullah Akın.

'The military run this town,' he told me, 'but I represent the people.'

We wandered into one small tea house where the local men (there were, of course, no women to be seen) were playing dominoes and backgammon as usual. Şerif had been coming to the tea house every afternoon for more years than he cared to remember. His age automatically gained him respect, and gave him authority as the local amateur historian.

'The Kurds have always fought against the centre.' He sniffed as he threw the dice across the board. 'It's in our nature. We've never liked other people telling us what to do and we never will.'

His fellow players grunted in agreement as more cups of tea arrived, and cigarettes were offered around the table.

We were talking quietly about the prospects for peace in the region – the fighting had died down, the roadblocks had been removed and the state of emergency was about to be lifted. People were more relaxed, a little more hopeful. Could it last?

There was a general sense of optimism but Şerif was more cautious, and he always kept coming back to the lessons of history.

'Listen,' he said, using his finger to drum on the table with an air of finality. 'None of us wants to go back to another war, we're sick and tired of it, but things have to be done properly.'

'And if they're not?'

'We don't want to think like that.'

He threw the dice again, before adding his final thought.

'Our young boys just want jobs and the chance to lead a normal life, but the other side can never crush us, you know, they can't break our spirit.'

It was the kind of sentiment I heard again and again in travels through Turkey's Kurdish provinces. Pride mixed with defiance. A romanticized view, perhaps, but heartfelt all the same. Even many of those who regarded the PKK leader Abdullah Öcalan as a buffoon at best, admired the way he had awakened Kurdish consciousness. With the help of a heavy-handed response from the Turkish military, he managed to turn a disparate collection of feudal tribes into a people with an identity they were prepared to stand up for. I never met many Kurds in the south-east who thought a separate state (landlocked and impoverished) was a good idea; but I never met any who thought they'd been treated well by the Turkish authorities.

As Şerif pointed out in the tea house in Batman, many people have tried to crush the Kurds over the years, but the Kurds have always survived. Only a fool would say they have prospered, but the world's 'largest nation without a state' is nothing if not stubborn. Today there are about twenty-five million of them, spread through often mountainous and inhospitable terrain between Turkey, Syria, Iraq, Iran and the Caucasus. Turkish rulers have always tried to control them – from Ottoman times through Atatürk's revolution to the present day – but the Kurds have always refused to conform.

At least under the Ottomans they were granted considerable autonomy, but the modern Turkish republic, with its instinctive urge to centralize, has been a bigger challenge. The Kurds quickly fell foul of early republican zeal as an uprising led by Sheikh Said was put to the sword. Said and his followers fought for Islam, not for Kurdish nationalism, but no one was surprised that the first insurgent threat to republican rule came from the badlands of the east. Kemal Atatürk had once spoken of plans to allow the Kurds to 'administer their own affairs in an autonomous manner'. But in his obsessive search for a single Turkish identity he changed his mind. They were all Turks, he told them, and for decades after his death that's how the Kurds were officially described – 'Mountain Turks' who would be assimilated over time into 'civilized society'.

Often it was done by overwhelming force: military officers who led the campaign against the PKK in the 1980s and 1990s had plenty of historical parallels to emulate. Thousands of Kurds were killed in the late 1930s in a ruthless scorched-earth campaign to try to pacify the central province of Dersim; thousands of others were deported, and their villages were razed to the ground. Kurdish names were banned, and Kurdish place names were changed en masse. Dersim became Tunceli, and memories of the assault were so devastating that Kurdish nationalism in Turkey was subdued for decades, even as it flourished across the border in northern Iraq. Until 1965, foreigners were not even allowed to travel to the south-east and Kurdish activists who emerged during the 1960s tended to get involved in left-wing politics rather than a fight for ethnic identity.

Forced displacement was followed by mass economic migration as people moved from the countryside to the cities in search of work. Some of them prospered in this changing Turkey. Millions of Kurds and Turks have intermarried over the years, and Kurds have always been able to rise to the highest echelons of society as long as they have been willing to suppress their ethnic identity. Some Kurds in western Turkey are trapped in urban ghettos, barely scraping a living while clinging stubbornly to their Kurdishness; but many others have joined the mainstream. A long line of cabinet ministers and successful businessmen can bear witness to that, as can Turkey's most famous singer Ibrahim Tatlıses – the 'Emperor'. I've seen Ibo's mournful ballads reduce grown men to tears, but when he tried to sing in Kurdish, nationalists called for a boycott of all his recordings and accused him of inciting separatism.

All the while, the Kurdish provinces were left to fester, with little in the way of education, health care or employment opportunities. Things are changing slowly, but even today much of the rural south-east remains a tribal society – the most conservative place in Turkey. Local landlords

and feudal clan chieftains still wield enormous power. They pay the
wages to agricultural labourers, and the bride price for young men to
get married; they adjudicate in family disputes and they can deliver
thousands of votes at general elections. Every political party knows the
reality: tribal leaders who own the land and even own the villages appear
on every election ticket.

'We love to talk about human rights because it's what everyone wants
to hear,' a leading lawyer in Diyarbakır told me ruefully. 'But we Kurds
have got the least democratic society in the country. We're far behind
everyone else, and plenty of people want to keep it that way.'

*   *   *

From inner city Istanbul to the Iranian border, Newroz has become a big
event in the Turkish Kurd political calendar. Conflict or no conflict, this
traditional New Year festival is now an annual focus of Kurdish protest
mixed with defiant celebration.

There have been some dark days of Newroz. In 1992 at least fifty
people were killed in clashes with the security forces in the border town
of Cizre; in 1999 there were more than four thousand arrests in Diyarbakır
alone; even in more recent years, with words like peace and democracy
on everyone's lips, there have been plenty of acts of defiance alongside
the officially sanctioned ceremonies.

Newroz is supposed to be a celebration of new life during the spring
equinox, but it has also become a battleground in which disaffected
Kurds assert their cultural identity, while the Turkish state imposes its
own law. Groups of Kurds gather around small bonfires to sing, dance
and jump through the flames, symbolically burning away the impurities
of the past. For years the state tried to suppress the festival completely,
before it suddenly decided to co-opt Newroz as an official pageant.

But in back streets and on patches of waste ground young boys still
burn tyres and bits of wood, and parrot what they've learned from their
elders.

'PKK, PKK,' they chant, and 'Long Live Kurdistan'.

The worst years of the conflict may be over, but the myths and the
memories have already been passed on to a new generation. The PKK
committed brutal acts of violence, and it still espouses an ideology well

past its sell-by date. But in Turkey's Kurdish provinces, and among Kurdish communities scattered across Europe, it has come to wield lasting influence. It has changed its official name to Kongra-Gel (the People's Congress of Kurdistan) and it says it wants a lasting peace, if only the Turkish state will grant amnesty to fighters who are prepared to lay down their weapons. But the state isn't interested – it thinks it won the war on the battlefield. The main concern now among diehard opponents of the PKK is that military victory is being slowly transformed into political defeat. The Kurds are starting to enjoy rights denied them for years, as reforms demanded by the European Union begin to take effect.

Ironically the seeds of the PKK were sown at the heart of the Turkish state, in Atatürk's capital, Ankara, where a young man named Abdullah Öcalan studied in the early 1970s. Born in a small town on the banks of the Euphrates river, like many urban Kurds he spoke Turkish first and foremost, and it would take many years before he could talk fluently in the language he decided to fight for. Öcalan was a ruthless opportunist who seized his chance. He saw Kurds beset by social injustice, economic deprivation and a lack of ethnic recognition. He mixed it all together into a potent brew – a violent Kurdish national liberation movement based on Marxism–Leninism, which grew quickly into the biggest armed challenge the Turkish state had ever seen.

Frustration among Kurdish radicals rose to boiling point amid the widespread political violence which scarred the years leading up to the 1980 military coup. When the generals took over and arrested thousands of leftists, Öcalan fled to Syria where he found a warm welcome for anyone willing to help destabilize Turkey. From his bases in Damascus and later the Bek'aa Valley, Abdullah Öcalan led the PKK into a full-scale armed insurrection. Using a mixture of extreme Kurdish nationalism and class war, the PKK took effective control of vast swathes of the rural south-east by the early 1990s, killing without compunction. Among their victims were local officials and their families, landlords, policemen, soldiers, school teachers, and fellow Kurds who were allied to the state. Anyone who represented Ankara and central authority, or the old feudal system, was in danger.

When the Turkish security forces hit back, they hit back hard – launching one of the largest counter-insurgency campaigns of modern times. At the height of the civil war, the Turkish army had more than a quarter of a million men in the south-eastern provinces. Several thousand villages and small hamlets were forcibly evacuated and destroyed, crops were burnt, herds of sheep and cattle were gunned down, and army commanders talked of 'draining the swamp to kill the mosquitoes'. Torture and mysterious killings were commonplace; arbitrary arrests, abductions and disappearances proliferated.

'For us it became a republic of fear,' said one prominent Kurdish activist, who lived through the worst years. 'Many of those who died were completely innocent, and while it was happening, the world looked the other way.'

The state also made sure it employed Kurds who opposed the PKK, to pit tribe against tribe. There was brutality on both sides, and blood feuds still fester. The village guards were armed and paid by the state, but barely trained. They are now one of the biggest stumbling blocks to lasting peace because they've taken the land of others, and they don't want to give it back. One of the most unnerving experiences I ever had in the south-east was when we drove up to what felt like an unofficial checkpoint, manned by village guards on a back road near Siirt. I think it was something to do with the way the loaded gun was pointing through the window of our car rather than at the ground. Discipline didn't seem to be a strong point, and there was lots of shouting and angry faces. They didn't let us pass, but we didn't care. It just felt good to be able to leave in one piece. Others wouldn't have been so lucky.

By the end of the 1990s, south-eastern Turkey was littered with abandoned villages and broken buildings. Their former inhabitants had been herded into vast new shanty settlements on the edge of towns and cities across the country. Some Kurds left the south-east altogether, in search of safety and of work. Istanbul is now the largest Kurdish city in the world – more than twenty per cent of its massive population claim some degree of Kurdish descent. Other displaced villagers streamed into the new slums of cities like Diyarbakır, where the population trebled to more than a million during the course of the decade. Typical of the new underclass were the men from Kelkum, a village which had been depopulated and torched by the gendarmerie at the height of the PKK rebellion. In the shadow of Diyarbakır's old city walls, they used to gather at the same place at the same time every day to swap stories, remember old times and dream of going home.

'We were all evacuated,' said one villager, a man with sad eyes, 'and no one has a permanent job here. Some of us try to sell goods on the street; some people even beg to make money.'

Several years on, the memories of what happened the day their village died, and the sense of dislocation, were as strong as ever. Conflict still raged in the minds of the dispossessed men from Kelkum, and some of them carried their physical scars with them as well.

'They just kept kicking me with their heavy boots, they beat the soles of my feet and they burned my body with cigarettes,' said Ahmet. 'I kept telling them I didn't know anything, but they kept doing it for three days. I don't know why they finally let me go. I thought they were going to kill me.'

What was most shocking about conversations like this over a period of years was how commonplace they were. You could walk into any café or market in the south-east and if people weren't too afraid to talk to a stranger, the stories would come flooding out. An entire society had been brutalized, and it hasn't been forgotten. While the world watched in horror during the 1990s as the former Yugoslavia convulsed in violence, the Turks got away with murder. By any standard it was a vicious conflict, but most of the killing was done by the forces of the state. According to official Turkish figures, the PKK killed 5,314 members of the security forces and 4,630 civilians between 1984 and the end of 1998. The overall death toll in the same period is estimated to have been somewhere between thirty and forty thousand. Most of the dead were poor Kurdish villagers who had joined the PKK and chosen to fight, or poor Kurdish villagers who were in the wrong place at the wrong time.

Fethi was one of the lucky ones, and from his cell in Diyarbakır's notorious city jail he had plenty of time to think about it. Fethi was a member of the PKK who turned 'confessor' after he was captured during an army operation in a neighbouring district. When I met him in prison he looked forlorn and nervous, but he said he was pleased to have put down his gun and survived. Formerly a student in Istanbul, he had fought against the Turkish army and represented the PKK in Greece before becoming disillusioned with Abdullah Öcalan's autocratic regime.

'There was a huge difference between the PKK we had in our heads and the reality of the PKK in the mountains,' he told me. 'Many people stay in the organization because they have no alternative; they have nothing else to believe in.'

The lack of an alternative may be the real key to the sorry recent history of south-eastern Turkey. As long as that vacuum was there and Turkey refused to do much about it beyond the use of overwhelming force, support for the PKK remained strong. Only recently have there been some signs of change. In the local elections in March 2004, the AKP polled well in the south-east, attracting support from traditional conservative Islamist voters, but also from other Kurds tired of war. Many people looked at the moves that had been made towards reform and democratization, and hoped they would usher in a new era of economic opportunity and personal freedom.

It still isn't difficult to find people in Diyarbakır or Hakkari or Şırnak willing to declare that the rebels remain their best bet. In some towns everyone seems to have a friend or a relative who has 'gone to the mountains'. For years no one else gave them any feeling of empowerment at all, and the PKK (the name Kongra-Gel hasn't quite stuck yet) still has totemic influence. But it doesn't speak for everyone, and if the current leadership of the PKK were to try to start another full-scale conflict, they would find that the number of people willing to support them has fallen sharply.

The focus now is on peaceful political change. On one steaming hot day on the outskirts of Diyarbakır I watched the mayor, Osman Baydemir, planting young saplings in the dry stony earth – a peace forest, they called it.

'We are all hoping that peace will endure,' he told the small crowd, as plain-clothes policemen filmed his every move. 'No one wants to go back to the bad days.'

Baydemir is leading a new generation of Kurdish leaders which has emerged to run local municipalities won by the pro-Kurdish party, DEHAP; and they sense that their time may have come. 'If DEHAP nominated a stone to be mayor,' I was told, 'the stone would win.'

The new generation still defers in many respects to the PKK, but it is a delicate balance. They want many of the same things, but their methods are very different.

'We have no organic or inorganic link with the PKK, and we don't support violence,' Osman Baydemir says in the most careful language he can muster. 'What we need is a solution to this conflict which involves everyone.'

As long as politics remains at the forefront in the continuing battle for greater rights, Kurdish eyes will remain focused not on rebel camps in the mountains of northern Iraq, but on the faraway offices of the European Union. It's been that way ever since Abdullah Öcalan was captured in 1999.

'It would be natural for them to try to establish peace here,' argued one displaced villager I met at the time on a Diyarbakır street corner. 'If anyone is interested in trying to do that, we would be very grateful to them.'

And with a wary nod he was gone. 'You never know who could be listening,' he had said over his shoulder as he walked away.

* * *

The Kurds, they say, 'have no friends but the mountains', and like any guerrilla force the PKK could always cling on in remote upland regions of the south-east. It was never completely defeated. But over time the vast numerical superiority of the Turkish armed forces proved irresistible, and by the summer of 1998 the fighting had died down sufficiently for the generals to launch their final charge. They rolled their tanks towards the Syrian border, and began rattling a few sabres. Turkish newspaper headlines spoke of 'meeting the Israelis on the Golan Heights', and the Syrians took the hint. President Hafez Assad quickly told Öcalan that he would have to go and the Kurdish leader was smuggled out via Greece to Russia, embarking on an extraordinary and ultimately unsuccessful odyssey.

For a while Öcalan was in Italy, where he tried to claim political asylum. The Italians didn't know what to do with him, but they made it clear that the Italian constitution wouldn't allow them to extradite anyone to a country where the death penalty was still in force.

'Let's abolish capital punishment to get him back,' a Turkish columnist wrote thoughtfully, 'then we can reimpose it again.'

Other reaction in Turkey was predictably apoplectic. Politicians muttered dark threats against their NATO ally, while Turkish businessmen launched an economic boycott. From shoe-shop chains to supermarkets, from raw

materials to industrial machines, Turkish companies suddenly stopped deal-
ing in Italian goods. Italian fruit was crushed underfoot in markets, and
Italian furniture was burnt on the streets. I even saw one angry young man
taking a sledgehammer to his beloved scooter, and begin bashing it to pieces.

Crowds gathered outside the Italian embassy in Ankara for days to lay
black wreaths and voice their fury. A bank of loudspeakers played patriotic Turkish songs, while the indignant battle cry of the protestors –
'Italya! Terörist!' – needed no translation.

'Damn the Italians,' said one tearful woman, holding a picture of her
dead son. 'I'm cursing them. They must be the most useless country in
the world.'

And many of her compatriots felt the same. Turkey wanted revenge
against Abdullah Öcalan, not some sort of equitable international compromise. The United States strongly backed Ankara's campaign to bring
Öcalan to justice, but Turkey's grim determination in the late 1990s to
deny the existence of any wider Kurdish issues hardly struck a chord,
particularly in Europe.

'The Turks,' confided one European diplomat in Ankara at the time,
'have become a bit like a bar-room bore sitting on a stool, telling anyone
who's unlucky enough to be within earshot how unfair life is, how misunderstood he is, and so on and so on.'

But on this occasion the bar-room bore had the last laugh. Italy
crumpled under pressure and asked Öcalan to leave. He became an
outlaw again. He tried to get to the Netherlands and an international
court, but his plane was turned away. Finally, after months on the run,
he was tracked down to the Greek Embassy compound in, of all places,
Kenya. The Turks were tipped off by the Americans and they sent a
plane full of commandos on a mission code-named 'Operation Safari'.
But no heroics were necessary. In the event the Kurdish rebel leader was
tricked into leaving the Greek compound in a Kenyan police vehicle. He
thought he was on his way to South Africa, but in a carefully coordinated
operation involving agents of various nationalities Öcalan was delivered
straight to the disbelieving Turks waiting on the tarmac.

Once their plane was safely in the air, the Turkish celebrations began.
A military intelligence video released to a gawking public showed Turks
wearing black balaclavas exchanging congratulations and 'high fives' as
Öcalan sat blindfolded and handcuffed. At one stage the blindfold was

removed, and in a close-up shot Öcalan was seen drenched in sweat, bewildered and nervous. 'Welcome home,' an agent says to him. 'Thank you,' says Öcalan, 'I love Turkey and I love the Turkish people.'

The mission to capture him was so secret that when the plane tried to land at Istanbul airport it was initially refused permission because it had no flight plan. It circled above the city until an urgent call from Ankara to the control tower gave the pilot the clearance he needed. Turkey's most wanted man was back in his home country; the government revelled in its triumph, but when it came to thanking its allies it was for once circumspect in victory.

'In the interest of not disturbing those parties who took part in this operation,' said the prime minister of the time, Bülent Ecevit, 'I will use a local expression: "Let us eat the grape and not ask where it came from."'

* * *

Öcalan feels like something of a forgotten man these days – the only inmate on the prison island of Imralı, in the middle of the Sea of Marmara. The PKK is still demanding his release from isolation, so is DEHAP, but while his lawyers and close family members are allowed occasional visits, no one else apart from his military guards has seen him for more than five years. I visited the island only once – for the first day of the Öcalan trial – and getting there wasn't easy. There was a retina scan, fingerprinting, and a thorough check for any suspicious trace of explosives. That was all before we were allowed onto the boat which would take us to one of the most heavily guarded prisons in the world.

Imralı was looking rather pleasant in the early summer of 1999 – a rocky outcrop topped with green, sitting in the middle of a calm blue sea. It had previously been a relaxed open prison, where inmates spent their time herding sheep or looking after the cattle. But they were all shipped out as soon as Öcalan was captured, and by the time we arrived for the trial he had been held in strict isolation for more than three months. Quite how a Kurdish snatch squad would try to rescue him wasn't clear, but the Turkish authorities were taking no chances. Our boat to the island was accompanied by a coast guard cutter and a frigate. Helicopters buzzed overhead and did some fancy low-level manœuvres to keep themselves busy.

As we approached the island itself I wondered who had placed fence posts at regular intervals along the shoreline and on the hilltops. Getting closer I realized the fence posts were armed, and they were actually Turkish soldiers. Öcalan's prospects of escape were not looking good. The court room where he was to be put on trial had previously been a prison cinema – rather appropriate for a scene which felt like something out of James Bond. It had been hastily converted, with wood panelling and a soothing shade of lilac on the walls. The turnstiles to get inside would have put most football grounds to shame.

As we took our seats, Abdullah Öcalan appeared suddenly and without ceremony through a side door. Wearing a grey-green suit and blue shirt, he looked relatively well and had clearly lost a bit of weight during his three months in custody. He was placed in a bulletproof glass cubicle designed, we were gravely informed, to withstand the impact of a small bomb. He glanced around the courtroom, shuffled on his chair and scratched his head. The small audience looked on, transfixed. Relatives of soldiers killed fighting against the PKK sat face to face with the man they held responsible for causing their grief. Some of them were draped in Turkish flags and holding photographs of lost husbands and sons.

Finally it was down to business – the serious business of putting Öcalan on trial for his life. On that first day he came across as a rather pathetic figure. There was no trace of the defiant revolutionary he imagined himself to be. He listened intently but impassively as prosecutors read out a damning indictment against him: murder, treason, armed revolt, extortion. It was all there, but the PKK leader didn't look too concerned. He apologized for any suffering he had caused, and declared that his trial had no legal value. Then he launched into a political defence – a rambling speech lasting for more than an hour which appeared to take even his own lawyers by surprise. He called for peace, and an end to armed struggle, but suggested that the Turkish state had to meet the PKK halfway.

'You can hang me if you like,' Öcalan told the court. 'But let me solve the Kurdish problem first – you cannot do it without me. My case should be the chance for a rebirth.'

Perhaps he had deluded himself into believing that his offer would be taken seriously, but the state had already decided that the evidence against him was overwhelming. A few weeks later the chief judge, Turgut Okyay, declared Öcalan guilty of thousands of murders. Judge Okyay looked across the courtroom and deliberately snapped a pencil in half – the traditional sign that the death penalty was being imposed. In the port of Mudanya, the nearest point on the mainland to the drama unfolding in the courtroom, relatives of dead soldiers – the Families of the Martyrs – reacted with unrestrained emotion. 'Death to Öcalan,' they screamed. 'Long Live Turkey.'

But it wasn't that simple. Within hours of the end of the trial, several European governments had called for the death penalty to be commuted, and a long process of legal appeals had begun. Many people thought Öcalan had simply been trying to save his skin during his trial, but this wasn't a sudden conversion. He had talked of ending the insurgency long before he was captured. Suddenly, in prison, he posed a different kind of problem to the Turkish state. After whipping up nationalist sentiment for years and portraying Öcalan as the devil incarnate, many Turkish officials realized that getting rid of him would create more problems than it would solve. They had no intention of allowing him to play a political role, but they didn't want to create a martyr, and cause a massive rupture in their relations with Europe.

For many Turks it was a galling process. The idea of Europe is usually associated in Turkey with progress and modernity. Öcalan on the other hand has been variously dismissed as terrorist, baby killer and outdated irrelevance. How, many people wondered, could Europe defend such a man? The answer, of course, was that Europe had no wish to defend him, but it did want some political steps taken to help solve the Kurdish problem, and it was steadfast in its opposition to capital punishment. Turkish nationalists who had joined the coalition government after the 1999 general election found it all too much to take. 'Damn the Europeans Who Prefer the Murderer of the Century Öcalan to the Turkish Nation!' said a typically angry headline in the newspaper *Ortadoğu*, the mouthpiece of the extreme right.

But beyond the slogans there was little else the nationalists could do, as the PKK for once showed some political common sense. Although the violence never died down completely, as the army continued to pursue the rebels wherever it could find them, the PKK did embrace Öcalan's language of peace; it declared a ceasefire and abandoned talk of a separate state. Instead it began campaigning for cultural rights in education and broadcasting – exactly what the European Union was asking Turkey to offer the Kurds in the first place.

To the barely concealed fury of parts of the Turkish establishment, the Kurds began to get what they wanted through the ballot not the bullet. Politicians from the pro-Kurdish party HADEP (now DEHAP) swept to power as mayors of towns and cities across the south-east. And within a few years the Turkish parliament took up the challenge of reform. Beginning in the summer of 2002, it abolished the death penalty – saving Abdullah Öcalan's life – and began making legal changes which Kurds could only have dreamt of a decade earlier.

There were and still are many attempts to knock things off course. After Turkey was officially accepted as a candidate for EU membership in December 1999 (there was no date for talks at that stage) the then foreign minister Ismael Cem suggested the time was right to allow TV broadcasts in Kurdish languages. A member of the public complained, and a state security court began investigating Cem on charges of encouraging separatism. A few weeks later the Kurdish mayor of Diyarbakır was hauled out of his car in the middle of the street and taken into custody, shortly after he held several days of meetings with European politicians to discuss Kurdish issues.

'Do we want to treat the PKK like the IRA, and HADEP like Sinn Fein in Northern Ireland?' wrote columnist Mehmet Ali Kışlalı in the newspaper *Radikal* at the time. 'If that's what anyone expects, they are living in a fantasy world.'

In fact moves to liberalize Kurdish freedom of expression have faced obstacles at every turn. In 2001 a Turkish court banned the Batman city council from using Kurdish words as street names – words which translate as 'Tulip' Street and 'High Pasture' Street were rejected out of hand. The highest administrative court in the land ruled that the names had been deliberately chosen to provoke a political reaction. They could, it said, lead to an 'erosion of cultural values'. Other street names to fall foul of the legal veto included 'Halabja', the Kurdish town in Iraq which was bombarded with chemical weapons by

Saddam Hussein, and 'Mahatma Gandhi'. The court ruled that the name of the Indian independence leader, synonymous around the world with peaceful protest, was likely to promote rebellion against the state.

Even newborn children have not been immune. In 2002 parents suddenly found themselves being warned that giving a child a Kurdish name would be 'interpreted as terrorist propaganda'. Children should be named, an Interior Ministry directive warned, 'in a manner appropriate to our national culture, moral principles and customs'. Subsequent legal reform should have got rid of the problem, but even now names which include the letters 'w', 'x' or 'q' – part of the Kurdish alphabet, but not the Turkish one – are routinely rejected.

* * *

Resistance to change is still a powerful factor, but change has come all the same, and with gathering speed. The regional state of emergency has been lifted, people are no longer routinely harassed and many road-blocks – once a tedious and sometimes frightening ritual of everyday life – have disappeared. A few years ago it was hard to find tapes of Kurdish music, sold surreptitiously on the streets; now Kurdish songs boom out from clubs and discos right across the country and no one pays it any heed.

Most significantly, the constitution has been amended to allow citizens to speak, broadcast and receive education in 'regional dialects'. Implementation of the new laws has been painfully slow, but several Kurdish language courses have begun to operate in south-eastern cities and in Istanbul, despite the bureaucratic obstacles strewn in their path. One private course had to delay its opening for several months because its door was a few centimetres smaller than official regulations demanded.

Local broadcasting is an equally sensitive issue. State television may have reluctantly begun its limited Kurdish coverage ('It smells of Turkish translation, it's half-hearted, there's no true Kurdish spirit in the pro-gramme,' said one disgruntled observer), but local channels are still struggling to gain approval. Gün TV in Diyarbakır operates from a tiny studio in the middle of a shopping complex. On the day I visited them a Kurdish musician from Syria had been invited to give a recital on his *saz*. He was allowed to *sing* in Kurdish (as long as he didn't sing anything from the long list of songs which have been banned by the state); but if he *spoke* a few words in Kurdish they had to be translated immediately into Turkish.

It all made for a very complicated programme. Six months earlier Gün TV had applied to the authorities to broadcast properly in Kurdish, and after a long silence they had received a letter saying their application was 'being evaluated'. A few days after my visit the station was shut down for a month by the authorities after one participant in a phone-in spoke in Kurdish and no one bothered to translate it.

'Things seem to be getting better, but not that much has changed for us,' Gün TV's young general manager Zeynel Doğan told me with a palpable sense of frustration.

'If the government had approached the Kurdish question with half the courage that it showed in confronting the state on the Cyprus issue, things would be different.'

To realize how daft the Turkish policy on broadcasting is you only need to stand in the middle of any sizeable community in the south-east and look upwards. Dilapidated satellite dishes, some of which look alarmingly like converted biscuit tins, cling to every balcony and sprout from every rooftop. It's been like that for years – even families who can hardly afford to feed themselves manage to scrimp and save to get hold of the ubiquitous dish. As long as local channels aren't allowed to broadcast in Kurdish everyone will continue to watch Kurdish satellite channels based in Europe. They are beyond the control of the Turkish authorities, and they regularly feature long statements from leaders of the PKK.

So a good deal remains to be done and the European Union has made it clear that it assumes the reforms introduced so far 'are only the beginning'. Full implementation will take a long time, and a change in mentality will take even longer. But why shouldn't local TV stations broadcast what they want, and why shouldn't optional language classes be introduced in public schools? European attitudes to minority languages should hardly constitute a threat to Turkey's national survival – after all the number of people in the EU speaking Breton or Welsh is continuing to decline. Turkish officialdom remains suspicious, but the Kurdish author, Edip Polat, who formed a Kurdish branch of the writers' freedom organization, PEN, is in no doubt that pressure from Europe has been the decisive factor.

'All this is happening because of the EU accession process. If the Europeans weren't taking an interest in what we are doing–' he laughed – 'we'd never have been able to open in the first place.'

Diyarbakır – the unofficial capital of the south-east – is now a strange mix. Alongside the street carts and slums, there are five-star hotels, shopping malls and burger bars – global culture has arrived. The only explosions heard at night in the centre of the city are from lavish firework displays celebrating another local wedding. And yet the Kurdish provinces remain the most impoverished region in the country, and many people still feel under siege. A big military operation in the summer of 2004 prevented thousands of residents in one neighbourhood from leaving their homes for ten days, and some reforms are only acknowledged in the breach.

In principle demonstrators can now hold protests anywhere without permission or harassment. In practice it's impossible, in a region still crawling with security officials who have made a career out of distrusting the people. The length of legal detention without trial has been cut from thirty days to a maximum of four, but access to a lawyer is often delayed, and many detainees say they are beaten. The Kurdish provinces remain the most fragile part of the new Turkey, and when the EU's Commissioner for Enlargement, Günter Verheugen, visited Diyarbakır in September 2004, the municipal government plastered the city with posters. 'Comrade Verheugen,' they said in Turkish, English and Kurdish, 'welcome to the greater Europe.' It was written as much in hope as in expectation. A plea that Europe won't forget them again.

* * *

High in the mountains of northern Iraq, close to the Iranian border, the tired cult of Abdullah Öcalan lives on. The PKK (Kongra-Gel) controls well-established camps scattered across this inhospitable terrain and early in 2005 Turkish pleas to the Americans to root them out were still falling on deaf ears. It means northern Iraq remains the wild card in the complex political equation surrounding Turkey and its Kurds. It may just be a passing phase, but the decision by PKK hardliners based in Iraq to resume the armed struggle in Turkey has raised many questions.

During 2003 and 2004 hundreds of rebel fighters are thought to have slipped back across the border into Turkish territory. The state of emergency may have gone, but parts of the countryside in south-eastern Turkey are still not at peace. Bomb attacks from Istanbul to the Mediterranean coast to small south-eastern towns – none of them huge but all of them destructive – have been blamed without real proof on Kurdish militants. The refusal of the state to countenance any kind of amnesty for surviving members of the PKK may have backfired – if we're regarded as outlaws anyway, they seem to have decided, then we may as well fight on.

There have been bitter ideological splits within the PKK leadership, who must be motivated by the fear of drifting into irrelevance. As the EU reform process begins to produce real results, no one seems terribly sure what the PKK is for any more. That's why some Turkish officials believe the remaining rebel leadership saw the political upheaval in Iraq as a chance to re-establish themselves as a military threat, or at least remind their old supporters that they still exist.

It won't be easy because there's no real stomach for a fight any more, and Turkish and Iraqi Kurds don't get on terribly well anyway. For years the Kurdistan Democratic Party, the Iraqi Kurdish group which controls the area next to the Turkish frontier, cooperated with the Turkish army in its frequent military operations in northern Iraq against the PKK. The leader of the KDP, Massoud Barzani, comes from a family of prominent tribal leaders and epitomizes the feudal structure which the PKK claims to despise.

But the Turkish establishment often fails to see the difference between Kurd and Kurd: it is terrified by the idea of a semi-autonomous Kurdish state within a new federal Iraq. All the old fears suddenly come flooding back – of the treaty of Sèvres, of partition and rebellion, and of threats to the 'indivisible unity of the nation'. There are certainly a few Kurdish nationalists in Turkey who still dream of independence, perhaps a grand federation with their ethnic brethren across the borders financed by the oil wealth of the province of Kirkuk. But most Kurds in Turkey simply want a better life, and a bit of respect.

Take the village of Kebapçi, a collection of broken-down houses on a small hilltop in the province of Mardin, surrounded by overgrown fields and uncultivated vineyards. When I first went there in 2001 it was completely deserted. Roofs had fallen in, many of the yellow mud-brick walls had collapsed, and weeds were growing in the few broken window frames which remained. For a long time people weren't allowed back to their villages unless they signed a statement declaring that it was the PKK which had burnt them out of their homes in the first place. Most Kurds weren't prepared to do that and their patience was eventually rewarded. With persistent encouragement from Europe, which regards a return to the villages as a crucial piece of reform, the government says it is going ahead with plans to resettle and compensate hundreds of thousands of people.

When I went back to Kebapçi three years later, about twenty people had returned to live in the few buildings which remained fit for habitation. They'd applied to the local authorities to get their precious electricity connection restored, and clubbed together to buy a handful of animals. Similar stories can be found across the south-east. Kurds and Syriac Christians (who were distrusted and victimized for years by both the state and the PKK) are coming back from exile in dribs and drabs, hoping to rebuild village lives which were hastily abandoned in the 1980s and 1990s.

But there are still plenty of isolated villages which have lost all electricity and telephone links, and even viable roads. Village schools had also disappeared after the teachers were killed by the PKK, and the buildings were burnt by the state. Hundreds of small hamlets are now uninhabitable during the cold winter months, and in many areas the village guards routinely threaten anyone trying to return. A detailed report from the pressure group Human Rights Watch in March 2005 argued that the number of displaced people going home was much lower than official figures suggest, and that assistance with reconstruction had been 'minimal or non-existent'.

Even in Kebapçi no money had arrived from central government to help the villagers re-establish their community, but they had already lodged an application with the European Court of Human Rights seeking redress.

'We used to have a good life here,' said Selahattin Kaya, gesturing at the empty fields. 'We grew tomatoes, peppers and potatoes; we had walnut trees, apricot and pear trees. Now they're all gone, and we're relying on Europe to help us bring them back again.'

A group of villagers gathered round. One of them showed me the bullet holes on a nearby wall – a reminder, he said, of the day the soldiers forced them out after a nearby clash with the PKK. We shared a plate of grapes and some strong sweet tea as the wind whistled through the buildings, throwing up clouds of dust. Unprompted, they all wanted to know when I thought they'd join the European Union.

'We're hoping we'll get some compensation eventually,' Selahattin said, 'and then we'll start to grow our vineyards back and buy some more animals.'

Another young villager appeared round the corner, back home after spending more than half his life in internal exile. Many Kurds will never go back to their villages – they've made new lives in the cities; others hope new horizons are finally opening up for them.

'My younger brother over there,' Selahattin said, 'he's going to go to university. He wants to become a teacher. It's good. In spite of everything, it shows we're making progress.'

5

OPEN WOUNDS: THE GREEKS AND THE ARMENIANS

The Greeks

More than fifty metres above the ground, the sounds of the city echoed around Istanbul's most astonishing building. It felt as if we were floating on thin air. Far below me, wandering between bright light and dark shadow, tourists crossed the ancient stone floor, surrounded by the accumulated memories of centuries gone by. I was standing on a narrow scaffolding platform, close enough to touch the tiny Byzantine tiles which adorn the inside of the dome of Aya Sofya.

'We've been restoring the mosaics, renewing the plaster, cleaning the marble,' the resident archaeologist, Sabriye Parlak, told me. 'It's a very old building and it's strong, but it needs constant attention.'

The biggest restoration project in more than a century has been taking place for years, but somehow Aya Sofya (Haghia Sophia to the Greeks) remains in limbo. Many parts of the complex are still closed off or in a state of disrepair, and Aya Sofya needs a lot more than a new coat of paint to bring it back to life. It is an iconic place for two peoples – Greeks and Turks. I find it hauntingly beautiful but flawed, a building caught up in a long history of old rivalries and competing cultures. In the first years of our new century relations between Greece and Turkey have improved dramatically, but Aya Sofya is still trapped by the political sensitivities of its extraordinary past.

When it was dedicated in AD 536, during the reign of the Byzantine emperor, Justinian, Aya Sofya was the wonder of the age. An architectural marvel, with its soaring arches and mighty dome, it was the spiritual home of Eastern Christianity: St Sophia's, the Cathedral of the Holy Wisdom. For more than nine hundred years it reigned supreme as the greatest church in the world, until the Ottomans claimed it for Islam and turned Aya Sofya into the Imperial Mosque. After the founding of the Turkish republic it became a museum and it remains one today, another legacy of Atatürk's reforming zeal. There are plenty of Islamists who want to reclaim Aya Sofya for themselves; at the moment Muslim prayers are recited in a small section at the back of the complex. But for the dwindling number of Greeks who still live in Istanbul, and for the thousands who now visit each year, it is a place of even greater importance – a reminder of their lasting links with the city they used to call Constantinople.

The Ecumenical Patriarch, Bartholomew I, is still based in Istanbul – the spiritual leader of more than two hundred million Orthodox Christians around the world. He and his patriarchate stay in what has become an overwhelmingly Muslim city, and they have no intention of leaving. Often the Orthodox Church has to battle against the odds – bombs have been thrown, threats have been made, and Turkey still refuses to recognize the patriarch as anything other than the local leader of a religious minority. But the Church remains in Istanbul to make an important point.

'Istanbul is still a Christian city too, and we want to share it,' an archdeacon at the patriarchate told me with quiet defiance. 'For us Haghia Sophia is still the great Holy Church of Christ. That's why we are here. It inspires us and it gives us focus.'

*　*　*

When Istanbul stood at the heart of the Ottoman Empire, it was the minority communities – Greeks, Armenians and Jews – which gave the city its unique cosmopolitan mix. The Greeks in particular were well educated, confident and prosperous. But history has been unkind, and the end of the empire hit the Greeks hard. A community which numbered hundreds of thousands at the end of the nineteenth century has shrunk dramatically. By the end of the twentieth century, there were fewer than three thousand Greeks left in Istanbul, most of them elderly, many of them poor, living on memories of the past. Greek schools and churches in the city are maintained with loving care and donations from abroad, but they are empty more often than not.

A few miles up the Bosphorus from Aya Sofya the small Church of the Virgin Mary in the village of Yeniköy is a pretty humble affair. Just down the hill from the old Orthodox cemetery, it sits unobtrusively in a residential neighbourhood – plain to the point of anonymity from the outside, but kept alive as a place of worship by the dedication of people like Laki Vingas, a local businessman. I visited the church on one of its most important annual occasions – a feast day in August when the icons are dusted down, the patriarch comes to lead the small congregation of worshippers and the sense of community is a reminder of days gone by.

'This is my father when he was young.'

Laki showed me a fading black and white photograph of Istanbul in the old days. His family has lived here on the shores of the Bosphorus for a hundred years, after migrating from the Greek islands. The current generation of the Vingas family are something of a rarity – Istanbul Greeks who still feel comfortable in the city. Laki's children speak both Greek and Turkish fluently and they regard this without hesitation as home. But Laki knows they could be part of a dying community.

'We have to be realistic, but we are determined to keep our identity,' he said, as we sat eating breakfast. 'That means keeping our church and our language alive.'

Greeks living in modern Turkey have never had to suffer the indignities heaped upon the Kurds – no one has ever tried to pretend that they don't exist. They are officially recognized as a minority in the republic's founding document, the 1923 Treaty of Lausanne, and their language has never been subject to the absurd restrictions under which the Kurds have been forced to labour for eighty years. But the Greeks have never been made to feel particularly welcome; and if the formation of the Turkish republic was a rude shock for the Greeks of Istanbul, for the Greeks of Anatolia it was a catastrophe.

The crushing defeat of the Greek Army in Izmir (ancient Smyrna) in 1922 was accompanied by widespread killings and a massive population transfer involving well over a million people. In 1923 Greeks from across

Anatolia – the merchants, tradesmen and professionals who kept many Anatolian towns running – were forced to swap places with ethnic Turks living in mainland Greece and the Greek islands. In one fell swoop, the long-established Hellenic culture of Asia Minor all but disappeared, leaving only ancient monuments and abandoned houses as a reminder of what had once been. Many of the ethnic Greeks who remained chose to convert publicly to Islam for self-preservation, and they kept their old faith to themselves.

In Istanbul the Greeks were allowed to stay under sufferance – many had nowhere else to go, but some were convinced that their control of much of the city's commercial wealth would afford them some kind of protection. For a while it seemed to work, they kept their heads down and got on with their lives as Kemal Atatürk signed a friendship treaty with Greece. But during the Second World War a punitive wealth tax directed specifically at Greeks and other minorities in Turkey brought many businessmen to their knees, and worse was about to come. Nationalists in both countries were spreading lurid stories about the growing communal tensions on the island of Cyprus, and in 1955 Istanbul was convulsed by riots. Mobs organized by the government rampaged through the city. Homes and businesses belonging to minority communities were left in ruins, and Orthodox graveyards were desecrated. Tens of thousands of Greeks fled in the following months, as the character of Istanbul began to change for ever.

'It was a terrible time,' Laki Vingas told me. 'For many Greeks in the city, it was the only life they had ever known. And it came to a very sudden end.'

As the situation on Cyprus deteriorated, so did the position of the Istanbul Greeks. News of massacres of Turkish Cypriots was greeted with fury and Atatürk's friendship treaty with Greece was abruptly cancelled in 1964. Many Greeks were expelled from Istanbul, their residency rights taken away. Some of them were given twenty-four hours to leave, and their property was confiscated by the authorities. In the space of a generation the community had been pushed to the edge of extinction. Only a few brave souls remained, under threat, facing discrimination and often in fear of their lives. In 1992 the pressure group Human Rights Watch described the Greek community in Istanbul as 'dwindling, elderly and frightened. Their fearfulness is related to an appalling history of pogroms and expulsions that they have suffered at the hands of the Turkish government.'

So they looked for support from their ethnic kin in Greece, which only made matters worse. As relations between Athens and Ankara stumbled along in the gutter, nationalists on both sides turned on the minority communities in their midst as an outlet for their frustrations. The discrimination suffered by the Greeks of Istanbul has been mirrored for many years by the treatment of ethnic Turks living in the region of western Thrace across the border in Greece. They have faced religious discrimination, a refusal by the Greek authorities to accept their ethnic identity, restrictions on freedom of expression and second-class status in education. 'The Greek state,' said Human Rights Watch, this time in 1999, 'has been unable for the most part to accept the fact that one can be a loyal Greek citizen and, at the same time, an ethnic Turk proud of his or her culture and religion.'

Politicians on both sides were stuck in a time warp, egged on by often hysterical nationalist rhetoric in the media. But sometimes ordinary people acting on their own initiative seemed to show much more common sense. Long before the current thaw in bilateral relations, I spent an unforgettable evening drinking Cappadocian wine on a rooftop terrace in central Anatolia, listening to Greeks and Turks getting to know the neighbours they never had. A Greek flag was (and still is) an unusual sight in Cappadocia, deep in the Anatolian heartland. But it was the first thing I saw – painted proudly on a board – when I arrived in the old town of Ürgüp. In this region of extraordinary rock formations and ancient underground churches, a minor political miracle was under way. After several years of informal contact, Ürgüp had been formally twinned with the Greek town of Larissa.

The two towns have a long and complex history. In the 1920s the Christians of Cappadocia and the Muslims in the Greek region around Larissa were forced from their homes as part of the state-approved population exchange (ethnic cleansing, as we call it today), which followed the Turkish War of Independence. It took nearly three-quarters of a century for a new generation to try to re-establish contact.

'I have been here many times now, my parents came from Cappadocia,' said Dimitrios Kappadokis, a Greek businessman who led initial efforts to forge links between the two communities.

'I want the Greeks and the Turks to be friends,' he added, 'I believe in peace.'

He had brought a tour party with him on that occasion, including an Orthodox priest making a pilgrimage to some of Christianity's earliest sites. Many of them had ancestral roots in Cappadocia, and some were coming back for the first time.

'We look the same, we know the same songs, and we eat the same food,' said Fazlı Çalışkan, a local Turk who doubled up as tour guide for the day, showing his visitors around the many ancient cave churches which dot the region.

'Before this we didn't know each other, and it was difficult for us to understand them. But when they came here, we saw them and we liked them. Our relationship started, and now it is growing.'

The 'twin towns' initiative which began so cautiously was designed to change perceptions, and it appears to have been a success. Delegations from both sides now make regular trips across the Aegean to visit the lands of their forefathers. Our host on the roof terrace that first night was Hikmet Can, a jovial local man whose grandfather had been forced to emigrate from Greece.

'Forget politics!' Hikmet said, raising his glass to a new Greek friend. 'Everyone knows Greeks and Turks find it hard to get along sometimes, but we don't have any difficulties here. Sometimes we disagree, but we all have a good discussion. It can be done.'

At the time it sounded rather too utopian, too much like the wine talking, but it turns out now that Hikmet was right. It can be done. But it took a massive tragedy to make many people see the light.

* * *

Güvenç Pembegül had been trapped under the rubble for four days when the Greek search and rescue team arrived at his home near the shores of the Sea of Marmara. Local residents could hear Güvenç crying out for help but they didn't know how to reach him. His father, a Turkish naval officer, was frantic – the Greek team was the first real chance he had of saving his son. The Greeks dug with their hands for fourteen hours, feeding the nine-year-old boy water and glucose through a long tube lowered down among the ruins. They got him to shout to them, or sing songs, anything to help them identify exactly where he was. When Güvenç was pulled out alive after a marathon effort, Greeks and Turks embraced and cried together – 'earthquake diplomacy' was about to be born.

When the first of those two terrible earthquakes ripped through north-western Turkey in August 1999, Greek rescue teams were among the first on the scene, searching through the rubble, and saving lives. They were followed by Greek doctors, structural engineers and humanitarian relief workers. A few weeks later Athens was hit by a smaller earthquake of its own, and Turkish experts were quick to repay the compliment. The earthquakes seemed to give the silent majority on both sides the signal they had been looking for. Thousands of people queued up to give blood or donate food, clothing and supplies. When faced with tragedy they helped each other without a second thought. Surely, the argument ran, it shouldn't be too difficult to get along when life returned to normal.

So it was that in 1999, for the first time in seventy-six years, the anniversary of the liberation of the city of Izmir from Greek control was a muted affair. There was no re-enactment of Turkish troops enthusiastically throwing the Greeks into the sea, no ceremonial lowering of the hated Greek flag. At about the same time a leading Greek basketball team came to play in Ankara, and they trotted out to the usual cacophony of boos and curses. But the Greek players had a new trick up their sleeves. They produced flowers which they threw into the audience, and the boos were transformed into a sudden roar of applause.

The change in mood was soon unstoppable as popular opinion in both countries began to delight in the novel idea of 'love thy neighbour'; sporting events, concerts and exchange programmes proliferated. It took a brutal shock to the system to have such an effect, but it was typical of the wear-your-heart-on-your-sleeve mentality of both countries: from bitter enemies to long-lost brothers in a matter of weeks. Others were understandably more cautious, but equally pleased.

'We hope the softening of tone between the two countries will not be temporary,' said Patriarch Bartholomew at the time. 'We hope it will produce sweet fruits.'

The effect of earthquake diplomacy was all the more remarkable because as recently as 1996 the two countries had come perilously close to war in a dispute about ownership of a couple of small rocky outcrops in the Aegean Sea, known as Imia to the Greeks and Kardak to the Turks. The rocks in question were uninhabited (unless you counted the goats), but for a while national pride was at stake, the media were beating the war drums, and the only diplomacy around was of the gunboat variety. At the last minute, the United States leant heavily on its NATO allies, and forced them both to step back from the brink. Without American intervention, shots would have been fired in anger, and things could have spun quickly out of control.

If the Imia–Kardak crisis gave anyone in authority pause for thought, they weren't always showing it in public. The then Greek foreign minister, the pugnacious Theodoros Pangalos, set out his stall the following year: 'We have nothing to do with Turkey,' he spat. 'A man can't discuss things with murderers, rapists and thieves.' Turkey responded by calling Pangalos a 'psychopath', and insults began to fly faster than the state-of-the-art aircraft which the two countries were using to engage in dangerous mock-combat over the Aegean.

But Pangalos soon received his come-uppance, forced out of government in disgrace after the Greeks were caught red-handed meddling in Turkey's most sensitive affairs. When it emerged that the fugitive Kurdish rebel leader, Abdullah Öcalan, had been given sanctuary in the Greek Embassy compound in Nairobi, many Turkish suspicions about their neighbours seemed to be confirmed. Greece, thundered the Turkish president, had 'just one more chance'.

The Öcalan affair could easily have pushed bilateral relations to a new low, but for once cooler heads prevailed. The newly appointed Greek foreign minister, George Papandreou, and his Turkish counterpart, Ismael Cem, found that they liked each other. There was military co-operation through NATO during the Kosovo crisis and high-level political contacts resumed on a much more practical footing, concentrating on issues like tourism and environmental cooperation where tentative progress could actually be made. A few months later, when the earthquake took its terrible toll, the politicians were ready to take advantage of the huge outpouring of popular sympathy.

* * *

Five years later, when Esra Erdoğan – the daughter of the Turkish prime minister – was married in a lavish wedding in Istanbul in July 2004, the guest of honour flew in from Athens. The Greek prime minister, Costas Karamanlis, had been asked to be a witness at the wedding, a sign of just how far the two countries have come.

'A few years ago nobody could have believed that this might happen,' he said. 'I wish happiness, peace and a lot of children to the married couple.'

It was a formal ceremony, embellished with all the razzmatazz of a society wedding: the bride sat resplendent in a full white gown and an Islamic headscarf covered in sequins. The presence of Karamanlis was in stark contrast to the absence of the Turkish president, Ahmet Necdet Sezer, who sent his regrets. The representative of the secular state couldn't bring himself to be seen surrounded by Islamic attire of all shapes and sizes, but the prime minister of Greece could. How much some things have changed, and how much others have stayed the same.

Tayyip Erdoğan and Costas Karamanlis have pushed rapprochement to a new level. A couple of months before his daughter's wedding, Erdoğan became the first Turkish prime minister in sixteen years to make the short flight across the Aegean to Athens. There's talk of a new 'strategic partnership' and deep cuts in defence spending are already beginning to bite. Bilateral trade is booming, as business delegations seek to make up for lost time, and a natural gas pipeline will soon make another permanent connection. Tourists from both countries are flocking across the border, following in the footsteps of the pioneers I met in Cappadocia. A genuine sense of neighbourhood solidarity is also emerging: Turkey helped protect Athens from the threat of terrorist attacks during the Olympic Games; and many Turkish football fans cheered as the Greeks defeated a succession of traditional European football powers on their way to an unexpected victory at Euro 2004.

It doesn't always work that way of course, even in the aftermath of earthquake diplomacy. Greece stormed out of one NATO exercise in the Aegean because of a long-running dispute about airspace, which still flares up on a regular basis; and as for football, well, it doesn't always bring people closer together either. When Fenerbahçe of Istanbul and Panathinaikos of Athens were drawn together in a European tie in

November 2002, rival fans exchanged insults and political taunts. Turkish fans bombarded the Greeks with coins, cigarette lighters and whatever else they could lay their hands on, while Greek fans threw plastic seats and cartons full of yoghurt at the foreign ministers of the two countries, who had made the rather unwise decision to tour the ground.

So there are still nay-sayers, and plenty of problems to be resolved. But at a political level, Greece has made a strategic decision to support Turkey's application for membership of the European Union after blocking it for many years. The Greeks are being pragmatic. They know they have to live in the same neighbourhood, and they would prefer to share it with a reformed Turkey which is allowed to join their club, rather than an angry, resentful Turkey which is turned away at the door. Already Greece has seen its policy bear fruit, most notably on Cyprus where Turkey has changed course dramatically. It's not now the Turks who present the main obstacle to a settlement; ironically, it's the Greek Cypriots.

* * *

Northern Nicosia, 24 April 2004. It was nearly midnight and thousands of Turkish Cypriots were on the streets of Europe's last divided city, waving flags, hooting horns and blowing whistles. There was cacophony. With the enthusiastic backing of the government in mainland Turkey, the Turkish Cypriots had just voted convincingly in favour of a United Nations plan to reunify the island after thirty years of division.

'We're Cypriots, we're Europeans!' a woman called Melek shouted, as she wandered past me with her children. 'They have to help us now.'

'Do you think they will?'

'Why not?' She beamed. 'Everything changes in the end, even on Cyprus.'

There was only one problem. The Greek Cypriots in the south voted 'no' to the UN plan in even more emphatic numbers – more than three out of every four votes cast. There was to be no reunification before Cyprus joined the European Union a week later, and that meant only the Greek Cypriots and their internationally recognized government got the full benefits of membership. The Turkish Cypriots, under economic embargo and diplomatically isolated from the rest of the world, are still missing out.

So the crowds in the Turkish-controlled north on referendum night had mixed feelings, happy that they had voted 'yes' but also looking for someone to blame. Under the Venetian walls of the old city a chant began to echo across the square: 'Denktaş istifa! Denktaş istifa!' – 'Get lost, Denktaş!' It was a less than subtle hint to the president of the self-declared Turkish Republic of Northern Cyprus, Rauf Denktaş, who led the Turkish Cypriot community for more than forty years before stepping down in 2005 with the island still divided.

Denktaş is a stubborn octogenarian lawyer with a passion for photography and caged birds, and he has made a career out of saying 'no'. He spoke out against the UN's efforts to bring Cyprus back together – 'it's a trap,' he told me – but his people ignored him. Luckily for Denktaş, he had an ally of sorts in the south. The Greek Cypriot president, Tassos Papadopoulos, a veteran hardliner, went on television with tears in his eyes to plead the case for a 'no' vote on his side of the island. The Turks, he suggested, couldn't be trusted, and he made sure that the 'yes' campaign struggled to be heard.

For the UN it was a huge disappointment, but for Turkey it was a great success. Since 1974, when the Turkish army invaded the north of the island, the Turks had been portrayed as the villains of the piece. They had sent in their soldiers in response to a Greek-backed coup aimed at uniting the island with Greece, and for years they had shown little inclination to change the status quo of enforced partition, or scale down their huge military presence. Now the government in Ankara had proven to the international community that it was willing to strike a deal.

Tayyip Erdoğan called it 'our greatest diplomatic triumph in fifty years'– a little exaggerated for the benefit of his domestic audience, but the sentiment was understandable. Turkey was finally able to break the logjam of international perceptions that it is primarily at fault for the division of Cyprus.

'We have shown the international community our good intentions,' the prime minister declared, and he expected something in return.

Erdoğan certainly made great efforts to ensure that Turkish Cypriots were in favour of the UN plan, and – even more critically – he managed to convince sceptics within the Turkish armed forces to put their doubts to one side. They had always treated Cyprus as a strategic and military issue; Erdoğan persuaded them that it was a political one. After the failed referendum, which would have been binding only if both communities had said 'yes', the generals arguably had the best of both worlds. The garrison of thirty-five thousand troops in the north (which would have been reduced over time to just a few hundred under the terms of the UN plan) was staying put, and Turkey had suddenly clambered onto the moral high ground in the continuing debate over the future of Cyprus.

The European Union was quick to react to the referendum results. At a meeting in Luxembourg just two days after the votes were cast, angry foreign ministers queued up to lambaste their Greek Cypriot colleague, George Iacovou, and proceeded to heckle him when he tried to defend his government's position.

'We wanted to sort this out before Cyprus entered the Union,' one minister confided later. 'They knew that and unlike the Turks they let us down. We won't forget it.'

But the Greek Cypriots are now in the EU, and that gives them a veto over any kind of change. Turkish Cypriots, who dreamed of direct trade with Europe, and the resumption of direct flights for holidaymakers, have been left disappointed. Economic sanctions against them haven't really been eased at all, and the Greek Cypriots are being obstructive at every turn.

The whole issue of Cyprus remains a nationalist rallying point, both for hardliners on the island and among their ethnic kin in Turkey and Greece. Everyone knows the dispute will eventually have to be resolved, and everyone knows what the outlines of a deal are going to be. Turkey will give back some of the land it grabbed, in return for recognition of the right of the Turkish Cypriots to run most of their own affairs. The UN will have another go at finding the right formula, and the new Turkish Cypriot leader, Mehmet Ali Talat, is in favour of reunification, but at the time of writing Cyprus remains a blot on Turkey's European landscape. The Turkish government knows it has to be flexible – extending its Customs Union with the EU to include Cyprus is just one example – but if it gives too much it will be hammered by nationalists at home.

It is awkward because – technically – Turkish troops are now occupying EU territory in northern Cyprus, and the Greek Cypriots have a long-term veto over Turkey's membership application. But many of the people who matter in Europe – the Germans and the British, for example – have been won over by Turkey's new willingness, after years of stonewalling, to try to find a deal. The Greek Cypriots and their obdurate political leaders are now identified as the biggest obstacle to a future settlement.

'The thing about the Turks,' mused a western diplomat in Ankara, 'is that when they say "no" they actually mean "no". And when they say "yes", they mean "yes". It took them a long time to change their minds about Cyprus, but I don't think there's any going back.'

* * *

When the humid heat of August arrives, and Istanbul starts to sweat, the well-to-do pack up their things and head for their summer houses. Some of them travel down the Aegean coast or take the short flight to the Mediterranean. But many of the old-timers still prefer somewhere a little closer to home. In less than an hour on a fast ferry, you can leave the city behind and reach the Princes' Islands, sitting snugly off the coast in the Sea of Marmara. The most distinctive of the islands is Heybeliada, known to the Greeks as Halki. It feels like a throwback to earlier times: wooden houses, horse-drawn traps, and on the hilltop the most important Greek Orthodox seminary in the world.

Every day the corridors of the seminary are swept, and the marble floors are polished; the classrooms and dormitories are spotless. But there have been no students here since 1971, when the Halki Theological School was closed on the orders of the Turkish government. Now the building is maintained as part of a monastery which has been a seat of learning for more than a thousand years. It still boasts one of the finest collections of ancient books in the world, but few people have the chance to read from the histories kept on the library shelves. For years, the school has been suspended in time.

The Ecumenical Patriarch, Bartholomew, spent eleven years on Heybeliada as a student and teacher, and he still visits the island regularly from his home on the mainland. With support from Europe and the United States, he has campaigned quietly for years to get the school reopened.

'This is a very special place,' he told me during a brief conversation one winter's day in the monastery gardens. 'A religious institution like ours needs its own place of education. How else can we train our future leaders?'

For a long time the Turkish authorities have refused to compromise, saying that the school has to become part of a faculty in a Turkish university before students from across the Orthodox world can be allowed back in. It's partly down to stubbornness, and partly down to prejudice, but strict laws which limit the influence of Islamic education are the biggest stumbling block facing the Orthodox Church. Many Turkish politicians still fear allowing the Orthodox seminary to reopen would lead radical Islamist groups to demand the right to train their own clergy as well, away from the all-seeing eyes of the state.

But times have changed. It helps that Greece and Turkey are no longer at daggers drawn, and the EU process is prompting reformers to break long-standing taboos. Some local Greeks are still pessimistic, but I think it is more than likely that students will sit once again in the classrooms at the Halki school in the next few years, the library will reopen and the next generation of Orthodox leaders will study in the same place as their forefathers. There may be protests, angry nationalists may burn the patriarch in effigy again, but the change will come regardless. The new Turkey is rediscovering old roots.

Istanbul may never return to the cosmopolitan days of old, but it can become a more diverse city again. For the tiny Greek community, a lot depends on politics and on how Turkey and Greece choose to build on their new relationship. Significant problems remain: neither the Cyprus conflict nor territorial disputes in the Aegean lend themselves to instant solutions. Tensions can still flare up unexpectedly. A start has been made, though, and for those who have had to live with the consequences of mutual dislike that is better than nothing. Others have an obvious interest in better relations between Turkey and Greece. Both the European Union and NATO have made it a priority issue for some time. But for Istanbul's Greeks, or for the Turks of western Thrace, it is much more than a policy preference.

'Minority communities are like eggs between two rocks,' Andrea Rombopoulos, the editor of a small Greek newspaper in Istanbul, told me several years ago. 'If the rocks move, the eggs break. But if Turkey and Greece can solve their problems, our community can survive in its current form. That's our hope – we were born here, we've grown here and we want to die here. This is our country.'

The Armenians

The elderly watchman who opened the door to the compound wasn't particularly talkative. In fact he said almost nothing at all. Why would he risk speaking to strangers? He was one of the last Armenians in Diyarbakır, and his church was falling down in front of him.

The roof had collapsed, and the altars had disappeared. All that remained of the Church of St Giragos were the huge arches of grey volcanic stone, standing defiantly in a bed of weeds and crumbling pillars.

'This must have been quite a place,' I said. No one answered. In the corner a couple of old *kilims* were rotting away. A startled bird flew from the remains of a low stone wall and the watchman slowly shuffled his feet.

All across eastern Anatolia there are isolated reminders of the people who used to live here; the people who have been airbrushed out of modern Turkish history. A hundred years ago more than two million Armenians called this region their home – thriving communities with beautiful medieval churches. Now only a few families remain – thirteen or fourteen in Malatya, a handful in Elazığ, a small community in Sivas, and one or two scattered elsewhere. In a village in Hatay near the Syrian border, you can find the descendants of the Armenians of Musa Dağ, who survived a famous mountain-top siege by Ottoman troops in 1915. But that's all; the rest are only memories.

Most of the Armenians who live in modern Turkey are residents of Istanbul – about seventy thousand people in all. They have flourishing churches and schools, and they are still the largest Christian minority in the country. They have their festival days and their own newspapers, and they intermarry with Turks and others. But theirs is a strange existence – a community surrounded by a wall of silence. There is almost no serious discussion in Turkey about what happened to the Armenians in the last years of the Ottoman Empire. It is the biggest taboo of all.

*   *   *

They were kept at a safe distance, but they were noisy enough. As Tayyip Erdoğan was negotiating his way towards acceptance of a date to start talks on joining the European Union, it wasn't the Cypriots or the Greeks or the Kurds who were demonstrating against Turkey in the park around the corner. Thousands of Armenians from across Europe had travelled to Brussels – by bus from Paris, by chartered plane from Stockholm and Athens – to make their voices heard. The Armenian diaspora is determined that Turkey should be forced to confront the darker side of Ottoman history, and it should be made to pay for it.

'No Justice, No EU', said one banner; 'Genocide', said another, in large black letters.

On the edge of the crowd, I found Laurent Leylekian, who runs the European Armenian Federation for Justice and Democracy. It is time, he argued, for Turkey to come to terms with its past.

'Many of our grandparents arrived here as orphaned children – even their names had been forgotten. We have to struggle for the memory of those they left behind.'

He paused as another chant rose from the demonstrators, followed by a burst of applause.

'It was genocide,' he insisted, 'and that has to be acknowledged.'

'And if they apologize, what then?'

'Well, then we have to think about compensation, that sort of thing. Someone has to take responsibility.'

Even the Turkish authorities admit that hundreds of thousands of Armenians died in what is now eastern Turkey during the declining years of the Ottoman Empire. What is bitterly contested, though, is the extent of the killing and whether there was a systematic campaign organized by the Ottoman government to wipe out the Armenian race. For several centuries Armenians had lived peacefully and prospered under the Ottomans. They were craftsmen, jewellers, silversmiths and traders. But towards the end of the nineteenth century the rise of competing Turkish and Armenian nationalist movements started to create serious unrest. As the minority community, the Armenians were vulnerable to attack and tens of thousands were killed in pogroms in the 1890s, and again in 1909.

Much worse was to come amidst fierce fighting on the eastern front of the First World War, when many local Armenians sided with the Russians against the Ottoman Turks. Even though Armenians fought in the ranks of the Ottoman army as well, the Armenian community came to be regarded as 'the enemy within' by hardline nationalists in the Young Turk government. In 1915 they ordered the mass expulsion of Armenians from eastern Anatolia. They believed with good reason that some Armenian nationalists were working with Russia to carve out a separate state. But everyone was made to pay.

On 24 April – the day now commemorated by Armenians as the anniversary of genocide – hundreds of Armenian politicians, intellectuals and community leaders were arrested in Istanbul. Most of them were subsequently killed. What followed in the east was almost unspeakable, but it was documented in detail by missionaries, diplomats and survivors. Men, women and children were machine-gunned in pits and ravines; rape and torture were commonplace and rivers were clogged with bodies; Armenians were taken out onto the Black Sea by the boatload and thrown overboard; sealed trains were packed with deportees who were sent to disease-ridden prison camps in the Syrian desert; others were forced to march southwards until they died by the side of the road. Kurdish tribes in eastern Anatolia acted with particular brutality, and even Turkey's wartime ally, the German ambassador in Istanbul, reported to Berlin that there was no doubt that the Ottoman government was trying 'to exterminate the Armenian race in the Turkish Empire'.

Many Turks don't know any of this; they're not taught about it in school, and it's not discussed much in the media. Instead they're told about the thousands of Turks who were killed in equally atrocious ways by roaming bands of Armenian irregulars. In the eastern town of Iğdır, the Armenian Genocide Memorial and Museum is not what the unsuspecting visitor might think. It was opened when I was living in Turkey in 1999, and it commemorates the deaths of local Turks. Of the Armenian dead, there is not a word. 'We are the victims,' the local governor complained at the inauguration ceremony, 'we are the ones who were massacred. But the Armenians are trying to show that the opposite is true.'

It's this refusal to deal honestly with the past which is so disturbing. The Turkish authorities accept officially that 'tragic events' occurred and that three hundred thousand Armenians died in 'widespread internal fighting'. But there is not a hint of regret or remorse for the lasting trauma of it all. It was self-defence, they say, and any Turks who divert from the official line (a handful of academics and Turkey's leading novelist, Orhan Pamuk) are dismissed as traitors. Armenians maintain that the number of people killed was far higher. They insist that the death toll reached one and a half million, in an organized campaign of genocide. And most scholars abroad – with some notable and vocal exceptions – agree.

Both sides produce stacks of documents to back up their claims, and pour scorn on the forgeries of their opponents. The Internet brims with vitriol. Even the most famous quotation used in this bitter battle is disputed. Nine days before he invaded Poland, Adolf Hitler addressed his troops on the eastern front, and argued that Nazi Germany could and would exterminate European Jewry. 'Who, after all, speaks today of the annihilation of the Armenians?' eyewitnesses quoted him saying, even though the words didn't appear in the official text of his speech.

Hitler's rhetorical question is now inscribed on one of the walls of the Holocaust Memorial in Washington, DC – an awkward piece of symbolism for those who deny the Armenian genocide. Efforts to get the US Congress to recognize genocide officially have been derailed by frantic Turkish pressure, and threats to withdraw American access to military bases on Turkish soil. Every year since he's been president, George W. Bush has issued a statement on 24 April acknowledging the 'annihilation of as many as one and a half million Armenians'. It was, he said in 2004, 'one of the most horrible tragedies of the twentieth century'. But for reasons of political expediency he doesn't use the 'g' word, and the diaspora feels betrayed.

Several countries have gone further than the United States. When the French parliament publicly recognized genocide in 2001 Turkey erupted in fury. The government threatened to break off diplomatic relations, universities suspended academic cooperation, and France – which just happens to be home to the largest Armenian population in Western Europe – was shut out of defence tenders and other lucrative projects. The crisis soon blew over, as it usually does, and many French politicians who voted in favour of the bill say they had no intention of condemning modern Turkey. But most Turks thought that was exactly what had happened.

It's where patriotism slides across the line into prejudice. Turkey needs to discuss the bad parts of its history as well as the good, and the slaughter of the Armenians in 1915 must be at the top of the list. Politics, say the Turks, shouldn't come into it – this is an issue which should be left to the historians. But whatever the old documents and diaries say, and whatever secrets may still lie hidden in the Ottoman archives, there is no dispute about the broad legal definitions contained in the UN Genocide Convention, which came into force in 1951. It defines genocide as acts 'committed with intent to destroy, in whole or in part, a national, ethnical, racial or religious group'. It is not confined to mass murder, and it doesn't even have to be carried out under government instruction.

The conclusion isn't a comfortable one for the Turks. If Slobodan Milošović can be charged with acts of genocide in Bosnia, and the Sudanese can be accused of genocide in Darfur, then the slaughter of the Armenians falls into the same category. But in a country where national pride is so important, and sensitivity to criticism from abroad is so acute, the Armenian genocide debate still stirs deep and lasting anger. It's as if admitting to the full severity of what happened under the Ottoman Empire would undermine the legitimacy of the Turkish republic ninety years later. It is a reminder of how history and identity are still so painfully intertwined.

*   *   *

'My history won't suddenly become true just because they accept it.'

Faces stare out from the walls of Hrant Dink's office in Istanbul. Black and white photographs of old Armenian communities from the Anatolian interior are carefully framed. His own family came originally from Malatya, a place he still visits from time to time.

'I'm well aware of my history and I'm a good grandson to my ancestors. It is my history and my pain, and I will carry it with me as long as I'm alive.'

As the editor of *Agos*, one of Istanbul's Armenian newspapers, Dink runs a spirited campaign for greater openness about the events of the past. He's not afraid to kick over a few statues either, and challenge the assumptions on which Turkey carefully constructed its modern identity. Take the case of Sabiha Gökçen – Atatürk's adopted daughter and

Turkey's first woman pilot. She remains a national icon and a heroine for secular feminists. But three years after her death in 2001, *Agos* published claims that Sabiha Gökçen was an Armenian by birth.

Nationalist Turks could hardly bear to contemplate the idea. The military suggested that *Agos* was trying to disturb the peace. According to the official history, Sabiha Gökçen was an orphan from the western city of Bursa, adopted by Atatürk in 1925. But an elderly Armenian lady in Istanbul insists that the official history is wrong. Sabiha Gökçen was her aunt, she says, and Atatürk had rescued her from an orphanage in the south-eastern town of Şanliurfa. Sabiha Gökçen's father, the story runs, was murdered in the massacres of 1915.

'We had a few threats from the nationalists, and a few protests outside the office.' Dink shrugs. 'But we have plenty of friends here, too.'

Some Turks say privately that they know what happened in 1915, but the ideology of the state has suppressed it. If Sabiha Gökçen really was an Armenian, it wouldn't be the end of their world. Most of the Armenians who still live in Turkey, even the outspoken ones like Hrant Dink, understand that. They don't share the fervour of the diaspora when it comes to the genocide campaign.

'The difference between us,' he says, 'is that we're living with the Turks of today, and they're still living with the Turks of 1915. I have a dialogue with the Turks and they don't.'

The battle against Turkey has become an obsession for many Armenians abroad. They are still pursuing the Turks of yesteryear, but they want modern Turkey to fail. On the violent fringe, revenge against their enemies was organized from the beginning. Two of the Young Turk leaders who ran the Ottoman Empire in 1915 were assassinated by Armenian gunmen: Talat on the streets of Berlin in 1921 – the trigger pulled by a man who had watched most of his own family die – and Cemal in Tbilisi the following year.

Half a century later the killings began again. In the early 1970s an Armenian extremist organization, ASALA, started to kill Turkish diplomats working abroad. The gunmen targeted ambassadors, junior diplomats, family members, drivers and security guards – anyone associated with the republic of Turkey. Bombs exploded at Turkish Airlines offices in Ankara, Istanbul and Paris killing many others. Over the course of a decade more than fifty people were murdered, before the leaders of ASALA died in Lebanon during the Israeli invasion in 1982.

The campaign of violence came to an end as a new generation of Armenian activists began to focus political pressure on Turkey around the world, but ASALA had a lasting impact – Turkey's determination not to give in to terror reinforced its refusal to re-examine the past. Understandably the Foreign Ministry in Ankara still harbours bitter memories of the gunmen, and the more the diaspora lobbied against them, the more the Turks grimly dug in their heels. The emergence of an independent state of Armenia in 1991, following the fall of the Soviet Union, hardly improved matters. When Christian Armenia won a military victory over Muslim Azerbaijan in Nagorno-Karabakh, the Turks reacted by closing their border with Armenia altogether.

*   *   *

The ruins of Ani – the legendary Armenian city of a thousand and one churches – stand on a high plateau above the Arpa river, surrounded on two sides by steep rocky gorges. There are only a few dilapidated buildings left within the huge sprawling walls, but they remain an imposing sight – the red stone cathedral, the citadel, churches, convents and a mosque, scattered across the empty meadows.

Time feels as if it is standing still in Ani, but things have moved on. The skeleton of the old city is now in a Turkish military zone right next to the Armenian border. On the river below are the ruins of a fourteenth-century stone bridge which used to be part of the Silk Road connecting Istanbul to the great cities of Central Asia. The bridge is broken – there is no connection here between Turkey and Armenia, and the terrible events of 1915 still cast a long shadow.

Ani is a symbol of the Armenian past in Anatolia, and of the stalemate which now prevails. There are closed borders and closed minds, and only very rarely do the two sides reach out to each other. A group of retired diplomats and academics met for several years in a forum known as the Turkish–Armenian Reconciliation Commission, quietly sponsored by the Americans. A legal opinion was commissioned from independent lawyers at the International Centre for Transitional Justice in New York. Their conclusion was that the events of 1915 did constitute genocide under international law, but that modern Turkey bore no responsibility for reparations. No legal, financial or territorial claim could successfully be made, the lawyers concluded, against any individual or state.

Nothing at the moment suggests that Turkey is willing to accept legal advice of this kind, but there have been some signs of a more open approach. In 2003 the government approved the screening of the film *Ararat* by the Armenian–Canadian director, Atom Egoyan, even though it shows Turkish troops in 1915 acting with appalling brutality, and it tells a story chillingly different to the one Turkish children are taught in school. But the government's decision came, apparently, too soon: ultra-nationalists threatened to attack any cinema where the film was shown, and plans to release it in Turkey were postponed indefinitely.

There will be further flashpoints in the future, and it may fall once again to the European Union to test the limits of Turkey's new approach to the world. The EU reform process has helped change Turkey in dramatic ways, and it is already provoking a backlash among those who were more comfortable with old certainties. But there is one more issue which the EU will in time want to discuss: the fate of the Armenians in 1915.

'France will pose this question,' the French foreign minister, Michel Barnier, said pointedly, just a few days before Turkey was given its European date.

'Reconciliation is the core idea of the European project. That's why Turkey will eventually have to come to terms with the past, with its own history, and recognize this tragedy.'

6

RIGHTS AND WRONGS

'This one is for electric shocks,' said Vedat Zencir, carefully turning a small handle. 'And that one over there,' he said, moving across the dimly lit room, 'is for hanging a suspect from the wall – like this.'

It was my first visit to Izmir and on a quiet side street in an old neighbourhood I was being shown around Turkey's most unusual museum. In a small humid basement, a grisly array of torture implements was unceremoniously displayed – a cage, a few chains, and some nasty-looking bits of wire.

It would be nice to report that this was a display of horrors from an earlier, more inhumane time, but it wasn't. The privately financed Freedom of Expression Museum was very contemporary. Upstairs, above the torture chamber, was another small display: books and newspapers which had been banned by state censorship, and photographs of dozens of writers and artists who were in jail.

'We just wanted to do something, we wanted to remind visitors what can happen here when people express their opinions,' said Zencir, the museum spokesman. 'Torture still takes place, and everybody knows it.'

Some time after my visit the museum was forced to close down – no, not a police raid in the middle of the night, just a simple lack of funds – but that cramped basement in Izmir stuck in my mind as an important symbol. Ordinary people were saying enough is enough – the state has to find a better way to go about its business. The desire for change was brought home to me again a couple of years later in Istanbul, when I interviewed a group of university students about their expectations for the future. We chatted for a long time, and they said pretty much what I expected them to say. Good jobs, more opportunities, a better democracy. But as I was about to switch off the microphone, I thought of one more question: what about human rights, I asked, what about torture?

I was half-expecting a defensive answer but a young man in the corner, who hadn't said much, was the first to speak.

'A lot of people get fed up with the foreign media,' he said. 'It's all "human rights this, human rights that" . . . it's not the full picture of Turkey. But we have had a problem, I know we have, and now we have a chance to do something about it.'

Other students at the table nodded. Some of them stared into their glasses of tea.

'Not for your sake,' said the girl sitting next to me, 'but for ours.'

For years Turkey's human rights record was a national disgrace. A decade ago deaths in custody were commonplace, torture was out of control and extra-judicial executions happened so often that they barely rated a line in the newspapers. But as it entered the twenty-first century, Turkey seemed to realize it could no longer afford to be so cavalier with human life if it wanted to receive the respect it thinks it deserves from its own people and from the rest of the world. Pressure from abroad – the ubiquitous EU process – has played an important part, but grass-roots protest from civil society has also bubbled up through the system to burst out in a flood of reform.

In a remarkably short space of time many laws restricting freedom of expression have been scrapped, and the government has declared 'zero tolerance' for torture. Pre-trial detention periods have been shortened; detainees have more rights of access to lawyers; and sentences for officials convicted of torture or ill-treatment have been increased. Turkey is beginning to shake off the image of malignant brutality portrayed in Ankara's least favourite film, *Midnight Express*. No one should be complacent, though. Old habits die hard, and most of the exhibits I saw in that sweaty Izmir basement are still in use in the darker corners of the state system.

*   *   *

So a story like this could still happen again. Süleyman Yeter was taken into police custody in Istanbul on 5 March 1999. Two days later he was dead. His body, which I saw before it was buried, bore clear marks of torture and physical abuse. The police said initially that he had died of a heart attack, but even they knew it wasn't true. Süleyman was a Kurd, and an Alevi; but most of all he was a committed communist, and it was that which brought him into conflict with the state.

I met Süleyman's family two days after he died, when his body was still in official custody. His mother had just arrived after a long and difficult journey from the east, and she had little information about her son's death; his aunt had heard about it on the radio. As we sat and talked, Süleyman's lawyer arrived with one of his friends, Bayram, who had been arrested in the same police raid on a radical left-wing newspaper.

'The last time I saw Süleyman he was in the cell,' Bayram told us. 'He was exhausted and he couldn't stop shivering. He said he'd been beaten, and they made him lie on a slab of ice while they hosed him down with freezing cold water. Then they came and took him away again, and that was that.'

The next morning I went with the family to the state mortuary. They were made to wait on the pavement for more than an hour as an extraordinary police presence built up around them. Only after a long bureaucratic battle was Süleyman's body finally released for burial. Before his funeral took place I saw for myself how he had been tortured to death. His body was carefully laid out in a local cemevi, and a doctor guided me through the clinical detail. There were broken bones in his chin and neck, a toenail had been pulled out; there was extensive bruising under his arms, and wounds on several parts of his body. Süleyman's friends said the police officers who were responsible had been out to get him for some time.

As the coffin was taken outside the long build-up of emotion suddenly broke into hysteria. People began crying and screaming, and Süleyman's mother tried to pull the green cloth covering off the simple wooden box. But a younger generation, more politicized, was about to take over the funeral. The coffin was draped in a red flag and fists punched the air; slogans were chanted and defiant speeches were made. The creation of another political martyr had begun.

Along the route of the funeral procession, hundreds of police officers in riot gear lined the streets. Water cannon and armoured cars lurked in the background.

'We can't take any risks,' an officer told me. 'These people are extremists. They will use violence if we give them the chance.'

But Süleyman's funeral was a peaceful affair. At the graveside his wife Ayşe, her face animated by angry passion, waved the imam away. Süleyman, she told him, was an atheist. He wanted no prayers.

Back in the capital Ankara, over the next two weeks, I asked for an interview about Süleyman Yeter with four different government ministers. They were all unavailable. I sensed no grand conspiracy, no cabinet cover-up. It was just that in 1999 the death of a radical left-wing union activist in a police cell in the country's largest city didn't seem to be that important. People were used to it, and there was a shocking sense of complacency.

Five years later, a police officer was finally sent to prison for his role in torturing Süleyman Yeter to death. Lawyers for Süleyman's family, who had to fight all the way to bring their case to court, said the punishment was far too lenient. The sentence had originally been ten years, but it was reduced to four years and two months on the grounds that it was impossible to determine which of the three men charged with torturing Süleyman had actually killed him. The officer found guilty, Mehmet Yutar, will serve less than half his reduced sentence; another policeman was acquitted in court, and the third is still 'on the run'.

Did Süleyman Yeter's family receive justice? Many trials involving police officers never reach any verdict because the legal process is allowed to drag on until cases have to be dismissed. Human rights activists say the authorities often treat public officials leniently, and that makes the declaration of 'zero tolerance' for torture ring uncomfortably hollow. At least in Süleyman's case, after a long legal struggle, a policeman was found guilty. But under reforms to the Turkish penal code, anyone now convicted of torture which results in death is supposed to be sentenced to life imprisonment.

'The verdict in our trial,' said the family lawyer, Keleş Öztürk, 'shows the resistance all state institutions display when it comes to torturers, especially if they happen to be police officers.'

It's a familiar story. There is a big difference between passing laws and enforcing them, and the message that things have to be done differently now has yet to percolate through every layer of the state security system. Turkey's independent Human Rights Association reported 692 cases of abuse in the first six months of 2004, and it is not entirely happy with the European Union's assertion that torture in Turkey is 'no longer systematic'. Electric shocks, sexual assault, beatings on the soles of the feet and 'Palestinian hangers' – a modern and more portable variant of the rack – all continue to feature in the list of complaints.

But indisputably things have changed. Until very recently there was an organized system to torture people and then to cover it up; most of that system has been dismantled. At the highest political levels torture is no longer tolerated. A new generation of security officials with a broader vision is moving into positions of authority. Police academies and military schools have included human rights lectures as part of their basic training for several years, and younger police officers have been changing long-established practices. Instead of handing out a beating to detainees, they hand out a cup of coffee and a few words of advice (inspiring the *Wall Street Journal* to come up with one of my favourite newspaper headlines on Turkey: MIDNIGHT ESPRESSO).

For an idea of how much things have changed you have to go to the people on the front line. People like Fazıl Ahmet Taner, who sits at his desk in a small office on a side street off Istiklal Caddesi – the busy shopping boulevard which runs through the heart of Istanbul. As a lawyer he's been fighting human rights cases for a long time, including his own. He was in prison for seven years between 1994 and 2001 without being found guilty of any crime. An initial confession that he belonged to an illegal organization was, he says, obtained under torture.

So Taner has seen and heard enough to be naturally sceptical of claims of progress, but he is very clear that the number of cases of physical torture has been reduced considerably.

'It really is quite striking. There's much less torture now, especially of political prisoners.'

Why has it changed so quickly, I wondered, if the same people are still in the system?

'Because it was a decision made at the top, under pressure from the EU. That was the crucial factor. But we still need far more social change in our society. We're a long way from where we want to be.'

'Do you think the worst is over?'

'I hope so, but it's still quite fragile. People are being abused psychologically all the time, and people are still beaten. That's a cultural reality. But it's not as bad as it was.'

The big problem is in police stations and isolated gendarmerie camps where there is insufficient supervision and too much 'freelance' activity.

'If you go in there,' said our driver as we passed one notorious gendarmerie headquarters in the south-east, 'you expect to be tortured. Anything else is a surprise.'

Changing the law doesn't immediately change attitudes – that will take many years, and plenty of torturers still work in the system. But the threat of exposure has made a huge difference. Under recent legal reforms, lawyers now have the right to visit all detainees. They may not always gain immediate access, but they keep trying. Hiding evidence of torture has become more difficult, and the days of blanket immunity have gone.

So it's not perfect, but the public now demands accountability. When volleys of shots rang out one night in November 2004 in the town of Kızıltepe near the Syrian border, the local authorities announced that two more terrorists had been eliminated. But Ahmet Kaymaz and his twelve-year-old son, Uğur, had simply been carrying blankets to a truck parked outside their house. Uğur ended up with thirteen bullets in his body. There were angry newspaper headlines and parliamentary investigations, followed by a lawsuit against four trigger-happy police officers. A similar incident in a remote eastern town a few years earlier – and there were many of them – would barely have been a footnote.

Even before the latest burst of reform, Turkey had a far more accountable system than some of its neighbours. Syria, Iran and Iraq spring to mind. But none of them wants to join the European Union. Turkey does, and it is by European standards that it will continue to be judged. Turkish officials now accept that, it is their choice, but they also believe the EU is not being entirely fair. Countries such as Greece and Spain were allowed to join the union to help strengthen their democratic credentials after military dictatorships. Turkey is being asked to make all the improvements first, before it can be considered for membership.

That's why some Turkish officials grit their teeth and grin when European do-gooders come visiting, and they talk openly about double standards. Scandinavians seem to irritate them in particular. Even Tayyip

Erdoğan sometimes lets the mask slip, and allows his nationalist alter ego to appear. In one interview, with the German newspaper *Der Tagesspiegel*, he accused human rights groups of being 'ideologically blinded'.

'I myself was in prison for four months just before taking office,' he said, 'and I know how things are. There is no torture in my country.'

It still isn't true, and everyone knows it. But progress in Turkey's EU application has – quite literally – saved a few skins.

*   *   *

Sometimes you come across things you struggle to understand. Watching Zehra Kulaksız die was one of them. In a small house in a run-down Istanbul neighbourhood she was starving herself to death as part of the longest-running hunger strike in the world. Her cheeks were pale and sunken, her lips were terribly cracked, and her voice barely rose above a whisper.

'I have to do this,' she said. 'It's the only way.'

I felt rather sick just being there. On the other side of Zehra's room was an empty bed with a red rose placed carefully on the pillow. Her sister, Canan, had died there the previous week. Both of them were teenagers.

Since October 2000 more than a hundred people associated with extreme left-wing groups have died in 'death fasts' to protest against prison conditions. It is an extraordinary statistic, and one which receives little attention either in Turkey or in the wider world. The number of people prepared to take part has dwindled dramatically, but the protest drags on. Many of the self-declared 'martyrs' have been inmates who have died in prison cells or hospital beds; others have been relatives or political activists who have starved to death in sympathy.

A week after I met her, Zehra Kulaksız was dead, having refused solid foods for more than five months. She was soon followed by Gülsüman Dönmez, who wrote a letter to her eleven-year-old son, Sinan, just a few days before she died.

'I love you more than life, and I don't know how to tell you how happy I am,' she told him. 'Only someone who is on hunger strike can know these feelings. I am smiling at death, my son.'

'These people are insane,' said one of my Turkish friends with feeling.

The group most of them belonged to, the Revolutionary People's Liberation Party-Front (DHKP-C), was also responsible for countless political murders, and attracted precious little sympathy from the rest of the country. But for a while the situation in the prisons was front-page news and there were heartfelt calls for 'something to be done'.

'They are the youth of our country and the basic fact is that they are dying,' a senior professor of medicine wrote in an open letter to the prime minister in 2001. 'My conscience is screaming that this should not be allowed, and I want my state to feel the same.'

Civic groups made heroic efforts to mediate, but concern about the 'death fasts' gradually faded, overwhelmed by a sense of hopelessness. There was to be, it seemed, no compromise.

When Selami Kumaz became the 117th person to die, in Tekirdağ prison in August 2004, no one really noticed. The hunger strike had long since developed into a grim ideological struggle in which martyrdom was at a premium, and individual lives were of secondary concern. The power of the state has been pitted against the intransigence of small nihilistic groups which want to destroy it. There are some things, it seems, that even the human rights lobby can't do much about.

'We don't give much publicity to the death fasts any more,' said one despairing activist in Istanbul. 'As soon as we talk about it, more people volunteer to die.'

The initial cause of the hunger strike has almost been forgotten. But the struggle passed a point of no return at about five o'clock in the morning on 19 December 2000, when the Turkish security forces stormed prisons across the country, determined to re-establish state control over dormitories run by inmates. Operation Return to Life had been planned for more than a year, and failure was not an option. At Bayrampaşa prison in Istanbul, heavily armed paramilitary police and soldiers took up positions on the roof and began trying to force their way into the dormitories by smashing holes in the walls and ceilings.

Detailed accounts from inmates who survived the assault were later brought out of prison by their lawyers.

'They saw us stand up and they started firing at us,' said Hamide Öztürk, a convicted member of the DHKP-C, who was in the women's ward. 'After the shooting they started to bombard us with all kinds of bombs. They threw smoke and sound bombs, nerve gas and pepper gas.

We constantly answered them with slogans and insults. They kept shouting, "Surrender or we will kill all of you." We said, "Come and kill us if you like, but we will never surrender."'

What happened as the day went on is the subject of bitter debate, but Operation Return to Life quickly became a killing ground. The authorities said the prisoners refused to give in and after several hours of clashes the DHKP-C issued orders for its members to practise self-immolation rather than surrender. One horrific television image showed a woman handcuffed to a wall with her flesh on fire. But the survivors, backed up by a report from forensic pathologists, insist that they were deliberately burnt out of their dormitories with incendiary devices, and many inmates perished in the flames. A series of legal cases involving hundreds of inmates and subsequently hundreds of members of the security forces rumbled on interminably.

At a price, the state had achieved its immediate objectives. Thirty prisoners and two paramilitary policemen were dead, but the DHKP-C's iron grip on the prisons had been broken. For years, they had been running dormitories of up to a hundred people as their own private indoctrination camps. The walls were covered with flags and slogans, and prisoners carried out their own military-style roll-calls every morning. Prison officials said they had been unable to enter some areas inside the jails for nearly a decade.

Now the most radical inmates – organized groups of leftists, Kurds and Islamists – have been moved to new maximum security prisons known as F-types, where they are kept in small cells which house between one and three prisoners each. For a few of them, the hunger strike is their last act of defiance. Small groups of inmates from the DHKP-C take it in turn to launch 'death fasts', refusing solid food for several months at a time. Many of them survive, and alongside the dead in this desperate dispute are hundreds of people who have ended up severely disabled after depriving their bodies of the most basic needs.

It was one of the most depressing stories I ever covered in Turkey because it was impossible to see where change would come from. The hunger strike could continue in one form or another for years – a reminder that extremist politics live on in the new Turkey, and there are groups on the very fringes of society who are utterly alienated from the state.

Overall conditions inside prisons remain poor – they are underfunded and overcrowded; many prisoners are still awaiting trial, or the outcome of trials which can drag on for years; and local human rights groups receive a stream of complaints from relatives that prisoners are beaten, victimized or held in isolation. Thousands of inmates are released in regular amnesties, which seem to be the only idea anyone has come up with for keeping the size of the prison population under control.

As for the F-type prisons – the source of so much controversy – they are modern and clean, but the authorities seem to be doing everything they can to impose a regime of isolation, without making it obvious publicly. Some of the more radical political prisoners refuse point blank to cooperate, but even those who want to work within the system struggle to claim the rights they should be granted under the law.

'At the moment it's not too good,' concluded one human rights activist, 'but it's not as bad as more and more people dying on hunger strike. That is simply pointless.'

*　*　*

It was a crime which shocked the country, but it was not altogether uncommon. What made it different was that Güldünya Tören had given an interview to a local newspaper just a few hours before she was shot dead by her brothers.

'Print my picture in your paper so the state will protect me,' she said, but it was to no avail.

Güldünya had already been shot once by her siblings, and left for dead on a street in Istanbul. After this first attack she was taken to hospital where she was supposed to have been under police protection. But there was no one to save her when her brothers returned; as she lay defenceless in her hospital bed, they entered the room and shot her twice in the head.

This horrifying crime was all about cleansing the family's 'honour' according to tribal customs. Güldünya Tören had become pregnant out of wedlock in a small village in the east of the country. She said she had been raped by the husband of her cousin. Frightened that she would be punished for her pregnancy, she appealed for police protection and was moved to a safe house in Istanbul where her baby Umut (Hope) was born and given up for adoption. After a while her family persuaded her that she had been forgiven. But they were lying. They had decided instead that it was time for her to die.

Mass migration has brought the gruesome phenomenon of honour killings into Turkey's big cities, but most murders like this take place in conservative rural areas far from the centres of power. Forty women were officially reported to have been the victims of honour killings in 2003, but the real number is far higher. Human rights activists are suspicious whenever they read of a young woman drowning in a river, or dying in the kind of agricultural 'accident' which happens when you get run over by a tractor. The killings are carefully planned at gatherings of the clan; a young male relative, often under age, is usually ordered to carry out the crime because a minor will receive a much lighter penalty if he gets caught.

Honour killings get a lot of publicity these days because they are so barbaric, and some Turks think they are publicized abroad in order to run their country down. But this is another story of the two Turkeys: there's the modern Westward-looking Turkey where many women are free to make their own choices, to explore their own sexuality, and to find the partner and the life they want; and there's the other Turkey where men dominate, women are treated as possessions to be bought and sold, and the laws of the land get no further than the front door. Amnesty International estimates that more than a third of all Turkish women are victims of domestic violence, ranging from regular beatings to rape and occasionally murder.

Migration has – if anything – made the problems women face more acute, as conflicting lifestyles collide. I was with a film crew once out in the countryside about fifty miles south of Ankara, not much more than an hour's drive from the capital's trendy bars and cafés. As the sun began to sink lower in the sky we were bumping along a back road near the town of Haymana when we spotted a shepherd looking after the sheep of a local landowner. His dog was alarmingly fierce, but Hasan was perfectly friendly towards strangers who came tramping across the field for no apparent reason. When I asked him about women who choose not to cover their hair, though, his answers were shocking in a country which aspires to Western modernity.

'They're all bitches and prostitutes,' he said in a matter-of-fact voice, 'that's what we're told.'

I don't really know what I expected him to say, but I was a little taken aback.

'Just a bit of hair like this,' Hasan said, tugging at his forelock, 'if just a little bit can be seen, it's like committing adultery. A woman shouldn't be naked.'

I was left to reflect on all the remote villages I've been to with uncovered women where we were greeted with warmth and hospitality. There doesn't have to be this gaping divide in Turkey, but there are deeply ingrained attitudes which treat women as second-class citizens and worse, particularly in Kurdish society. They put a rather gloomy perspective on the extensive reforms which – in this area of the law as in so many others – have changed things on paper dramatically.

The civil code, for example, no longer states that 'the husband is the head of the family'. A range of provisions which used to give men the final say in deciding where a family should live, how children should be brought up, how money should be spent, and whether women could get a job have been removed. Family courts have been created to ensure that property and assets are divided equally in the event of divorce – something which is becoming more and more common amid the stresses and strains of city life.

The new penal code, approved in 2004, has also taken some important steps towards better legal protection of women. There is a promise of longer sentences for honour killings and the notion that 'honour' is any kind of legal justification has gone; rape within marriage has been criminalized, and for the first time rapists will no longer be given reduced sentences (this really used to happen) if they agree to marry their victims. Sustained domestic violence has been defined as a form of torture, and sexual harassment in the workplace has been designated a crime.

Legal change has come because women decided to get organized and launch a vigorous campaign for equality. A group called Flying Broom chose the best name, and it does some of the most valuable work. From its headquarters in Ankara Flying Broom runs an annual women's film festival and a nationwide network of grass-roots correspondents to report on women's issues. Slowly but surely they are making contact with women across the country.

'We have to make women more visible,' said Flying Broom's national coordinator, Halime Güner, 'we have to turn all these campaigns for women's rights into a national action plan.'

I sometimes wonder what connection these determined republican activists can make with young girls in distant villages who can neither read nor write, or women in conservative city districts just round the corner, who aren't even allowed out of their house without permission. But they have made a difference. Some of the reforms which have been pushed through parliament in the last few years, often against the natural instinct of conservative deputies, would have been quietly shelved if a coalition of women's groups hadn't been furiously working the phones and lobbying for change.

Most of the penal reforms were overshadowed anyway in the public mind by the great adultery debate, as the AKP tried to throw a bone to its more conservative constituents. A previous law banning adultery had been annulled by the constitutional court in 1996 on the grounds that it was only ever used to prosecute women. But Tayyip Erdoğan argued that the new proposal – which set out identical penalties for men and women – would be used to protect women, and strengthen the family.

'The family is a sacred institution for us,' he said. 'The stronger the family, the stronger the country. If the family is weakened, the country is doomed to destruction.'

Many people still wondered what he meant by 'family'. It's quite normal for men in conservative Turkish regions to take a second or third wife. Many members of parliament and even ministers have done it, so have criminal court judges, on the grounds that Islam allows them more than one wife, even if Turkish law doesn't. Atatürk banned polygamy, but a man can still marry a woman in an official state-sanctioned ceremony and then take other wives in traditional religious ceremonies. They are technically illegal, but they remain socially acceptable in many parts of the country. It all puts the idea of adultery into a rather different context.

The strangest thing about this sudden fight over the meaning of family values was the timing: right in the middle of an intense phase of diplomacy with the EU. Conspiracy theorists thought it was an artificial crisis manufactured by the government to draw attention away from other shortcomings. But women's groups were outraged and they marched noisily on parliament to make their point, while many newspaper columnists pointed out that the adultery proposal had nothing to do with European norms, and was much closer to the Islamic model of countries like Saudi Arabia.

'The West is not perfect,' Erdoğan responded sharply, before he suddenly agreed to drop the whole idea. 'If we took the West as a model of perfection in everything, we would have to deny ourselves and we would perish.'

Homosexuals had also hoped to benefit from the reform of the penal code. There are thriving gay subcultures in the big cities, and leading entertainers and TV personalities are openly gay. But popular prejudice is still strong: some homosexuals risk losing their jobs if their sexual orientation is disclosed, and the army and police are notoriously hostile. Gay activists had lobbied for new legislation which would have made discrimination 'on the basis of sexual orientation' a criminal offence. It was included in an early draft, but later dropped by conservative members of the AKP. If Turkey's moral majority couldn't criminalize adultery they were hardly likely to hand victory on a plate to the gay lobby.

All in all, the political battles surrounding the new penal code were a reminder for many people that while the AKP government has a well-earned reputation for crusading reform, a significant number of its supporters are not exactly bastions of modern values.

'They are incredibly conservative,' muttered a rather feisty female journalist I know. 'When you look at some of their people in parliament you think, "My God, where did they come from?" and you can see that the idea of women's rights is utterly alien to them.'

Little wonder then that many modern women idolize Atatürk. They believe, with good reason, that it was his revolution that gave them the freedoms they enjoy. He was a staunch advocate of the emancipation of women who, they will remind you, had the right to vote in Turkey before their counterparts in France. Today among the metropolitan middle classes there is genuine equality – men and women work together in shops and offices and relax together in bars, clubs and restaurants. Attitudes to sex among the younger generation have become much more liberal, to an extent which would probably surprise many of their parents; Internet chat rooms are full to the brim; and in some sections of society it's no longer unusual to meet unmarried couples living together in the big cities.

Women still make up only about a quarter of the labour force, and they are very poorly represented in politics, but for those with the right education and access to opportunity nothing is impossible. Women routinely rise to the top in their chosen professions as corporate executives and academics, doctors and lawyers; and in the 1990s Tansu Çiller became Turkey's first female prime minister. Television screens are dominated by glamorous young women reading the news, competing in fashion shows and dodging the paparazzi. In sport, music and the arts, a growing number of Turkish women are living the lives they choose.

* * *

'Maybe they see these things on TV, and that's good, but it's like looking through a window into another world.'

There are no fashion shows for the women Zozan Özgökçe meets every day at the new offices of the Van Women's Association. At the far eastern end of the country, in a provincial city with a troubled recent history, opening any kind of private organization used to be fraught with difficulty. But the laws have been relaxed, and in Van there are now several human rights groups, an environmental association and a philosophy club as well. Civil society is booming, but women are still struggling to catch up.

'Look,' Zozan said as we wandered along the street. 'Tea house – men only. Internet café – men only. Where are the women? Indoors, working in the house.'

When we got to the office a woman and her family appeared in the doorway, looking for legal advice. Her husband had been killed in an accident and since then she'd had no compensation and no income.

'As soon as we opened, we had women coming in here asking for help,' Zozan's colleague Gülseren said. 'From the first day. Some of the men get angry, the rest just think it's a joke. They say they want a men's association too.'

We digressed briefly to talk about the popularity of a recent hit song 'Katula Katula', which comes down hard on any man who seems to be losing control of his woman. A real man is like old-fashioned 'stone-oven' bread, the song suggests, rather than the fluffy artificial stuff produced for the modern palate.

'Stone ovens,' Zozan said, suddenly serious again. 'Do you really think anyone would jump into an oven of their own free will?'

According to official figures about sixty young girls have committed suicide in Van in the last few years. The police say some of them have jumped into ovens, or thrown themselves down the steps into the coal store.

'I think we all know what really happened,' Zozan said, 'but there are never any witnesses.'

Women need better protection, and if all the legal changes which have been made in the last few years were actually implemented it would be a profound social revolution. Stone-oven Man wouldn't know what had hit him. But there is stubborn resistance to change, and in most villages around Van reform has had no effect whatsoever. Many rural women are never aware of their rights, or have no way of claiming them if they are. Getting organized, say women like Zozan and Gülseren, is just the first step in a very long process of change.

It didn't happen quickly enough for Nazime Alır, whose face stares out from the cover of the first issue of the Women's Association magazine. At the age of twenty-one she was burnt to death in her village when her husband poured diesel over her and lit it with a match. Before she died, she'd been to the police, to the governor's office and to the head of the village. We can give you food, they said. I don't want food, she'd replied, I want protection. When Zozan and her colleagues visited the village, everyone they spoke to said they knew Nazime was going to die, but nothing had been done. Her husband was still 'at large', but he'd been seen regularly around the village.

We got into Zozan's car for a quick tour of the city and a visit to the lake. Almost every vehicle we passed was driven by a man.

'You know,' she said, as we parted company, 'there are lots of sayings in our language we want to get rid of . . . "A husband can beat you and love you", "Men who don't beat their daughters will beat their knees". We can't change most of the older women. They accept their situation, including all the violence, because they don't know anything else. So we have to create a new generation, we have to start doing it in schools, and that's where education comes in.'

* * *

Small red flags with pictures of Atatürk emblazoned upon them were fluttering in the breeze. Children holding posters and banners were standing in the snow, stamping their feet to keep out the cold. The military had organized a public address system, two sheep were about to be sacrificed and a rather reluctant-looking posse of traditional dancers was poised for action. All in all, it was an important day in the town of Erciş, just over an hour's drive from Van on the northern shores of the lake. Education is the key to changing Turkey for good, and in Erciş another new school was about to be opened.

Educating the masses was one of Atatürk's battle cries in the early years of the republic, but many of his successors failed to make it a priority. Now they have no choice. So many things depend on improving education: better rights for women, better protection for children, and the country's ability to create jobs for its young population in the face of stiff global competition. There are no quick-fix solutions, but in the last few years remarkable progress has been made. 2004 was the first year in Turkey's history when more money was spent on education than on defence. It is funding a quiet revolution which is sending hundreds of thousands of children, most of them young girls, to school for the first time.

'It's still not easy to persuade all the parents,' said one of the young teachers in Erciş, Ramazan Karabörk, as we sat in his freshly painted classroom. 'We go to their houses and we talk to them. But when it comes to the girls, some of them don't see the point.'

So the teachers have to convince the families first. With the support of organizations like UNICEF, local campaigns have been launched to fight back against poverty, tradition and social prejudice. Parents are being taught that education is a good investment because it will mean more income in the future. It is compulsory, they are told, and it is free. In places like Erciş there has been real success – more girls are studying than ever before – but in other areas attitudes have hardly changed at all.

I arrived at the new school with the minister of education, Hüseyin Çelik, in a convoy of cars containing local dignitaries and villagers hoping for a favour. The national anthem was played, and the dignitaries made speeches. 'Study hard,' the minister told wide-eyed children in blue uniforms as he toured the classrooms, 'this is your school now.'

Hundreds of new schools have been built in eastern Turkey in the last few years, funded by the government and by grants from the World Bank, to replace isolated village schools which were falling down. Children from outlying areas come into town to study and they stay in dormitories during the week to make sure they're not simply kept at home. Boarding schools aren't a recent innovation – the minister himself is a product of the system – but the scale has suddenly become far more ambitious.

'It's a massive task,' Çelik told me, 'but you have to do something massive if you want to change your country. That's what we're trying to do.'

The foundations were laid in 1997 when the length of compulsory primary education was suddenly extended from five years to eight. Pupils are now supposed to stay at school until the age of thirteen at least. Attendance figures have risen dramatically, but in some rural areas more than half of all young teenage girls are still not enrolled. Many families believe early marriage is far more important than allowing their daughters to study, and as the girls get older the conservative instincts kick in. Some traditional fathers don't want their daughters travelling on school buses with boys, others object to the ban on wearing the headscarf in schools.

'Some of them,' added Ramazan Karabörk, 'are just looking for excuses. They refuse to let their daughters have an education – full stop.'

So there is a long way to go. There are already plans to increase the length of compulsory schooling again – to eleven years, to bring Turkey into line with European norms. But the system isn't ready yet. Investment in infrastructure and teaching has been insufficient for years, and the money which is being thrown at the problem now hasn't yet redressed the balance. Many schools in big cities have to teach kids on a double-shift system, because that's the only way they can fit them all in. There is still a huge imbalance between the first-class education given to the sons and daughters of the elite, and the struggle facing so many others in decrepit schools with overcrowded classrooms and poor facilities.

New schools like the one in Erciş, built with a private donation from a local businessman, are a small step forward. But changing the education system is not just about how many schools you have, or even how many pupils you get to fill them. It's also about what children are taught and the way in which they learn; and the next stage of reform is perhaps the most controversial of all. The school syllabus is being rewritten from start to finish – a highly political exercise – and teaching methods are being overhauled to encourage children to think for themselves. The old dogmatic methods, which don't prepare students for the modern world, are gradually being pushed aside.

The political columnist, Cüneyt Ülsever, once explained to me how he thought the old system worked.

'The teacher is always right. He or she has the knowledge and there is only one knowledge. The student's role is to memorize the knowledge, and to ask no questions.'

'And what does the knowledge say?'

'Well, two plus two equals four of course, but in general it tells you that the state is more important than anything else in life.'

From social science to religious studies, text books tend to stress the role of the state, the importance of the military and the existing order of things. It's all about legitimizing the system, and the teachings of Kemal Atatürk pop up in all corners of the curriculum. 'As Atatürk said,' children are helpfully informed, 'physics is a good science.' In fact the founding father seems to have a view on just about any subject you might wish to study – all you have to do is learn what he said. A lot of this will have to change if Turkey wants a modern education system, but as with anything affecting Atatürk and our old friend, the state, it is a sensitive business. There are plenty of bureaucrats who will fight tooth and nail against any major change.

A new curriculum has already been agreed for the first few years of primary school, but the more difficult debates are still to come. If there is supposed to be greater emphasis on critical thinking and analysis, will there be a point at which dissenting opinions suddenly become unwelcome? Will anyone be encouraged to think about the Kurds or the Armenians? Teenagers take a compulsory national security course, for example, which is usually taught by serving or recently retired military officers. Radical reform in that part of the syllabus may prove rather difficult. Already gone from the old system, though, are some of the references to the enemies Turks face in every direction – the Greeks and the Russians have suddenly become neighbours instead.

Once again, I fancy further change will come through a combination of pressure from without and pressure from within. Many parents virtually bankrupt themselves to get their children into university, and they will demand an education system which pays a proper dividend. In the final year of high school, many students hardly bother to turn up for classes at all. They are too busy attending private study centres called *dershanes* where, for exorbitant fees, they cram in the information they need to pass the highly competitive university entrance exam.

The exam is all about solving specific problems: right or wrong, true or false; original thought isn't necessary. It means the first year at university becomes a kind of conversion course, where students have to be taught how to evaluate and criticize ideas for the first time. The brightest of the bunch can adjust fairly quickly, but many students graduate from Turkish universities barely equipped with the analytical skills they need to compete in the global job market. The lucky ones who study at the elite private universities, where independence of thought is actively encouraged, are part of a privileged minority.

Discussion of taboo subjects is spreading slowly to other universities, but education will continue to be highly politicized. Kurdish language courses, disputes about the headscarf, better access to university for graduates of religious high schools – all the political fights in the country are reflected in the education system. Raising standards is far more important, though, and behind the headlines something significant has been set in motion. Changing the way people think must sound terribly subversive in some quarters of the Turkish establishment; but it is beginning to happen, whether they like it or not.

I met several teachers who still harbour doubts about members of the AKP government, and wonder if they're just putting on a show to impress their new European friends. School inspectors say they are still encouraged by the bureaucracy to be as tough as possible on anyone who steps out of line. But in Erciş, Hüseyin Çelik sounded like a man on a mission.

'If we want to become part of the wider world,' he said, 'we need a broader perspective. It is a mentality revolution, but no one should see it as a threat. They should see it as a great opportunity.'

*   *   *

Turks love little children. The sternest of policemen can't help breaking into a smile at the sight of a small baby. No one seems to mind if a waiter abandons his job for half an hour to play with a child who's just come through the restaurant door. Families dote on their kids, and spoil them rotten. It is, I think, a Mediterranean thing. But there are still plenty of children who have been failed by the system, who remain beyond the reach of the most ambitious education reforms. More than a million kids have to go out to work every day, trapped by the desperate poverty of their families.

I met Leyla at the height of summer in a field near the Syrian border. It was early and the sun was still low in the sky, but the heat was already intense. She was doing what the rest of her family was doing – tearing white buds of cotton from the plants all around her and stuffing them into the sack which was hanging loosely from her back and dragging along the ground. Other children were scattered across the fields, working from dawn until dusk to earn the equivalent of a couple of dollars a day. Leyla's hands were blackened and calloused. She was only ten years old.

'It is hard work,' she whispered, as her uncle warned her to concentrate on the job at hand. Leyla couldn't read or write, and she had never been to school.

A couple of hours further down the road I came across two more children, even smaller, a boy and a girl with torn clothes and snotty faces. They were both about seven or eight, and they were working their normal beat on a busy street corner in the city of Adana. As cars paused at the traffic lights, these two tiny kids who were scared of strangers tried to make a little money by wiping filthy bits of rag across windows they could barely reach. Occasionally someone took pity on them and gave them a coin; more often than not they were waved away. They were Kurdish migrants who spoke little Turkish, the poorest of the urban poor, and they didn't even seem to know what school was.

Children like Leyla and the two little window washers represent perhaps the biggest challenge of all. It's hardly a problem unique to Turkey, but the gap between rich and poor is vast and growing wider. There is plenty of poverty in the big cities in the west of the country, but as a general rule the further east you go the poorer it gets. In 2003 per capita income in the south-east was about one-tenth the level of the richest region around the Sea of Marmara. Travelling to parts of eastern Turkey can feel like taking a step back in time.

By every indicator the eastern provinces are struggling: average income, rates of illiteracy, levels of unemployment. Successive governments have promised concerted action but it hasn't been enough. A repressive security presence and the threat of violence from the PKK have combined to keep most would-be investors well away. It is striking how many western Turks have never ventured very far past the capital, Ankara, let alone all the way to the eastern borders. 'You've actually been to Şırnak?' they might ask in astonishment, as if they were talking about another planet. 'What was it like?'

Migrant agricultural labourers like Leyla's family are nearly all from the east. Constantly on the move, they follow the crops wherever they can find them. If they're not picking cotton in the burning southern heat, they're harvesting potatoes and sugar beet across central Anatolia, or collecting hazelnuts on the Black Sea coast. It's all back-breaking work, and their nomadic lifestyle is unremittingly hard. They pitch tents made of canvas, wood and plastic in temporary encampments next to isolated roads, with no running water and the most basic of food supplies.

'If we had any land of our own,' said Leyla's uncle, but he never finished his sentence. He just shrugged his shoulders and went back to work.

Patterns of rural life have changed across the country but it is the south-east which has suffered the most. A couple of generations ago villagers produced nearly everything they consumed, but that doesn't happen any more. Forced displacement and evacuated villages have simply added to the sense of trauma, throwing hundreds of thousands of people into poverty almost overnight. Families which used to be self-sufficient are crammed into urban ghettos where they have to scrimp and save, beg, steal and borrow, just to find the cash to feed themselves. Many people complain of depression and lethargy; they can't afford to buy books and uniforms to send their children to school, and they end up sending them onto the streets to earn extra money instead.

They can only dream of having what Abdullah Çetin has got – a piece of land, and plentiful water to help him grow his crops.

'This used to be nothing but dust,' Abdullah said, as we squelched through the mud next to a long concrete irrigation channel. 'Look at it now. It's all because of the water. The water has saved us.'

We weren't all that far from the ancient town of Harran, where strange conical mud-brick houses sprout from the landscape, in the region which used to be known as the Fertile Crescent. For years, centuries even, the Harran plain was anything but fertile – a forgotten backwater. But now nearly fifty thousand families live and work on newly irrigated land.

Abdullah Çetin and his neighbours have been thrown a lifeline by the largest development scheme in Turkish history. The massive South-Eastern Anatolia Project (known by its Turkish acronym GAP) is Ankara's answer to regional poverty and underdevelopment. Harnessing the waters of Turkey's two great rivers, the Tigris and the Euphrates, everything about GAP is big. It covers nearly ten per cent of the country, it aims to create nearly four million jobs, and when it's finished it will include twenty-two dams and nineteen hydroelectric power stations.

The centrepiece of GAP is – appropriately enough – the biggest thing of all. The massive Atatürk dam on the Euphrates is an imposing wall of concrete, curving across an isolated valley. It is a source of pride for many Turks, a symbol of modernity which always pops up in official brochures and public relations films. When Turgut Özal inaugurated the dam in 1990 he declared that the days of the impotent Turk were over; so my first reaction must have come as a bit of a disappointment to the engineer who was showing me around.

'It really is very big, isn't it,' I said. Low marks for originality, but he nodded all the same. It was a pity, I went on, that the World Bank hadn't agreed to finance it, because of concerns about the amount of water GAP would provide to Syria and Iraq downstream. No comment. And then, of course, there were all the towns and villages which were going to be flooded by future projects. No comment again. This, I was told politely, is a dam, not a political statement.

The questions haven't gone away though. Syria and Iraq still worry that Turkey could in effect turn off the tap in any future conflict; they say GAP will cause water shortages and pesticide pollution downstream. Absolutely not, insist Turkish officials – the dams allow them to manage water flows more professionally, and they have always given their neighbours more than they need. Back on the Harran plain, Abdullah Çetin was less diplomatic but just as determined.

'This is our water, Turkish water,' he said, as he watched the precious liquid dribble gently onto neat rows of tomato plants. 'We can do what we like with it.'

GAP has also been controversial in Europe, where a big campaign by environmental and human rights groups persuaded foreign banks and companies to withdraw support for the Ilisu dam on the Tigris. The Turks still want to build the dam, but if they do they will flood the lower levels of Hasankeyf, the oldest continuously inhabited town in Anatolia, and displace thousands of people. Critics also worry about the damage GAP is doing to the region's ecosystems, and some Kurdish activists say it's all a wicked plot to cleanse them from their ancestral homes.

The Turks are undeterred and they hope to finish the construction phase of the GAP project by 2010, at a cost of more than thirty billion dollars. If all goes to plan, it will provide more than a fifth of Turkey's electricity needs and irrigate 1.7 million hectares of new farmland. But the people who run GAP have also taken heed of some of the criticism. Having started life as a civil engineer's dream – big dams and big money, a typical top-down project dominated by the Turkish state – GAP has changed. It has evolved into something more inclusive, and it now concentrates on the human aspects of development just as much as on concrete and kilowatts.

Local community centres promote literacy among women, and teach villagers about child nutrition and better sanitation. They provide access to computers and basic skills which can help women earn money of their own. There are job-training schemes for everything from bee-keeping to photography to cultivating mushrooms. The long-term benefits of big dams remain a subject of heated debate all over the world, but GAP has improved many people's lives.

'We started to listen to the people,' said Olcay Unver, the man who ran the GAP administration for many years. 'Now they tell us what they want as individuals, and we try to respond.'

'What about all the criticism? Do you ever feel you're misunderstood?' I asked.

'Sometimes,' he said with a slight smile. 'But this is Turkey. It goes with the job.'

* * *

This is Turkey. *Burası Türkiye*. It's always been one of my favourite Turkish expressions. Deftly employed with a sympathetic shrug of the shoulders, it can be used to explain away almost anything. 'What can I do; what can anyone do?' the shrug implies. 'This is just how things are.' In a country where fatalism is so deeply ingrained it is hugely appropriate, but still I wonder whether it needs updating. More and more people in today's Turkey believe they can change their lives for the better. From torture victims to tomato farmers, they no longer accept that 'this is just how things are'. Broadly speaking most Turks want what everyone else wants – nice houses, good health care, better education and more job opportunities.

For many thousands of people who are beaten and abused every year, either by officials of the state or within the family home, the struggle is still a more basic one. It's about protection from violence. But for millions of Turks who don't suffer so directly, the idea of human rights means something rather different. It's about aspirations and opportunities, the hopes and dreams of a better life. Some of them are cruelly disappointed, and the have-nots still outnumber the haves. But Turkey knows it needs to banish inequality as fast as it can, and it knows that access to information and technology has made expectations rise. That's why everyone talks so much about development; and at the heart of development there has to be a stronger economy, which rids itself of an alarming reputation for boom and bust.

7

IT'S THE ECONOMY, STUPID

Monday 19 February 2001 began like any other Monday morning –
there was heavy traffic on the bridges across the Bosphorus, concern in
the papers about American-led bombing raids in neighbouring Iraq, and
an apparently routine meeting of the National Security Council in
Ankara. There was nothing to suggest that Turkey was heading for
another calamity – something which would force thousands of businesses
into bankruptcy and throw hundreds of thousands of people out of
their jobs.

I was sitting on the floor trying to fix a wheel back onto my chair
when the prime minister, Bülent Ecevit, appeared suddenly on the small
TV screen in the corner of my office, talking about a 'serious crisis in the
state'. He'd just had a huge row with President Sezer in the National
Security Council, and had stormed out of the room. With Turkey's
omnipresent military leaders looking on in stony silence, the president
had been haranguing the government for pursuing corruption allegations too slowly.

'You're sitting on the mud,' the president had insisted. 'We can clean
it up if you're not going to do anything about it. Why are you so scared
of investigating corruption?'

A copy of the constitution was thrown back and forth across the table
before Ecevit and members of his cabinet walked out. An angry prime
minister then went on national television to announce that he'd been
insulted, and his aides let it be known that he expected an apology. Was
the government about to resign? Would political instability ever go

away? The markets, already unnerved by a financial wobble a few months earlier, took one look and didn't like what they saw. Within minutes, the Istanbul Stock Exchange went into meltdown and Turkey was plunged into the worst economic crisis in living memory.

Sezer and Ecevit had already had several high-profile disagreements following the president's unexpected election by parliament a few months earlier. But this was more than a clash of personalities. It was a fundamental disagreement about how the state system should operate. President Sezer had reactivated a rarely used State Inspection Board to investigate the political plunder of public banks over the previous decade. The prime minister had already appointed investigators of his own, and he was angry that the president seemed to be 'inspecting his inspectors'.

Both men had reputations for honesty in a dirty political world, and the veteran Ecevit – a poet and translator of Sanskrit in his spare time – obviously believed his integrity had been called into question by the ferocity of the president's criticism. His mistake, however, was to go public in full view of volatile financial markets. Here was an old-style politician failing to understand the speed of a modern economy, where big decisions are taken at the click of a mouse. Turkey would pay a heavy price for his indiscretion, as its volatile economy lurched towards collapse.

By the end of the day several billion US dollars had been wiped off share values, and several billion more had been sold from the precious foreign exchange reserves of the Central Bank to try to stabilize the situation. Some interest rates soared to absurd levels of several thousand per cent. Economic confidence was in tatters, and banks were soon struggling to meet their debt repayments. Before the week was out the government was forced to abandon exchange rate controls, allowing a huge devaluation of the Turkish lira. The national currency – already the butt of many local jokes about the six zeros on every bank note – promptly lost a third of its value against the dollar. That in turn triggered an upward lurch in inflation, a brutal recession and an almost unbearable dose of economic misery for ordinary Turks.

'They're trying to impose an economic solution on a problem caused by politics,' raged an exasperated Turkish friend of mine, who worked at the time for a leading financial institution in Istanbul. He was normally a mild-mannered man, but he was finding it hard to contain his anger. 'When are they going to learn? When? This is the wrong medicine for the illness, and now the pain is going to get worse.'

Well, they did learn. There had been plenty of economic crises before, but no one in the country has forgotten the events precipitated in February 2001. Rich, poor, secular, religious – everyone took a hit, and many people are still struggling to recover. It was another turning point in the transformation of Turkey. The cosy alliance of politicians, bureaucrats and businessmen who had carved up the spoils between them for decades, with no questions asked, could never rest quite so easily again.

* * *

'Our people won't be able to pay their bills, and families will have to rally round and help each other.'

It was one month after the economic crisis struck, and Mehmet Edip Ağaoğulları had just fired seventy people from the cooking-oil factory he ran in the north-western city of Edirne, in the heart of Turkey's sunflower belt. Production levels at the factory had slumped to twenty-five per cent of normal levels, and across the city more than three and a half thousand jobs had already been lost.

'Everyone is tightening their belts,' he said, 'and there's nothing we can do.'

In a nearby tea house I listened as Muammer Erat and his friends talked about their predicament, and railed against the political system. Muammer had just lost his job at the cooking-oil factory after working there for more than eighteen years, and he felt let down by the people running the country, and by economic forces he didn't fully understand.

'There are no other jobs,' he said, 'and there's nothing else I can do. I'm looking, but it's impossible. When you're old they don't want you, and I'm not well educated.'

The speed with which the economic crisis spread was extraordinary. It was as if a house of cards had just collapsed. What was happening in Edirne was happening across the country. Turkey suddenly became a cash-only economy. There was no credit available, even between long-standing business contacts, because no one knew who might be unable to pay. It wasn't just the poor who were suffering – countless small businesses went bust as people stopped buying all but the bare necessities; companies relying on imports were in deep trouble – they couldn't afford them any more; and many middle-class Turks who had followed the fashion of taking out a mortgage denominated in foreign currencies, usually the Deutschmark, lost their houses after the repayments became unaffordable overnight.

I watched angry demonstrators take to the streets in exasperation: shopkeepers who hadn't made a single sale for days were joined by taxi drivers who could no longer afford the price of imported fuel. Nearly a quarter of the fourteen thousand journalists and technicians working in the Turkish media were fired as big media barons trimmed their margins; more than two hundred thousand workers in the shoe industry alone lost their jobs. One small businessman in Ankara, a florist named Ahmet Çakmak, briefly became a popular hero. Burdened with hard currency debts he couldn't repay, he launched a one-man protest, hurling his cash register down the steps of the prime ministry building as Bülent Ecevit was leaving his office.

In big cities like Istanbul and Ankara, where rich and poor live cheek by jowl, a crime wave followed as some people began to steal to survive. Others set up makeshift stalls on the pavement to sell valuable possessions, and the number of prostitutes working on the streets suddenly increased. Popular disgust at the way politicians reacted to the economic crisis intensified as Turks began to realize the extent to which long-established corruption had contributed to their current plight. State-run banks controlled by whichever political party was in power had run up losses of more than twenty billion dollars, by handing out bad loans in return for political favours.

'That's the real crime,' said an Istanbul shopkeeper, Mehmet Aktaş, as he flourished a hand-written poster saying GOVERNMENT RESIGN. 'We don't trust any of them any more. Why should we?'

Another man walked by, shouting angrily and swinging his placard like a weapon. YOU'RE SUCKING OUR BLOOD, it said.

Many people only managed to get through the first few months of 2001 because extended families and religious communities rallied round. As the rumblings of social unrest grew louder, the National Security Council even felt the need to issue a formal statement rejecting speculation that an 'interim regime' of technocrats backed by the military could be on the way.

'The trouble with Turkey,' the veteran Istanbul businessman, Ishak Alaton, told me at the time, 'is that it's probably the worst-managed country in the world. And that has got to change.'

It was true, and finally everyone knew it. The cycle of short-term boom and spectacular bust had to come to an end. People had been talking about Turkey's huge economic potential for years, but lasting success had always been just around the next corner. When Turgut Özal liberalized the economy in the 1980s he unleashed the tremendous dynamism of the private sector. But it came at a price: sloppy standards, crony capitalism, a wink and a nod and a quick fix of the books. Throughout the 1990s economic growth was often impressive, but it was built on deeply unstable foundations. Various governments tinkered with economic reform, but they were ignoring the root of the problem. At the beginning of the new century the country could no longer muddle through with crisis management, populism and corruption running out of control.

So Bülent Ecevit – bruised and battered both by the markets and by popular discontent – brought back a Turkish economist, Kemal Derviş, from a comfortable job at the World Bank in Washington. His task was to hammer out terms with the International Monetary Fund for the latest in a long line of painful economic rescue packages. The new deal, when it finally came, was worth a massive nineteen billion dollars, and this time there was to be no quick fix.

'We can't dynamite the future to save today,' Derviş told parliament, as anti-IMF protestors demonstrated on the streets outside.

Kemal Derviş's intervention may well have been the turning point for the economy, but he didn't have long to work his brand of magic. Ecevit's political party, the Democratic Left, was soon in a state of collapse and at the 2002 general election none of the three parties in his unwieldy coalition won a single seat in parliament. A generation of politicians was swept onto the sidelines and the AKP emerged victorious with a huge majority as Turkey's first single-party government in a decade.

It was perfect timing. The AKP came to power just as pressure at home and abroad for dramatic change had reached its peak. At last political and economic reform began to move hand in hand, and the new government took over the tough economic restructuring programme Derviş had agreed with the IMF, without having to shoulder the blame for introducing it in the first place. It suggested that Tayyip Erdoğan had one indispensable asset: he's a lucky politician, in the right place at the right time.

The big business and finance community in Istanbul was initially sceptical of Erdoğan's ability to manage the economy properly, but it was won over by his actions – a willingness to take advice, and a grim determination to follow the rules set down by the IMF, even when they hurt. Austerity (including deep cuts in public spending) is a painful process, and unemployment in Turkey continues to be a massive problem. The IMF's economic medicine has been desperately hard for most ordinary Turks to stomach. But despite the lack of new jobs, the results in the first three years were generally impressive: the first signs of economic stability, and even (whisper it softly) sustainable economic growth.

There are plenty of sceptics out there who argue that the recovery is fragile and unbalanced, and that a sudden flight of foreign capital could see Turkey become the next Argentina (which defaulted on debts worth more than one hundred billion dollars in 2001). Even technocrats admit that the country isn't out of the woods yet, but Turkish officials are increasingly convinced that the days of skyrocketing inflation and interest rates are gone for good. The banking system, the source of so much of the trouble, has been overhauled and freed from political plunder: under the watchful eye of an independent regulator, there are now about fifty banks operating in the country; five years ago there were more than eighty. Reform is beginning to have a real impact.

There have been some significant landmarks along the way. In early 2004 the inflation rate dropped into single figures for the first time since September 1972, something many of the Turks I know thought they would never see in their lifetime. And on 1 January 2005 the symbol of a new era was launched: new coins and bank notes with Atatürk's face staring sternly from every one of them. One new lira is worth one million old lira. Turkey's billionaires' club suddenly became considerably more exclusive, but there were few complaints. Computer screens in banks had been running out of space for big transactions and taxi meters had to be constantly updated to fit in all those zeros. Introducing the new notes was an important psychological step in a campaign to restore public confidence in a currency which had taken a beating for years.

'We're very happy to have rid Turkey of this shame,' the prime minister declared as he spent the first of his new money in a local shop. 'We're happy to bring back the dignity of the Turkish lira.'

* * *

The optimism doesn't convince everyone. At the offices of Turkey's popular cartoon magazine, *Leman*, weary scepticism hangs heavy in the air. In a room on the top floor I met Mehmet Çağçağ – one of the leading cartoonists – flicking through a pile of back issues and giggling occasionally at the characters he'd helped to create.

'It's bittersweet,' he admitted, 'it's about people finding things to laugh at as they struggle to survive.'

Leman has returned repeatedly to the economic problems faced by ordinary urban Turks in the last few years. Turkey is renamed 'Unemploymentistan', and cartoons show trainee pickpockets being put through their paces on a military assault course, or a man being carried around on the back of a friendly slab of stale bread. There is also an endless variety of cartoon characters queuing: to try to find a job; to pay another bill; to get on a bus; or to eat a free meal during Ramadan.

'For many Turks,' Çağçağ said, 'this is the reality of daily life.'

Insecurity is now a permanent condition. Union membership has been declining dramatically for years, and the idea of a guaranteed job is disappearing fast. Millions of people still work for the state, and whenever you go into a government office there always seem to be huge numbers of people hanging around in ill-fitting suits. But a radical pruning of the civil service is on the cards. Quality not quantity is the order of the day.

The old system was all about political patronage, and crowd-pleasing schemes designed to win votes. But it was erratic and unaffordable, and parts of it had begun to change well before the AKP appeared on the scene. Long gone is the most generous state pension scheme in the world which, a decade ago, allowed men to retire at the age of forty-three and women at thirty-eight. To no one's great surprise they discovered that it was running up a massive deficit, and everyone simply picked up their pension and tried to keep working anyway.

Many Turks still earn their money wherever they find it, and try to juggle more than one part-time job if they can, but the squeeze is on. Even firms that have recovered reasonably well from the calamities of 2001 are now employing fewer people.

'We're more efficient than we used to be,' I was told by a local businessman who used to live up our road. 'If we weren't, we would have gone bust.'

Efficiency is now the name of the game, and in an economy financed by billions of dollars from the International Monetary Fund that means privatization (fewer old jobs) and foreign direct investment (hopefully more new ones) have moved to the top of the agenda.

Privatization has always been a delicate subject in a country which is so sensitive about the symbols of statehood. Turkish nationalists in politics, the bureaucracy and the military don't want vital national interests falling into the wrong hands. Little by little, though, in the face of legal challenges and bureaucratic resistance, underperforming state enterprises have been sold off: oil refineries, sugar factories, the state tobacco producer and parts of Turk Telecom and Turkish Airlines are all coming under the hammer. It's been a slow stuttering process, and there's much less global demand for big privatization projects than there used to be. The huge financial gains other countries made from selling state assets in the 1990s, at the height of the stock market boom, are no longer instantly available.

There are plenty of other pitfalls for would-be foreign investors in Turkey as well, and many of them have taken their money elsewhere. According to the United Nations Conference on Trade and Development, Turkey ranked fifty-seventh in the world in 2003 for attracting foreign direct investment. That put it behind such investment superpowers as Sudan and Bermuda, with a total of five hundred and eighty-six million US dollars. 2004 was better, but Turkey has attracted less in twenty years than countries of a comparable size have done in one.

'In a word, pathetic,' said a banker in Istanbul.

'Why so bad?' I asked, and he just rolled his eyes and launched into a long list: corruption, high taxes, red tape, a reputation for legal minefields and huge difficulty in getting justice done quickly if disputes arise. New laws have been passed to reduce bureaucratic procedures and give foreign investors the same legal status as Turkish companies, but suspicions about the objectivity of the bureaucracy and the judiciary still give many people pause for thought. Judicial corruption, in particular, is a huge problem.

'If you know where to spend it,' I was told, 'this is the best legal system money can buy.'

Permits don't arrive on time, and legal disputes drag on and on. Far smaller countries have had far more investment because they are seen as less of a risk. Many Turkish businessmen hope EU membership talks, and the continuing partnership with the IMF, will change that perception, but they may not see instant results.

The official aim is to attract fifteen billion dollars of new foreign investment between 2005 and 2007, but integrating Turkey with the world economy is a slow frustrating process. Memories (rose-tinted for some) of the closed economy of yesteryear live on, and inertia still seeps through the system. In March 2004 Tayyip Erdoğan met senior executives from foreign companies based in Turkey to hear about their problems. The prime minister promised action to help them but, according to one insider, six months later nothing had been done. Politicians can issue instructions, but there is still resistance to change at the very highest levels of the bureaucracy.

'Promises, promises,' sighed my source, 'Turkey is a land of promises.'

The strange thing is that everyone knows why foreign investment hasn't been flooding in, and yet few people seem prepared to do anything about it. Ties between Turkish political and business leaders are still strong, and local companies are often favoured in public tenders. It leaves me wondering whether there really is a critical mass in politics or in the bureaucracy which actually wants the foreign investment to arrive.

'People always try to do things "alla turca". They don't trust foreigners and they don't really want them doing business here,' said one European businessman based in Turkey. 'So a lot of foreign business plans are designed for short-term profit and nothing else. You make your money and run.'

In some of Turkey's big manufacturing industries, international companies have reduced the risk by forming joint ventures with local partners. In the car industry, Renault has a long-standing partnership with OYAK, the armed forces pension fund, while both Fiat and Ford are in business with Koç Holding, Turkey's largest family-owned conglomerate. Many of the vehicles are manufactured for export but there are also ambitious plans to expand the domestic market, in a country where less than one person in ten owns a car. In many rural areas good-quality roads are almost deserted, and if economic development takes off international car makers will see Turkey as a lucrative market for growth.

Still, in many quarters, suspicion of any foreign involvement in the economy runs deep. Take, for instance, the law passed by the AKP in 2003 which allowed foreign nationals to buy land in Turkey. Amid a flurry of legal challenges, the opposition Republican People's Party calculated that two hundred and seventy-seven thousand square metres of land were bought by foreigners in the first year after the law was passed and – horror of horrors – nearly a third of that total was bought by Greeks.

'Our lands are slipping away under us,' thundered a leading opposition deputy, Haluk Koç. 'Some people may describe our warning as a medieval mentality, or paranoia, but it's not. Saying that the Turkish economy is heading towards total foreign domination, and saying it without resorting to arms or violence, is being patriotic.'

* * *

In a factory on the edge of Istanbul, hundreds of workers in burgundy T-shirts keep the production lines humming along. Circuit boards and screens roll past them as they put the finishing touches to one of Turkey's most successful new exports. A man with a toy hammer turns on the remote control and gives each new television a quick whack to make sure it's as childproof as possible. Remarkably, in 2004, more than fifty per cent of all the TV sets sold in Europe were made in Turkey – most of them by two companies, Vestel and Beko Elektronik.

Beko produced seven million TVs during the course of the year and it exported nearly all of them to hungry European markets. Some of them were sold under their own brand names; others were made under licence for more established European companies. Beko has already bought the famous German brand, Grundig, to give it a firm foothold in the German market.

'It used to be Turkish delight and Turkish carpets,' Beko's energetic vice president, Erem Demircan, told me. 'Now it's Turkish televisions. No one in Europe is thinking about getting their televisions from anywhere else.'

Since 1996 Turkey has had a Customs Union with the EU, which abolished all tariffs on industrial goods. For a while, Turkish industries suffered badly as imports from Europe shot up. But the good ones adjusted, survived and began to flourish. The Customs Union still has its critics, but more than seventy per cent of Turkey's trade is now with the enlarged European Union. It's not just TVs. Fridges, washing machines, cars and buses are all being manufactured in Turkey, where labour is relatively cheap, and they're flooding into Europe. Turkey's textile and clothing manufacturers are also doing a roaring trade, supplying high-quality brand names. They're confident that they're flexible enough to fight off stiff competition from China and other Asian producers.

It means that big Turkish companies are well placed to become regional economic leaders. From Istanbul, container ships reach Felixstowe in seven days; and fleets of articulated lorries carry Turkish exports to cities across Continental Europe in just forty-eight hours. Turkish manufacturers can send truckloads of goods to growing markets in the Balkans faster and more cheaply than their German or Italian competitors. And if stability ever comes to Iraq, Turkish companies will be in pole position to increase all kinds of trade across their eastern borders as well. Turkish products, from satellite dishes to microwave ovens, have already poured into Iraq since the fall of Saddam Hussein. When I was in Baghdad shortly after the end of the American-led invasion, the only cold beer in town was Turkey's finest: Efes Pilsner.

The inferiority complex which used to haunt many Turkish companies in the face of international competition has gone. Lack of quality is no longer an issue, partly because they have also had to change the way they operate at home. In the bad old days of inflation and a banking system rotten to the core, many of them made more money from financial investments than from the products they were trying to sell. In 1999, Turkey's five hundred biggest firms made a staggering eighty-eight per cent of their profit from lending money to the government. Now they have to prove that they can be competitive in the real world.

Some of them are failing, but many are succeeding. In the aftermath of economic crises, there's a consumer boom in Turkey as well – a growing middle class is eager to acquire white goods, cars and personal computers. Even in the remotest of towns every other building seems to house an Internet café, and knowledge of the outside world is spreading fast. Across the country, regional centres of economic power are booming and new shopping malls (that sure sign of globalized culture) are springing up everywhere. About a third of Turkey's people live in the five biggest metropolitan areas, and within a few years affordable mortgages will be widely available for the first time. The rural economy of the 1960s has changed out of all recognition.

Another sign of a country on the move was the decision by Turkish Airlines to plump for dramatic expansion – signing huge deals to buy more than fifty new aircraft from Airbus and Boeing, to meet the demand for more flights on domestic and international routes. More Turks are travelling than ever before, and more foreigners are visiting the country for business and pleasure. Tourism has taken off in recent years and it has become a leading earner of foreign exchange, bringing in more than thirteen billion dollars a year.

Turkey is now trying to get away from the image of a backpackers' paradise and concentrate on people who have money to spend. Coastal cities like Antalya on the Mediterranean are growing at a remarkable rate, and there's been a boom in the construction of luxury yachts and marinas. Spending a week sailing from bay to bay in the blue waters around Bodrum is one of life's better experiences, and with five thousand miles of coastline there is plenty of scope for expansion. The Turks are still some distance behind other Mediterranean holiday destinations like Greece or Spain, but the industry has proved remarkably resilient.

'What are they going to throw at us next!' exclaimed the travel agent near our office, when I went in one day to pick up some tickets. She listed the obstacles one by one: earthquakes, war in neighbouring Iraq, bombs in Istanbul, and threats of revenge after the capture of Abdullah Öcalan.

'If we can survive all that,' she said, 'we can survive anything.'

I told her she needn't worry because if the product is good enough it will always sell, and Turkey has got everything you could ask for in a tourist brochure. As well as beaches and blue seas, and the historic centres of cities like Istanbul, there are almost too many special places to mention: the weird and wonderful rock formations of Cappadocia, the breathtaking empty beauty of eastern Anatolia, the lush mountains and Alpine valleys near the Black Sea coast, and one of the most extraordinary collections of archaeological sites anywhere in the world.

Millions of Europeans are beginning to discover all this for themselves. They come to Turkey every year and form a very different impression of the place and the people than the one they may have had in their heads. Conservative? Insular? Here instead is all the outgoing natural charm of some of the most hospitable people I've ever met. One of the reasons why the Turkish earthquake in 1999 received so much more attention in the Western media than similar tragedies across the border in Armenia or Iran was that millions of people had been there. Turkey felt more familiar, closer to home, part in fact of the Western world.

And the effect of tourism cuts both ways. Turks are meeting other Europeans in ever greater numbers – not just those who can afford to travel abroad, but the one and a half million people who are employed in the tourism industry as well. Mehmet works in a small fish restaurant on the Datça peninsula, the beautiful stretch of coastline where the Aegean meets the Mediterranean. Before a relative helped him get his seasonal job as a waiter, the only time he'd been more than a hundred miles from his small town in the interior was when he was sent to the Georgian border on military service.

'If I was back at home, I wouldn't be doing anything much.' He grinned as he came to the end of another shift.

Turkish pop was booming out of a bar down the road, and there was the sound of raucous laughter. The harbour lights twinkled in the distance and yachts bobbed up and down on the water.

'Here I meet more people, and I see more things. It's a whole new world for me.'

*　*　*

But the old world is still there. You don't have to travel far from any of Turkey's big cities to sense the huge change of pace. Drive out of Ankara, and the endless rows of new concrete buildings suddenly disappear, the traffic thins out dramatically and the hustle and bustle is gone. Instead small villages dot the horizon, the sky looks bigger, there are rolling fields and plane trees, tractors and flocks of wandering sheep. This is rural Anatolia and until the 1960s this *was* the economy. While the ruling classes in Ankara were obsessed with Soviet-style five-year plans and massive state-run industrial giants, the vast majority of the people lived off the land. Many of them still do. Migration to the cities has already produced dramatic social change, but about a third of the population still depends on agriculture to make a living.

And that's a problem. Not far from the small town of Gordion, home of the famous knot cut by Alexander the Great in 333 BC on his way to conquer Asia, local farmers are wrestling with a more modern conundrum – the chill wind of competition. Anatolia may well have been the place where organized farming first began some ten thousand years ago, but a tradition which stretches back through generations of agricultural life is under serious threat. There are too many farmers in Turkey, way too many, and the state can no longer afford it.

'People are selling their land, selling their tractors,' said a local official, as he tested the quality of a new consignment of wheat which had just been brought in from the fields. 'They are struggling to survive.'

IMF reforms have already hit the agricultural sector hard. For years crops like wheat (or tobacco or sugar) were purchased at set prices by the state, and the prices were generous. It doesn't happen any longer and farmers are feeling the pinch: new farming techniques and changing economic priorities have driven many small agricultural communities out of business. In the south-east, the livestock trade has been decimated by war. But the government still wants to make further radical reductions in the number of people working in agriculture and there is no painless way of doing it.

'We used to be self-sufficient,' said Sait Akyar, as he sat under the shade of a tree on a country road, waiting to sell his trailerload of wheat. 'But they've annihilated our economy by importing cheap surplus crops from other countries.'

It's not all bad news, because Turkey has many of the natural advantages it needs – good soil, a good climate and plenty of water. It could become a regional breadbasket one day if reform is handled in the right way. Small pockets of success – such as organic farmers exporting high-quality produce to Europe – are already up and running. For the moment, though, economists insist that agriculture is the most backward sector of the Turkish economy, and change has to come.

That's why the farming sector – outmoded, overmanned, and inefficient – is often quoted as an almost insurmountable obstacle to Turkey's full integration with Europe. It's partly a question of scale. If Turkey joined the current European Union it would add thirty-nine million hectares to the EU's agricultural area: an extra twenty-three per cent. Eight million people work on the land in Turkey, more than in all the countries of the EU combined. Trying to accommodate all those Anatolian peasants within the EU's comically inefficient Common Agricultural Policy (the CAP) would break the bank.

Judging Turkey by today's standards, though, is a bit of a red herring. By the time it could conceivably be ready to become a member of the EU, in ten to fifteen years, the CAP will probably have been consigned to history, or at the very least radically redrawn. Turkey will be an entirely different country by then, and anyone who tells you they know what the EU will look like in 2020 is either a fool or a convincing liar. But the Turks are well aware of one thing – no new member state in the future will get the kind of money that has been doled out in the past.

Agriculture is by no means the only challenge ahead. Turkey lags far behind European levels in things like food safety and environmental protection as well. Highly infectious animal diseases like foot-and-mouth are a constant problem, and a study conducted by the World Bank says the bill to bring Turkey's environmental standards up to scratch could be as high as forty-nine billion euros – an enormous sum. Technical issues like these will take years to resolve. Questions of human rights and democratic reform tend to grab all the headlines, but the nitty-gritty of joining the EU means there are eighty thousand pages of rules and regulations which Turkey will have to implement and adopt. In that sense it's not so much a negotiation as a dictation of terms. And if there's one thing your average Turk hates, it's someone else telling him what to do all the time.

So there could be some rude shocks in store, as Turkey begins to discover what sharing sovereignty means in practice. Immediately after his country was officially named as a candidate for EU membership in December 1999, President Süleyman Demirel let it be known that he no longer wanted a sheep sacrificed every time he opened a new factory or shopping centre. It is a long-established custom in Turkey to kill a sheep, or sometimes a goat or if you want to go right over the top a camel, to celebrate the inauguration of a big project. Demirel, though, was quick to point out that hidden among all those pesky EU regulations is one which forbids the slaughter of animals in the street.

Turkish newspapers can't get enough of the EU effect. Cartoonists depict well-known politicians transformed into true Europeans by shaving off their moustaches, or tulip-shaped tea glasses replaced by the good old British cuppa.

'We won't be able to drive straight through red lights?' asked one newspaper column in mock astonishment. 'What on earth do you mean?'

Not only that, but a shell-shocked public has been informed that an even greater Turkish tradition could be under threat. Kokoreç is a sandwich sold from small roadside stalls which is made of sheep's intestines soaked in fat. It may sound disgusting to the uninitiated, but add a little tomato and oregano and flavour generously with hot spices, and it tastes rather good. Alas, it too may be against the rules – a breach of European health standards. Kokoreç fans are aghast, as Turks begin to learn for themselves the power of a European bureaucracy which would change their lives in ways great and small.

So is there anything in it for Europe? Well, yes – the dynamism of Turkey's private sector and the flexibility of its labour markets fit the European model rather nicely. And if Turkey's economy takes off it will eventually produce millions of hungry new consumers who covet European goods. But what might head in the opposite direction? Never mind all those fridges and TVs, one of the biggest negatives for Turkey in Europe is the spectre of mass migration. There's already talk in the corridors in Brussels that some permanent safeguards should be built in to any future Turkish membership of the EU to prevent hordes of Anatolian villagers descending on London, Paris and Berlin.

It is an issue which understandably raises hackles in Turkey, and it's hardly in keeping with the laws or even the spirit of the EU's single market, which guarantees the free movement of labour. Previous experience also suggests that it's unlikely to happen. Where are all those Greeks and Portuguese who were going to head north when their countries joined? What happened to the hundreds of thousands of Poles and Lithuanians who were going to flood into Britain at the earliest opportunity? Most of them simply stayed at home.

In any case, demographic forces may be on Turkey's side. In the long term Europe needs to import labour to survive – its ageing economies and creaking pension systems are crying out for an infusion of youth. In Italy and Spain villages are fading and dying because birth rates have fallen dramatically and there are no young people left. Managed migration is a must, and Turkey can provide. Nearly thirty per cent of its population is under the age of fifteen, and while the education system has its well-documented problems, more and more students are attending universities and technical colleges, the best young graduates are providing home-grown expertise in middle management, and a large labour force is willing to travel to find work. Their only problem is that Europe has yet to decide whether it is willing to accept them.

In other words, the size of its population is one of Turkey's biggest obstacles, but also one of its biggest opportunities. In the short term, it is a huge domestic challenge for Turkey's leaders. Vitality and youth are all very well, but the number of people of working age is increasing by about a million a year, far more than the number of new jobs on offer. Look again at the sullen faces in all those tea houses – youth unemployment is rampant, and it has become a recruiting sergeant for radical politics, for the criminal underworld, and for the unrelenting growth of the black economy.

* * *

Shortly after the collapse of the Soviet Union in 1991, ordinary Russians did what their political masters had been dreaming of for centuries. They invaded Istanbul. Hundreds of thousands of eager entrepreneurs, many of them women, arrived by ferry and chartered plane. In bags, boxes and bulging suitcases, they took all they could carry with them to the vast new consumer market back home. By the mid-1990s the suitcase trade was worth more than eight billion dollars a year. Barely taxed and lightly regulated, it helped export garments and household materials from the old Istanbul neighbourhood of Laleli to every corner of the former Soviet Empire.

There have been difficult times since then, but Laleli remains a visible symbol of the strength of Turkey's unofficial economy. It was hit hard by the Russian economic crisis in 1998, and then by aggressive competition from countries in Asia where prices were often cheaper. After that Laleli was buffeted by Turkey's own economic freefall, but the suitcase trade survived. The streets are still dominated by leather and clothing shops, there are signs in Cyrillic script, and women from Ukraine and Belarus hawk fur coats on the pavement before turning to Laleli's other main trade, prostitution, once night has fallen.

It's impossible to give an accurate estimate of just how big Turkey's black economy is, but it could be worth nearly as much as the official economy. Up to five million people probably make their money outside the law, and millions more operate in the grey area in between. Red tape and high taxes have persuaded thousands of small firms to go underground in the last few years, and even registered companies routinely dodge whatever they can. The state loses enormous amounts of revenue every year, a loss it simply can't afford.

You don't have to look very hard for the evidence, either. One of the striking things about Turkey's big cities is how unplanned they are. Houses and offices of all shapes and sizes are built everywhere – on precipitous slopes, on patches of waste ground, anywhere their owners can find precious space. Half-finished new houses and apartment blocks litter the outskirts of every city and in Istanbul, Ankara and Izmir alone there are more than seven hundred and fifty thousand unlicensed (i.e. illegal) buildings.

Some of them are small shacks known as *gecekondu* – literally 'built overnight' – crammed with new arrivals to the city; others are regular apartment buildings or office blocks. All of them share one thing in common – they pay no taxes: nothing for a construction permit, no estate tax, no planning permission, and they are often badly built. The earthquake in 1999 would have claimed far fewer lives if the black economy hadn't taken such a firm hold of the construction sector.

Integrating the unofficial economy with the real economy, and persuading people to pay their taxes, is one of modern Turkey's most difficult challenges. It's all about changing people's attitudes, and breaking ingrained habits about rules which are routinely broken. But inevitably the black economy is not just the preserve of individuals and small businesses struggling to make ends meet. A shocking report by the Ankara Chamber of Commerce in June 2004 said the Turkish mafia was tightening its grip on many areas of economic life. Activities related to organized crime, it said, generate more than sixty billion dollars a year – equivalent to a quarter of the entire national income.

The biggest business is the traffic in women and children, and the smuggling of drugs and guns. The mafia (a pretty loose term in Turkey embracing anyone with a couple of heavies and a proclivity for dodgy deals) is also involved in the procurement and sale of organs such as kidneys, which are purchased from impoverished donors for tiny sums and sold for huge profits. Dirty money is laundered through a variety of front organizations: casinos in northern Cyprus, football clubs and holiday resorts.

But organized crime has also infiltrated much more prosaic areas of daily life. Street vendors selling fish or kebabs pay protection money for the most lucrative pitches. Illegally produced coal and smuggled cigarettes are sold under the watchful eye of the gangs. They tow cars, they print pirate copies of books and CDs, and they intimidate urban landowners into selling small plots which are turned into parking lots or yet more illegal buildings. According to the Ankara Chamber of Commerce, the mafia also fixes Turkish football matches and makes a fortune betting on the results. And finally, of course, the criminals take full advantage of the habit Turkey just can't kick: corruption.

* * *

'That may be difficult,' Mahmut said, with considerable understatement, but I wasn't in the mood to listen. When I was getting ready to leave Turkey after four years I decided that I simply had to take my beloved Jeep with me. We'd shared a lot together – trundling through earthquakes, up snow-bound passes and across flooded river beds. I couldn't just abandon it, bureaucracy be damned. I had a sneaking feeling that the combination of the Turkish traffic police and the Turkish customs could be a bit of a challenge, but I reassured myself: how hard could it be?

'Right,' said the man behind the counter. 'First you have to pay your overdue taxes.'

'Which taxes?' I asked.

'The overdue ones,' he replied helpfully.

'How much?'

He pushed a small computer printout towards me: seven billion lira.

The Turkish lira had certainly taken a bit of a battering in recent years, but that was a lot of tax.

'That's about four thousand pounds,' I blurted out, to no one in particular.

The man behind the counter was unimpressed with the speed of my currency calculations. He lobbed a cube of sugar into his tea glass and stared at the ceiling. After double-checking my figures on a piece of paper, I staged a strategic retreat and sought out one of those mysterious men who always appear at times like this – a fixer, an agent, someone who knew the system. The problem, he explained, was that when Jeeps like mine were imported into the country they were given the wrong weight as part of a scam to avoid customs duty. Now I would have to pay large amounts of overdue tax, because no one could really be sure how heavy the vehicle actually was.

'Well, why don't we weigh it?' I suggested brightly.

But it wasn't that simple. We haggled. We pleaded. We pulled out small tufts of hair. When I left the country the Jeep was still sitting in a warehouse and it took several more months of bargaining to set it free. 'Fees' had to be paid . . . not nearly as much as seven billion lira, but I'd been done all the same. I'd fallen foul of the system, even as I was taking my leave.

I really shouldn't have been surprised because corruption in Turkey is still endemic, particularly at local and municipal levels. Here's a typical story, told to me in confidence: a businessman who had been given a huge road contract was asked by some associates of the local mayor to 'make a donation' to pay for the lavish wedding plans of the mayor's daughter. Fifty thousand US dollars was deemed to be an appropriate sum. The contractor pointed out that he hadn't been paid for his work for the previous nine months, and if the payment came through he would be happy to make a donation. The mayor wasn't impressed with this show of disrespect, so he sent out his inspectors the following morning. They decided that the quality of the road repair wasn't good enough, and they ordered the contractor to start again from scratch.

'Corruption is so much a part of life here that it's become accepted business practice,' was the comment of one leading businessman. 'It's very difficult to know how to stop it.'

A man who owned a small electrical shop near my office in Istanbul told me another familiar tale. A few months earlier a local policeman had come into the shop and bought a fridge and a washing machine. He said he was in a bit of a hurry, and he promised to pay for his purchase later. The money never came, and the policeman threatened serious trouble if the man tried to complain.

'There's nothing I can do,' the shop owner said. 'He thinks he's entitled to have it.'

Corruption has spread right through the system – from the solitary bank note slipped across a counter to get a bureaucratic signature, to the million dollar 'fee' which helps secure a big construction or energy contract. Everyone knows it; it's no longer a surprise. But some things are starting to change. In the last few years Turks have watched with growing satisfaction as businessmen and bureaucrats previously considered untouchable have been hauled before the courts on charges of fraud and abuse of power. It's a slow process, but it's beginning to happen at every level of the system. A policeman in our neighbourhood once tried to give his new boss a share of the monthly bribes collected by the traffic police – money for soup, they call it. His boss called his bluff and the officer, still protesting his innocence, was suspended and shamed.

Then there are the big fish, like the once-powerful Uzan family, who reigned apparently supreme over the Turkish business world for more than a decade. They set up the country's first private TV station (in a handy partnership with Turgut Özal's son) and established a media empire; they had a finger in every pie and grew fabulously wealthy; and they borrowed nearly three billion dollars from Motorola and Nokia in the late 1990s to boost their own company, Telsim, at a time when Turkey was the fastest-growing mobile phone market in Europe.

The money was never paid back, and much of it vanished. The Uzans bought private aircraft, luxury yachts, and properties across the globe, including seven apartments in New York's Trump Tower alone. (Why on earth, you might ask, did Motorola and Nokia lend the money in the first place? As *The Economist* put it so elegantly: 'When companies are blinded by their own saliva, they can make foolish decisions.') Charges were filed against family members in New York and London, and the net began to close at home. In 2003 two utility companies were taken over by the state, and then the Uzans' flagship bank, which the banking authorities declared a threat to national financial stability. The following year more than two hundred other Uzan companies were seized, in an effort to recover debts totalling nearly six billion dollars.

The most prominent member of the family, Cem Uzan, had already formed a right-wing nationalist political party which polled well at the 2002 general elections, but not well enough to give him parliamentary immunity. In October 2004 he was sentenced to eight months in prison for insulting Tayyip Erdoğan during a political rally at which he'd called the prime minister 'treacherous and godless'. Other charges followed, and video tapes were recovered containing material which had allegedly been used to blackmail the Uzans' political and business rivals; but it was Cem who claimed political victimization, saying the government was trying to destroy his family.

Dispassionate observers looked on with satisfaction as more and more of the untouchables began to feel the heat. Even those who have reached the very top of the political tree no longer seem immune. In the autumn of 2004 a parliamentary commission ruled that the former prime minister, Mesut Yılmaz, and his economy minister should be tried for alleged corruption in the sale of the state-owned Türkbank. Other former ministers are also facing their day in court; and, notably, so are senior military officials, including a former commander of the navy, the highest-ranking military officer to be prosecuted on corruption charges in decades.

But is all this enough? Is much of it politically motivated? Does the punishment fit the crime? Cem Uzan is still free on an appeal which could last for years, and he dismisses a fifteen-month jail sentence handed out in London for contempt of court as a plot against Turkey and the Turkish people. Other prominent figures who have been accused in the past have somehow always wriggled free.

'The corrupt politicians who are known to be corrupt still function, and the ex-politicians who are known to be corrupt still remain out of jail. No one gets properly punished,' argues Metin Munir, who writes for

the *Financial Times* from Istanbul. 'Maybe it will get better, but one certainly doesn't get the impression that there's a real battle against this
horrible thing, which eats away at the nation's savings.'

They won't come close to eradicating corruption, but that's hardly a
disqualification for joining the European Union, as anyone with a passing knowledge of Italy can testify. What has changed since the economic
crisis of 2001 is that, at the very top end of the scale, Turkey has run out
of money. In the old days corruption was endemic because there was so
much cash sloshing around the system. When huge infrastructure projects were built, particularly in the energy sector, a significant slice of the
money spent went into the pockets of the politicians and the bureaucrats
and the contractors. Now there isn't as much money to go around and
hey presto there's less corruption. But it hasn't been stamped out, and it
never will be.

During long years of negotiations on joining the European Union,
though, the pressure for change will intensify. Those in Turkey who
favour EU membership know the system has to be cleaned out, and that
many attitudes have to change. A more open society is a prerequisite, and
most Turks want one whether they join the EU or not. But however
strong the pro-reform lobby is, they also have powerful opponents.
There are influential people in all walks of life who've gained enormous
wealth and prestige over the last few years through questionable means.
They won't give it up without a fight, and they certainly don't want to
share it with outsiders.

* * *

As we approached Konya from the flat salt plains of central Anatolia, the
gleaming skyscraper in the distance caught my eye. In an old conservative city, the spiritual home of the Whirling Dervishes, it looked out of
place, even out of proportion. But the tower was an appropriate symbol
of a new business elite which had emerged in the Turkish heartland. It
was the headquarters of Kombassan, one of the country's largest business
groups. Their shops don't serve alcohol, their factories have prayer
rooms and for years they made a thumping profit. This was capitalism
with an Islamic face.

'We are religious people, we are believers,' Kombassan's combative chairman, Haşim Bayram, acknowledged, when I met him on the top floor of the tower. 'But these are personal beliefs not corporate ones. There is a difference.'

If you listened to the warnings of the generals in the late 1990s, or to the complaints of the traditional business establishment in Istanbul, you might have been forgiven for thinking that companies like Kombassan posed a threat to the survival of the state. The political battle between secularists and Islamists was firmly entrenched in the world of big business as well, and the rise of Islamic or 'green' capital was a significant factor in the 'soft' coup which forced Necmettin Erbakan and the Welfare Party out of government in 1997.

In a string of central Anatolian cities like Konya, companies which placed emphasis on Islamic ethics established a strong sense of loyalty among their employees, and quickly became a major force in their local communities. Kombassan built a shopping centre and restaurant complex next to its corporate HQ, and a children's park named after the wily Erbakan. It was never ashamed of its roots.

'We work hard for our shareholders,' Bayram said, 'and they trust us.'

What made things a little more murky was the way the money was raised in the first place. Billions of dollars were invested in companies like Kombassan, and most of it came from the savings of Turkish workers abroad. The sales pitch was an explicitly religious one – attracting people who avoid conventional banks because they believe earning interest on loans is against the teachings of the Koran. But Kombassan has fallen from grace in the last few years. It suffered badly during the economic crisis in 2001 and a chain of retail clothing stores it bought in the United States went bankrupt. It has been pursued though the courts by financial regulators and a growing number of its small shareholders has been demanding their money back.

That is what green capital was all about – the money which pious Muslims used to keep under their pillows or stashed away beneath the floorboards. It was a highly unregulated business, and the men in uniform smelt a rat. Another front in the fight against fundamentalism was opened, official investigations were launched, and several Islamist companies were charged with breaking the law. Some of them had, and they collapsed. Others which were deemed to be too Islamist to be trusted have been shut out of public auctions and defence tenders (which is a shame for military conscripts stuck in the mountains who are denied access to all the best biscuits.)

I never found a great deal of evidence that Islamic money was supposed to be funding a revolution, but there is little doubt where the sympathies of this new breed of Anatolian businessmen lie. Plenty of them raised their money in more orthodox ways than Kombassan, but they all see themselves as outsiders trying to redress the economic balance. The rise of Anatolian capital is part and parcel of the battle of ideas which will help determine Turkey's future direction: how to reassert Muslim identity in a deeply conservative country without destroying the established order.

It's also part of a profound revolution in the way the Turkish economy works. Until the 1980s, the economy was closed to the outside world, and strictly controlled by the state. Ankara, as the bureaucratic centre, and Istanbul, as the home of capital, had the whole thing stitched up between them. But once the controls were loosened, a new entrepreneurial class emerged in the provinces, hungry for success. With Turgut Özal's government encouraging the development of export industries and foreign trade, companies in cities like Denizli, Gaziantep, Konya and Kayseri began to ignore Istanbul entirely, and produce directly for the global market.

Now these former regional backwaters have become centres of economic power in their own right, ringed by industrial parks, increasingly troubled by pollution, but growing richer all the time. Some people have dubbed them the Anatolian Lions, others call them the Anatolian Tigers (Turkey has no indigenous species of Big Cat) – and a conservative pro-Islamist business elite has moved to Istanbul to challenge the power of Turkey's established business leaders in the big city.

Turkey's main business organization TUSIAD (The Turkish Businessmen's and Industrialists' Association) has always been a leading supporter of the EU membership process. It was one of the first organizations to call for radical democratic reforms if Turkey was going to make any progress. It lobbies skilfully in Brussels, Washington, Paris and Berlin.

The new elite organized themselves under a new organization MUSIAD. The 'M' in their acronym stands for 'Müstakil' (Independent), but for a long time it might as well have meant Muslim. When MUSIAD was first set up in 1990 its founders said they wanted to create an 'Islamic economic system', and their sights were set on Turkey's fellow Muslim neighbours to the east.

Just as many Islamist politicians have changed their tune, though, so have many Islamist businessmen. Time and money have mellowed the radical streak. They still trade heavily with the Middle East, but MUSIAD has close relations with the pro-European AKP government and they feel like they're part of the new establishment. Tayyip Erdoğan has been careful to cultivate the link. When he broke with the more radical approach of Necmettin Erbakan he knew he needed a support base outside the world of politics, and big holding companies like Yimpaş and Albayrak were there to provide. The dynastic alliance with Albayrak was cemented when Erdoğan's daughter married a member of the Albayrak family.

By 2004 MUSIAD had grown into an economic giant – representing more than seven thousand companies with a combined annual revenue stretching into billions of dollars. They have embraced the idea of looking West, as long as they can retain their Muslim identity and their social conservatism. You can export hip-hugging jeans to Europe during the day, but make sure your daughter wears her headscarf when you get home. But faced with the choice of going the whole hog, and joining the EU itself, some of the organization's leading members are still not so sure.

'I'm happy for us to be good neighbours. But there's no reason why we have to share the same house.'

Erol Yarar was MUSIAD's founding chairman, and it proved to be a rather hazardous business. At one stage he received a twelve-month suspended prison sentence for 'trying to change the constitution illegally'. From an industrial park on the Asian side of Istanbul, he exports a variety of products to more than thirty different countries around the world. Europe is an important market, he told me, but so are the Middle East, North Africa and Russia.

'Some people in this country have an unhealthy obsession with Europe,' he said with a twinkle in his eye. 'It's been like that for a hundred and fifty years. Why can't we do business with the West but keep our own culture? It worked pretty well for the Japanese.'

It always struck me as rather good news that Islamic capital was becoming more bourgeois. If more Islamists have a stake in the system there should be fewer people willing to toy with radical ideas for over-throwing it, whether they want to join the EU or not. As economic success has spread to different corners of the country, the new Islamist middle class has begun to demand a range of financial services which are compliant with their religious beliefs. Many of them have turned to Islamic banks, known as Special Finance Houses, where customers don't receive interest for the money they invest – instead, rather like at Kombassan, they follow Islamic law by sharing profits and risks.

Turkey's first Islamic bank was set up in the mid-1980s, but the industry has grown quickly in the last few years. Under reforms demanded by the International Monetary Fund in 2001 it became part of the mainstream banking system, and there are now five Islamic banks with more than two hundred branches. By 2015 they could account for ten per cent of the total assets held by the Turkish banking sector, controlling funds worth more than twenty-five billion dollars. They look set to become significant financial players.

The secular establishment has grown more accustomed to the new breed of Islamist business, but it still has its concerns. Part of it is motivated by ideological differences, but old-fashioned business rivalry also comes into play. The Turkish armed forces may have stepped back a pace or two from the front lines of political life, but they still have a major stake in the Turkish economy. Alongside the massive defence budget, they have more direct interests which make some military leaders rather sensitive to sudden economic change.

The armed forces pension fund, OYAK, does a little more than manage retirement plans for generals who want to put their feet up by the coast. It runs its own business empire, and it has become one of the most influential corporate players in the country. It owns a bank, and a multitude of companies involved in manufacturing, construction, agriculture and financial services. It's one of Turkey's largest car makers, and it controls a substantial share of the domestic insurance market. It's a major house builder, and one of the biggest private electricity producers in the land. Many of its investments take the form of partnerships with multinationals or with leading Turkish conglomerates.

OYAK is a highly professional well-managed company, but it always struck me as a bit of an oddity, blurring the lines. It has a massive guaranteed income generated by salary deductions from one of the largest armed forces in the world. It pays no taxes, it is free of government control, and its profits pay for pensions and other generous benefits for the men in uniform. The military also controls a corporation called the Foundation for Strengthening the Turkish Armed Forces which helps run a host of defence-related companies. Eighty per cent of its income finds its way back to the soldiers. The net effect is that the economic interests of the armed forces are part of the status quo. No wonder they got a little nervous when they thought Islamic capital was getting too big for its boots.

* * *

There's a shop in the covered bazaar in Istanbul which sells old hats from central Asia. It's no bigger than a phone box and almost impossible to find. The first time we stumbled across it we bought a couple of hats after much discussion and debate, and I was about to pay the old man who ran the shop when I realized I'd run out of lira. I only had some dollars and a few pounds.

'Sorry about this,' I said, knowing that he'd much prefer the dollars anyway. 'Will you take any other money?'

'I take! I take!' He beamed, slapping me on the back. 'Any money, any money. All money is good!'

He obviously liked the sound of it because it became his catch phrase. Wandering around the carpet shops in the bazaar was a regular weekend hobby and we used to go back to the hat man every few months. As soon as we'd appear around the corner he'd recognize us immediately and shout it out again. 'All money is good!'

I think he was right. I'm not sure that most Turks care much whether military money or Islamist money or foreign money enables them to find a job. The political sensitivities will linger on, but in the end Turkey's ability to succeed will depend on how well it manages to develop its economy, and the colour of the money doesn't matter. Economic liberalization and the rise of Anatolian capital have helped spread the wealth a little wider and a little deeper, but it has been a long time coming. It's now nearly fifty years since the need to escape from poverty forced millions of poor Anatolians to leave their towns and villages for the first time in their lives and head for Europe to find work.

8

EURO-TURKS AND EUROPEANS

One of the first things Hilal did after I met her was to stop at a red light on a pedestrian crossing. There were no cars in sight.

'Shouldn't we cross the road?' I suggested politely.

'I'm a law student,' she replied with a smile, 'and this is Germany. We have to wait.'

It was hard to imagine anyone being quite so patient in Istanbul, whether there had been any cars coming or not. But we were in Cologne, and Hilal was a second-generation German Turk, brought up in the heart of Europe.

'I could never go back and live in Turkey,' she told me, as we strolled down a street packed with Turkish supermarkets and cafés. 'It's too different. I'm not German of course, but this is my home.'

As Turkey and the European Union continue their delicate diplomatic dance, and debate rages about the true meaning of European identity, millions of Turks (and Kurds) have already arrived. Germany has the largest Turkish community in Europe – more than two million people – and cities like Cologne feel like test beds for the integration of the future. It's easy to be terribly gloomy about the whole thing. There are plenty of long-standing problems: racism and alienation, high unemployment and cultural misunderstandings. Many older Turks living in Germany don't speak any German, and hardly mix at all with their German neighbours.

'I don't think they ever thought they were going to stay,' Hilal said, as two elderly women wrapped up in headscarves bustled past. 'By the time they realized what was going on, they were too set in their ways.'

But change is happening here too. A new generation of German Turks has emerged, more confident about who they are, and creating their own distinct identity. It is a gradual process, and some people don't seem to want any part of it, but more and more Turks are finding their own place in mainstream society. Turkish businessmen are beginning to make their mark, there are now more than one hundred and twenty thousand mixed marriages, and (what greater proof do you need?) in restaurants and fast food stalls across the country *döner kebab* has become a German national dish.

* * *

The history of Turks living in Germany began in the 1960s when West Germany needed labour – willing hands to help keep its post-war economic miracle on the move. In October 1961 it signed an agreement with Turkey for the dispatch of thousands of Turkish 'Gastarbeiter' or 'guest workers' to help fill its coal mines, steel mills and car factories. From villages and small towns in a country which had little contact with the outside world, they came to bustling industrial cities on the Rhine and the Ruhr and worked for companies like Volkswagen, Siemens, Krupp and Thyssen. The culture shock was profound.

It was a turning point, though, in the way Turkey related to the rest of the world. Despite their nomadic roots, the Turks had never been a migrant nation. There was no mass movement of Turks to the new world across the Atlantic or to Christian countries in Europe. They stayed in the Ottoman realms, and when the empire collapsed they regrouped in the newly formed Turkish republic. It was to be a self-reliant nation, beholden to no one, and travel abroad was virtually unheard of. All of a sudden in the 1960s tens of thousands of the least-educated workers in the country pitched up in Germany. They might as well have landed on another planet.

Initially it was just the men who came to work, away from the poverty back at home. But they were soon joined by their families; they put down uncertain roots and had children who were born in Germany. New Turkish communities sprang up across the country: in Cologne and Essen, in Stuttgart and Frankfurt and in Berlin's Kreuzberg district.

People from the same regions of rural Anatolia tended to settle close to one another in their new homes – village communities were rebuilt in a very different setting, reinforced by arranged marriages and extended family ties. The Turks kept themselves to themselves.

Other countries followed the German lead in importing Turkish labour – Belgium, the Netherlands, Austria, France and Sweden – and nearly four million ethnic Turks now live in Western Europe. Back in the 1960s it was assumed that nearly all the guest workers would pick up their pay cheques and eventually go home when the great industrial boom began to decline. But they stayed on. Ties to the old country remain strong and the majority are still Turkish citizens; but many of them only return home for good when they die – their coffins transported back to village cemeteries across Anatolia.

Their sons and daughters, and their grandchildren, have much more semi-detached relations with Turkey. Ask people running shops and small businesses around Weidengasse in the centre of Cologne where their families come from and you get a roll call of central Anatolian provinces: Konya, Sivas, Erzincan and Aksaray. But many of the memories of these ancestral homes are only partial – gleaned from brief holidays or stories passed down by their elders.

'I'm a Turk and I'm from Tokat,' said Özgür in his busy little grocery store, 'but this is my village now.'

Around the corner at the Ankara hair salon a couple of middle-aged men were having a shave, and behind the counter Serpil was bemoaning the state of the German economy.

'It's tough at the moment,' she said, 'but we'll get through it. I've been here for thirty years, since I was a child, and it's difficult to think of anywhere else as home.'

On the other side of the road the Bosphorus restaurant had just opened for lunch. I asked the owner, Ali Bey, how he thought German Turks viewed themselves, nearly half a century after their grandfathers first arrived.

'We're the people in-between,' he said. 'They still regard us as foreigners here, and when we go back to Turkey they call us Germans. But I'm optimistic; I think things will get better here if we give it a few more years.'

Things are certainly beginning to change, as Germany starts to have an open debate about multiculturalism, but negative images are not hard to find. For years the stereotype of Turks in Germany has been nourished in dreary ethnic ghettos like Chorweiler on the edge of Cologne: all dilapidated housing, insular communities and smoky cafés. Young women are forced into arranged marriages and young men hang around on street corners with nothing to do. Unemployment among German Turks is much higher than average, and levels of education are low.

At the local train station I met Faruk and his friend standing on the platform with time on their hands. There were problems with crime and gangs, they agreed, and there were no jobs to be found. Faruk said he'd dropped out of school early and he'd been in trouble with the police 'once or twice, nothing serious'. He spent most of his time listening to German–Turkish rappers who mix the sounds of East and West and sing about exclusion and alienation.

'They talk about things we understand,' Faruk said. 'They know what it's like.'

This is where the experiment seems to have gone wrong. Racial tensions bubble just beneath the surface, and break out into the open all too often. There have been plenty of attacks by right-wing German extremists since the infamous case in 1993, when arsonists in the city of Solingen killed five members of a Turkish family who had lived in Germany for more than twenty years.

'There are still people like that; people who hate us,' Faruk said blankly, 'but I don't really care what they think. We've been here long enough. They have to get used to us.'

Many Germans know little about the Turkish communities in their midst, and only a few get past the condescending assumption that they all come from the same deeply conservative Muslim stock. Headlines about 'honour killings' in Berlin (such as the shocking death of twenty-three-year-old Hatin Sürücü, who was murdered in a hail of bullets at a bus stop, allegedly by her three brothers) hardly help matters. But the complex fault lines which cut through Turkish society have been exported to Germany as well. Alevis have become a highly organized political group and are starting to receive far more recognition of their separate identity in Germany than they do in Turkey. The extreme left is also active, and so are the Kurds. About a quarter of the Turkish citizens in Germany are Kurdish and the PKK raises a great deal of money from voluntary donations, protection rackets and a host of dubious money-making schemes.

As for the original generation of guest workers, they never really integrated at all. It was too big a step. They never learnt German, and no one in authority saw the need to try to teach them. Like other immigrant communities across Europe they still live in parallel societies, making little attempt to accommodate German customs or culture. They watch a wide variety of Turkish TV channels via satellite, they read German editions of all the main Turkish newspapers, and many of them worship at mosques run by an arm of the Turkish state.

The Turkish Islamic Union (DITIB) is the largest immigrants' organization in the country, and it actively encourages its members to think of themselves first and foremost as Turks. DITIB is financed by the Directorate for Religious Affairs in Ankara with the aim of providing pastoral care for Turks abroad (as well as keeping a watchful eye on them). Its imams are paid by the Turkish state – sent to different postings on short tours of duty as if they were religious diplomats. There are about seven hundred of them in Germany alone, but few of them speak decent German. Their sermons are delivered in Turkish, and they support the officially approved principle of (Turkish) state control over religious matters.

Given current concerns over the potential spread of radical Islam and firebrand preachers among European Muslims, DITIB may well be considered a good thing; it's certainly not pushing political Islam. But it does little to encourage integration either, in its obsessive advocacy of Turkey's national interest, and it fails to reach tens of thousands of Turks who worship at independent mosques. Islamist Turks are extremely well represented in Germany, and some of the younger generation have reacted to their exclusion from the mainstream by turning back towards stricter and more political versions of Islam, in a search for their own identity.

The Fatih mosque just outside the centre of Cologne looks more like a warehouse than a house of prayer – as grey as the skies above. In fact it used to be a coffee factory. There are no minarets, and no call to prayer echoes around the surrounding streets. It is all terribly low-key. Elderly men with neatly trimmed beards and skullcaps mutter Islamic greetings as they go in to pray. A small travel agent advertises cheap flights to Adana, Izmir and Istanbul. The mosque is affiliated to Milli Goruş, the Islamist group with close ties to the former Turkish prime minister, Necmettin Erbakan, but it doesn't exactly come across as a hotbed of dangerous intrigue.

'We're not financed by the state,' I was told, 'but that doesn't make us a threat to anyone. If the Turks in this country weren't so divided we'd all be better off.'

The president of the mosque, Hüseyin Koçum, a worker at the local Ford factory, was in the middle of organizing an exchange programme. If he was an extremist he was hiding it pretty well. A group of young Germans were coming to visit the mosque, he explained, and he had agreed to send some Turkish teenagers to look around the local church.

'We may not all be the same,' he said in a soft voice, 'but we all have to live in the same place. We're believers here, and we want to live in peace with our neighbours.'

Milli Goruş, though, remains a bit of an enigma. It controls several hundred mosques across Western Europe, and when it holds political rallies it manages to fill football stadiums with flag-waving enthusiasts. But the German intelligence agencies have kept a cautious eye on it for a long time, describing it in one report as 'a foreign extremist organization . . . opposed to integration'. There's no doubt that it wants Turks in Germany to be more Islamic, which is awkward, but that doesn't necessarily make it a threat to the state. In fact, after the AKP took power in Ankara, Turkish embassies across Europe were asked to improve links with Milli Goruş as it tried to present a more moderate face to the world.

But there is a violent Islamist fringe in Germany which has done a great deal to give ordinary Turks a bad name. The Caliphate State, which was based in Cologne until it was banned by the German authorities, was dedicated to the overthrow of Turkey's secular republic. Its leader, the self-styled caliph, is a rotund radical preacher named Metin Kaplan, who has already served time in Germany for inciting murder. Kaplan became the first Turk to grace the cover of Germany's leading news magazine, *Der Spiegel* – hardly the role model many of his compatriots would have wanted. He was extradited to Turkey in October 2004 after a long legal battle, and he could spend much of the rest of his life in prison.

Kaplan is facing trial as the alleged ringleader of an extraordinary plot to fly a small aircraft packed with explosives into Atatürk's mausoleum in Ankara in 1998, during ceremonies marking the sixtieth anniversary of the founding father's death. If the plan had succeeded, prosecutors say, it could have wiped out Turkey's entire political and military leadership. There was also talk of seizing a prominent mosque in Istanbul and fighting to the death against the security forces. I was living in Ankara when the plot was uncovered, and I remember at the time it all seemed terribly far-fetched. After 9/11, and the emergence of possible links between the Caliphate State and al-Qaeda, it became plausible to say the least.

* * *

'If we only concentrate on the bad things, we'll never get anywhere.'

Kemal Şahin arrived in Germany as a student from Turkey more than thirty years ago. His first business venture was a small gift shop on a busy commercial street in Aachen, selling knick-knacks and T-shirts to tourists who'd come to visit the former capital of Charlemagne, the founder of the Holy Roman Empire.

'I worked sixteen to eighteen hours a day,' he recalled. 'I sold the T-shirts, I bought the supplies, I did the secretarial work and in the evenings I drove the van taking more T-shirts to all my other customers. It was hard work.'

Now Şahin has an empire of his own – the largest Turkish-run business outside Turkey. The corporate group which bears his name, Şahinler Holding, enjoys sales of more than a billion dollars a year in textiles, clothing and tourism. He is a success story, still quite rare, from a generation of Turks who came to Germany to seek their fortune. He is also the founding President of the Turkish–German Chamber of Commerce in Cologne, and like most of his fellow Turks, he hasn't taken German citizenship.

'My cultural mentality is still Turkish,' he explained, 'but my business mentality is German. And I'm not alone. There are more than sixty thousand German–Turkish entrepreneurs in this country.'

You don't have to look too hard to find them. They run all those grocery stores, restaurants and travel agents which are dotted around the Turkish quarters of German cities. Most of them opened only in the last fifteen years. Before that everyone assumed they would be going back to Turkey. They'd only come to work, they bought cheap furniture, everything felt very temporary; but in the 1990s things changed and the business community began to boom. Turks are also moving into the professions as doctors, lawyers, accountants and computer consultants, and German banks have taken on German–Turkish staff specifically to deal with what's been called the 'Turkish economy'.

'Turkish businesses have become a flourishing part of German society,' Kemal Şahin argued. 'As they become stronger and stronger, they will help us break down many barriers, and smash the ghetto mentality.'

He makes it sound terribly simple, but there's no reason why it shouldn't be true. Similar stories are emerging in other walks of life. There are politicians like Cem Özdemir, a German member of the European Parliament who describes himself as a 'cultural Muslim' and would rather be identified by his Green politics than by his Turkish ethnicity.

'I grew up in a Protestant neighbourhood,' he said, as we waited for a cup of coffee in a bar at the European Parliament in Strasbourg. 'That is just as much part of my identity as being Turkish or Muslim.'

Özdemir is a prominent example of the growing number of German Turks who have arrived in middle-class society and don't feel the need to organize on an ethnic or religious basis.

'We are neither typical Germans nor are we like our parents when they came over here thirty or forty years ago. It's a patchwork identity which we have to define ourselves. We don't want it imposed from above.'

German Turks who are making their mark in the arts have been exploring the dilemmas of this dual identity for some time. There are writers, musicians and film-makers like Fatih Akın, whose film *Head On* (about second-generation Turks rebelling against the strict values of their parents) won the top prize at the Berlin Film Festival in 2004 and broke mainstream box-office records in Germany; there are also entertainers like the stand-up comedian Kaya Yanar, the first German Turk to have his own TV show – *What You Lookin' At?* – with its cult characters like Hakan, the nightclub bouncer, and Yıldırım the driving instructor. Yanar gently lampoons other immigrant groups as well and gets away with things which German comedians simply can't say.

Football is another great leveller, as it is for immigrant communities across the Continent. A new generation of young Turks is making its mark in the Bundesliga, and even the stiff suits in the Turkish Football Association have recognized the potential of the Euro-Turks in Germany. A scouting network brings players like Ümit Davala and Tayfun Korkut back home and puts them in the national team. Mixing German organization and training methods with natural Turkish flair has been a highly successful formula, and players who were born and raised in Germany helped Turkey reach the semi-finals of the World Cup in 2002. Home-grown Turkish players, who used to look like fish out of water when they went abroad, have also started to prosper at major European clubs.

The success stories may still come from a minority of the Turkish community, but optimists will tell you that Turkey's progress towards EU membership talks has boosted the feel-good factor. There are certainly more people travelling back and forth between Turkey and Germany than ever before. Flights are packed and German number plates are a common sight in the most out-of-the-way places in rural Anatolia. In the summer season I've been overtaken more than once by convoys of cars packed with people, bags and boxes tearing down empty roads at fearsome speed towards towns and villages where friends and relatives still live.

It means there are now Turkish networks stretching across the Continent and plenty of enterprising businessmen are using these extended family ties to good advantage. Some of them produce clothing or other items in Turkey and sell them in Germany. Others cater to the huge number of German tourists who head for Turkey's Mediterranean shores every summer. All this helps to change perceptions. It's estimated that twenty million Germans have been to Turkey in the last few years, and the more they know about the delights of Antalya and Istanbul the less prejudice they feel towards the Turks they see on the streets at home.

The first generation of German Turks were from the uneducated rural poor – no wonder they found integration too hard to contemplate. But the second and third generations are beginning to find a distinctive voice. Some people in Ankara dream of a powerful ethnic lobby emerging within the European Union to argue Turkey's case, and in Germany it may already be happening. Turks are a growing political force as more and more of them take on German citizenship – well over half a million of them voted in the national election in 2002. After his narrow victory Gerhard Schröder was nicknamed the 'Chancellor of Kreuzberg' because without widespread Turkish support he would almost certainly have lost.

Many German Turks were keen on Schröder because he was keen on Turkey's bid to join the EU. It's not just about solidarity with the old homeland; it's a decision which they believe will say a lot about Europe's attitude to them.

When I wandered into Ahmet Lal's jewellery shop in Cologne he was weighing up the pros and cons of packing up and going back to Turkey.

'Just look at the growth rates they've got over there,' he muttered.

Even if he stayed in Germany, though, he would take it as a personal affront if Europe ever turned Turkey down.

'How do you think I'd feel?' he asked, tapping his finger for emphasis on a glass display cabinet. 'I'd feel rejected; I think a lot of people would. It probably wouldn't make an enormous difference to my life. But psychologically, yes, it would be a big disappointment. It would say we weren't really welcome here after all.'

* * *

Theo van Gogh was murdered as he cycled to work in Amsterdam. The controversial Dutch film-maker, an outspoken critic of the treatment of women in Islam, was shot several times. His throat was slashed so violently that he was nearly decapitated. His killer then thrust two long knives into van Gogh's chest, pinning a text to the lifeless body which urged Muslims to rise up against the infidels.

Eight months earlier nearly two hundred people were killed when bombs detonated by mobile phones ripped through commuter trains travelling into the heart of Madrid. There had been no warnings. The government initially put the blame on Basque separatists, but many people felt instinctively that this was the work of Islamic extremists, and so it proved.

Neither of these gruesome events – the carnage in Spain and the murder which shook the Netherlands – involved Turks in any way. Muslim groups in Europe were quick to condemn the killers. But, without question, Turkey's efforts to join the EU have reached critical mass at a difficult time. The long process of membership negotiations is beginning just as many Europeans are questioning the basis of the multicultural societies they have grown up in. There are fifteen million Muslims in the EU already, but a violent minority is starting to grab all the headlines.

There is a feeling of uneasiness, a feeling that a new form of intolerance has taken root in the heart of Europe . . . didn't some of the 9/11 hijackers hatch their plot in Hamburg? Turkey is being swept along uneasily and unfairly as part of the same debate. When Tayyip Erdoğan was in Brussels, negotiating the date for opening membership talks, protestors in Copenhagen made a point of their own. TURKEY IN THE EU? read the sign they hung around the Little Mermaid, the bronze statue on the seafront which was inspired by the fairy tales of Hans Christian Andersen. The Mermaid herself was invisible, covered from head to toe in a traditional black Muslim *burka*.

Opponents of Turkey's European bid talk a lot about its size and its poverty – they conjure up images of millions of new migrants heading westwards while billions of euros of taxpayers' money are drip-fed in the other direction. But the real argument is about Turkey's cultural identity. If it is proving so difficult to integrate the Muslim minorities in our midst, they argue, then what business do we have inviting an entire country of seventy million Muslims to join us as well? It is, it seems to me, an argument based on fear, but it is proving persuasive. Public opinion in several countries – France and Austria in particular – is openly hostile to Turkey joining the EU.

So the closer Turkey comes, the louder is the clamour of voices raised against it. The French prime minister, Jean-Pierre Raffarin, wonders how wise it is to allow 'the river of Islam to enter the river bed of secularism' in Europe, while cultural conservatives in the Catholic Church believe Turkey lacks something else quintessentially European – its Christian tradition. When Pope Benedict XVI was still known as Cardinal Joseph Ratzinger, Pope John Paul II's strict enforcer of Catholic dogma, he had no problem with the idea of Europe as a Christian Club.

'Turkey has always represented another continent in the course of history, in permanent contrast to Europe,' he said in one widely quoted interview in 2004.

The future pope's thoughts were echoed in the musings of the Dutch

European commissioner, Fritz Bolkestein, who warned of the 'creeping Islamization' of Europe. To allow Turkey in, Bolkestein added, would mean the defeat of the Ottomans at the gates of Vienna in 1683 'would have been in vain'.

'Perhaps,' the then Cardinal Ratzinger concluded on behalf of them all, in remarks which must have gone down a storm in Ankara, 'Turkey could try to form a cultural continent with some neighbouring Arab countries instead.'

It's always struck me as a little odd that Europe's social conservatives want to keep the Turks out because they are too socially conservative. 'Maybe if we all converted to Christianity . . .' suggested one of my friends in Ankara, as we sat in the pub. But there is another debate which the Turks really can't do much about. Many of the opponents of full Turkish membership cling to the grand vision of a federal Europe. Enthusiasts of an ever-closer political union based around a Franco-German core, they see the dream slipping away already as the EU enlarges beyond their reach. Turkey, they fear, will be the final nail in the coffin. These Turco-sceptics talk instead of a 'privileged partnership' with Turkey, a term dismissed in Ankara as a 'no' dressed up to look like a 'yes'.

So the debate about Turkish membership of the EU has become all existential. What does it mean to be a Turk? What does it mean to be a European, and what kind of Europe do we really want? Many ordinary Europeans recoil instinctively from unreconstructed Islam and its attitudes to women and personal freedoms. But if the sceptics worry about civilizations clashing noisily in their midst, then so do Turkey's supporters. They take the same concerns and wrap them up in a very different package.

'To modernize an Islamic country based on the shared values of Europe would be almost a D-Day for Europe in the war against terror,' Germany's foreign minister, Joschka Fischer, argued in one BBC interview. 'It would be the greatest positive challenge to these totalitarian and terrorist ideas.'

Tony Blair has been another outspoken supporter of Turkish membership, if the Turks meet all the relevant conditions. For a start he knows there would be no need to worry about a federal 'United States of Europe' if Turkey were part of the equation, but there's more.

Throw him a question on Turkey's prospects, and he goes into one of his evangelical moods.

'Turkey is a country with a long and proud history,' he told one press conference I attended, 'and it is a Muslim country too. To all those people who thought that the European Union couldn't reach out in this way, I think we have shown that we can . . . it is a huge demonstration of our confidence in the new Turkey which is taking shape, and which will eventually take its place in the family of the European Union.'

For Western leaders who believe they must wage a long struggle against violent Islamic fundamentalism the AKP government is a beguiling prospect. Democratically elected pro-Western Islamists, in a secular state, with a market economy to boot . . . the PR men couldn't have done any better. That's why there has also been consistent American pressure on the EU to get a move on, pressure which has sometimes been counterproductive. As the host of one European summit where Turkey was high on the agenda, the Danish prime minister, Anders Fogh Rasmussen, received a phone call from George W. Bush, urging him to speed up Turkey's admission.

'If you're so keen on us letting the Turks into the EU,' the plucky Dane replied, 'why don't you let Mexico into the United States?'

I think it comes down to whether you're an optimist or a pessimist about the ability of Western societies to integrate different cultures and faiths. Some people will read that, snort and argue that optimism has nothing to do with it: you're either a naive idealist or a hard-nosed pragmatist. The debate is heating up, and there is clear reluctance in several EU member states. For now Europe's ruling politicians have decided that Turkey deserves its chance; but both they and the Turks themselves need to do a lot more to persuade the public that this is a good idea, and that looking outwards in a globalized world is their best bet.

* * *

Understandably, many Turks don't much like being treated as some kind of geopolitical laboratory animals. (Take a bit of Islam, add a little democracy, light the blue touch paper and stand well back.) They have a point: in reforming itself, Turkey is answering a popular clamour for change, not trying to win an international talent contest. But at the same time everyone acknowledges that the carrot of EU membership has been an indispensable part of the equation. In both Ankara and Brussels it has become an article of faith to compare the way the 'soft power' of the European Union is transforming Turkey with the way the 'hard power' of the United States has brought chaos to Iraq.

Television debates and newspaper columns in Turkey study the European tea leaves almost every day. The tabloids are still full of fallen film stars and B-list Turkish celebrities, and many people in small Anatolian towns admit they know little about Europe. But for the chattering classes it is an all-consuming topic. To join or not to join? Do they want us or not? It has become a national obsession. Most of the media is relentlessly in favour as long as Turkish pride is preserved. Some of the coverage is sensationalist, while some of it goes into mind-numbing detail. You can probably find out more obscure information about the European Union in a week of watching Turkish television than you can in a year in Britain.

Influenced by all the political and media comment, opinion polls suggest that a healthy majority of the population are in favour of the drive towards Europe. If you tell someone for long enough that they will be richer, freer and happier when they sign on the dotted line it tends to have that effect. A few lone voices worry that too much EU too soon will be disastrous for Turkey's poor, who could be swept away by stronger competitors in the single market. But there are also ardent Euro-sceptics who think Turkey can be its own master; among them are the diehard Kemalists who fear their core values are in great danger as the old system is gradually dismantled.

So while opponents of the EU process in Turkey agree that something pretty significant is going on, their take on the 'soft power' of the EU is rather different. 'During the negotiations,' said a typical commentary in the Kemalist newspaper, *Cumhuriyet*, 'many extra conditions will be added on. The plan to divide the country and break it into pieces, which was done by force in Yugoslavia, and which is being done through occupation in Iraq, will be accomplished in Turkey by civilians, without a shot being fired.'

The education system and the political culture feed this siege mentality, preserving long memories of past betrayals neither forgiven nor forgotten.

Ask any Turkish student about the Treaty of Sèvres (that failed attempt to dismember the Ottoman Empire and leave the Turks with a small parcel of land in Central Anatolia) and they will be able to quote chapter and verse; many of them will launch into an earnest discourse about the wrongs of an obscure document which outsiders have long forgotten.

In the late 1990s I was told by the veteran Turkish politician, Bülent Ecevit, who was about to become prime minister again, that many influential Europeans want to recreate the 'spirit of Sèvres', and Turkey has to be permanently on its guard. He is not alone in believing that plans are afoot to tear the country apart – rights for the Kurds and recognition of Armenian genocide are all part of the same dark plot. Cyprus is another touchstone issue which is guaranteed to produce some crunch moments over the next few years. Even Tayyip Erdoğan has, to the alarm of some EU officials, spoken of the European effort to 'divide the country'.

Turks have always had something of an 'us against the world' attitude to life – it's one of the things I like about them. But when it crosses the line from stubbornness into paranoia it does make it rather too easy to accuse *yabancilar* – foreigners or outsiders – of discrimination, or even outright malice. For a long time that allowed Turkish politicians to ignore their own failings and inadequacies, and took attention away from the massive programme of social and economic reconstruction which Turkey needs. When you look at the scale of change Turkey still faces over the coming decade, you wonder whether sensitivity within the EU about its Muslim identity might have worked in its favour. A Christian country of comparable size with the same multitude of problems would probably have been turned down flat.

'Do you think you'll ever join the EU?' I asked a man with a bushy moustache, who was quietly smoking a water pipe. I was in a café in Trabzon on the Black Sea coast, doing what journalists do, taking a rather random pulse of the people.

'I'd like to finish this first,' he said, waving the pipe at me before taking another long slow puff.

'What, before you answer the question?'

'No, before we join. I think I'll have time.'

His friend cackled with laughter, and I ordered some more tea.

Is it ever likely to happen? With the best will in the world, it will be a mighty struggle, and an immensely revealing one. There is a genuine groundswell of enthusiasm for the idea of Europe because it seems to offer so many people the hope of something better. It will be put to the test in the coming years, and maintaining the breakneck pace of reform will be difficult. In the meantime there are politicians and generals, businessmen and academics, bureaucrats and trades unionists, from the left and the right, who have their doubts. All of them will continue to have their say in the battle for Turkey's future.

They are not in the majority at the moment, but they could still win the day. It is just possible that Turkey will reform itself beyond recognition, and then decide that it no longer needs the EU. An economic partnership yes, but a fully fledged union . . . well, no thank you. If that were to be the case, Turkey will have changed for its own sake, and it will emerge as a more confident and more dynamic nation. If the Turks were to be rejected, though – if they were not allowed to make the decision for themselves – then the chip on the shoulder would grow a little bit bigger, and more extreme Islamist and nationalist politicians would be quick to take advantage.

* * *

When I worked in Istanbul my office was not all that far from Ali Sami Yen, the concrete hulk of a stadium which is home to Galatasaray, 'Cim Bom', one of the giants of Turkish football. Home games were a microcosm of Turkish politics: passionate, biased, sometimes dirty and always colourful. There was the bare-knuckle local rivalry with Fenerbahçe from just across the Bosphorus, and with Beşiktaş from just down the hill; there was the disdain with which provincial teams were sent packing; and then there were the big European nights when the pride of the Turkish nation appeared to be at stake.

Sometimes it turned nasty, tragically so when two Leeds United fans were stabbed to death down the road near Taksim Square. But most of the time the WELCOME TO HELL banners hanging around the stadium were just part of the game, the perception rather than the reality. All the trappings of knockabout politics were there: the war of words in the tabloids, the cartoons showing arrogant European crusaders, and the overinflated egos in the directors' box looking down intently as the game was won and lost.

Those European nights mattered so much because Ali Sami Yen was another arena in the battle for acceptance. Try suggesting to a Turkish football fan, tongue firmly planted in cheek, that they shouldn't really be playing in Europe at all ('What about the Middle Eastern Premier League?'), and they will indignantly take the bait. Why? Because even if they know you're joking, and you're not really Benedict XVI in disguise, they wonder deep down whether you really mean it.

And so it is with politics. The questions keep nagging away, but no one is quite sure what the answers are. Does the EU have either the courage or the inclination to follow through on its initial invitation to Turkey to join the club? Would such a decision make the Union impossible to manage? Does Europe really want to extend its reach to the borders of Syria, Iraq and Iran? Can it, above all, overcome profound doubts about the wisdom of handing a leading role in European affairs to an overwhelmingly Muslim nation?

And as for the Turks, are they prepared to make all the far-reaching changes which Europe demands? Will they really want to join if and when they jump through all the hoops which are strewn in the path of would-be members? Do they fully understand the loss of sovereignty which EU membership implies? And does it make good economic sense for this rapidly changing society to throw in its lot with an ageing Union of shrinking populations and slow growth?

'We've got a decade to sort all these things out,' a senior Turkish diplomat said with feeling. 'It should be an interesting ride.'

9

CROSSROADS

My favourite road in Istanbul is the one which leads down to the village where we used to live. Escaping from the madness of the city traffic, you plunge suddenly down the steep hill towards the Bosphorus: past the park, past the cemetery, past the makeshift shanties and the walled compounds. At one end of our street is the local mosque, at the other an old Armenian church.

Below us, across the road, is the water's edge with the fishermen casting their lines and the children playing on the swings and slides. From our windows we used to watch the tankers and freighters, the trawlers and passenger ferries, heading north towards the Black Sea or south towards the Mediterranean. In the distance the mighty span of the Bosphorus Bridge glimmers in the sunlight, as cars press forward impatiently on the road between Europe and Asia.

The village has its own chaotic rhythm. There are the small cafés next to the candle shop on Old Cupboard Street, where the local men sit and talk, smoking and arguing. Tea on the ground floor, something stronger in the room upstairs. Hasan, the barber, waits by the window with his fearsome pair of scissors. The car park attendant is slowly getting drunk again. There are fish restaurants and a fancy French pâtisserie; old wooden houses clinging to the hillside in various states of disrepair; supermarkets, corner shops and vegetables sold off the back of a lorry. Poor Anatolian migrants live just around the corner from the wealthiest people in the country; top-of-the-range luxury cars compete for space with rickety carts; gleaming mansions sit in the same street as small wooden shacks.

It all became reassuringly familiar very quickly and yet the image of
Istanbul, seen from outside, can be one of barely suppressed anarchy.
There have been some grim headlines in recent years – bomb blasts and
hotel sieges; hunger strikes, an economic crisis and football fans stabbed
to death in the streets. There are miles and miles of grim new suburbs,
pockmarked with the soulless architecture of rapid development. There
is real anger, real poverty and a growing gap between the haves and the
have-nots. But Istanbul is one of the most alluring places I've ever lived.
There's a surprise around every corner, and just when you think you've
got to know your neighbourhood, you discover something new.

Some of the old-timers bemoan the loss of the 'real' cosmopolitan
Istanbul. Millions of Anatolian peasants have migrated into the city in
the last three decades, turning a mighty imperial capital into a vast
sprawling village. The minorities who flourished here for centuries – the
Greeks, the Armenians and the Jews – are only just clinging on. But cities
are never stagnant, never standing still, and Istanbul has the strength
to survive.

It is one of the great crossroads of the world, still full to the brim with
indelible images: the palaces and mosques; the hustle and bustle of the
bazaars and markets; skyscrapers and shanties; trams and buses jam-
packed with faces; people hurrying in every direction and ferries
steaming out of the Golden Horn, bringing traders from Turkmenistan
and Bosnian businessmen with a bargain in every pocket.

After more than two years living in the capital Ankara – high on the
Anatolian plain hundreds of miles from the sea – it was the water which
I loved most about Istanbul. The Bosphorus is the city's heart, lungs and
transport artery all rolled into one. It is why this place has been fought
over for centuries. As the last rays of the sun began to set on the Asian
shore, we would stroll down to the promenade. If the fishermen had had
a good day there would be a steady stream of customers. Small boats
moored on the water sell sea bass, mullet, and in the winter season my
local favourite, *hamsi*, a type of anchovy which washes down well with a
bottle of rakı and an aubergine salad.

In the fading light the Bosphorus becomes a vast kaleidoscope of
glinting waves, constantly forming and reforming, reinventing itself just
like the city it struggles to nourish. Istanbul is a great European city and
a great Muslim city all rolled into one, as good a symbol as you can find

of a country wrestling with its identity. It's a place which never fails to remind you that Turkey's extraordinary geographical position – sitting so strategically between Europe, the Middle East and the former Soviet Union – is a huge challenge and a huge opportunity.

* * *

Abu Kalam Ajad emerged from the rubber dinghy like a wounded animal – slumped on all fours, bewildered – his face cautiously scanning the shoreline in front of him. A 27-year-old from Bangladesh, he was found alive nearly thirty hours after he'd been plunged into a nightmare.

Huge waves and high winds had sent the Georgian-registered cargo ship *Pati* thumping into the rocks on the southern Turkish coast, spilling its human cargo into the sea. It was New Year's Day just off the resort town of Kemer, a popular place for British and German tourists to soak up the summer sun. Abu Kalam remembers people swimming and people sinking, and he was one of the lucky ones. Smeared in oil to keep warm, he survived until he was spotted in a rocky inlet and rescued by Turkish naval commandos. Other young men, from India and Pakistan, died in the water a long way from home. They knew they were on a dangerous journey, but they must have dreamt of success.

Abu Kalam said he entered Turkey by crossing the border from Kurdish-controlled northern Iraq. The mountains are dotted with smuggling routes, the back roads of the lucrative trade in human beings. But Turkey is just a staging post: once Abu Kalam got to Istanbul he gave all his remaining money to smugglers who promised to get him into Europe. While European leaders grow increasingly concerned about how to keep illegal migrants out, the number of people heading in their direction is rising all the time.

Turkey sits on Route One of this great flood tide of people: between Europe and Asia; between the Christian world and the Muslim; between the rich and the poor. For Turks, there are many advantages: potential trading partners in every direction, and a cultural history rich enough to make archaeologists go weak at the knees. But there are disadvantages as well: because of its porous eastern borders, and its proximity to the EU, Turkey has been a natural centre of the smuggling trade for years. Just stand on the Aegean coastline after dark and stare out at the twinkling lights of the Greek islands. They seem almost close enough to touch, and they draw would-be migrants like moths to the flame.

The heart of Turkey's trade in smuggled people, though, is to be found in the back streets of Istanbul, in down-at-heel neighbourhoods like Aksaray, where Eastern European prostitutes mingle with touts and traders in the grimy lobbies of cheap hotels. In the windows of local travel agents, signs advertising VISAS are prominently displayed, and they're not talking about credit cards. There's nothing illegal about helping a traveller obtain a visa, but everyone knows that many businesses operate at the dubious end of the market where gangs from Pakistan and Iran rub shoulders with the Russian mafia. All of them make vast profits from tens of thousands of illegal migrants who want to get to Europe.

It doesn't take long to find an offer to travel on one of the many smuggling routes which this city provides. In a back room of a small hotel, a woman from the Caucasus runs what is clearly a profitable business. We are introduced by a mutual acquaintance, and ask whether she can help an Iranian friend of ours get to Bosnia. She has a few questions of her own, and she sounds a little suspicious. We never find out her name.

'Why Bosnia?'

'He has relatives there.'

'When does he want to go?'

'As soon as he can.'

Finally she picks up the phone to call a contact – the man with the visas.

Before getting on to our business, she asks a question for another would-be client. How easy is it to get someone into the United States? Via the Bahamas, they agree, appears to be the best bet. After a brief conversation she says a visa and a ticket for Bosnia can be ready the following day for one thousand US dollars.

'Does your friend want to go further?' she asks.

'Perhaps.'

'That can also be arranged, but it will cost much more.'

For those who are ready to part with their life savings, anything is possible. Dodgy tickets on cheap flights to the Balkans are not the only way of getting into Europe illegally. Thousands of people arrive in

Turkey from the east every week, and many of them come to Istanbul for another throw of the dice. Some are smuggled onto rusting cargo ships bound for Italy; others try their luck under cover of night at Turkey's long land border with Greece and Bulgaria. I once came across a bedraggled group of about sixty Iraqi Kurds sitting on the forecourt of a police station near the Greek border. They'd been caught down by the river where three of their friends had drowned in freezing waters. Minefields also claim many anonymous victims.

No one knows how many people get through, but the security forces are overwhelmed by the weight of numbers. Corruption is rampant, and the gangs wield enormous economic power. From policemen to politicians, from the customs to the coast guard, everyone has their price. Egged on by Europe, though, the Turkish authorities have made a remarkable effort to crack down on the smuggling trade. In the past decade, a staggering number of illegal migrants have been caught on Turkish soil – more than half a million people in all.

Many of them come from Turkey's eastern neighbours in the Islamic world: Iraq, Iran, Afghanistan and Pakistan. There are also thousands of disaffected people from the former Soviet Union on the move, from Moldova, Russia and Ukraine. Some of them have been captured several times in a constant game of hide-and-seek with the authorities. When they are deported or released, they have only one aim in mind: to try again and again, until they reach the promised land in Europe.

So the smugglers are feeding a growing demand. They have the power to corrupt, and the ruthlessness to abandon those whose luck deserts them. Getting to Europe is a hazardous business, and there is no guarantee of success. Some people arrive in Turkey and then get stuck, forced to eke out a life outside the system in grinding poverty. I met Nashmi Rashidi when she was living illegally in Turkey with her husband and two young children. They had paid several thousand pounds to buy false Iranian passports, and bribe their way across international borders via Iraq and Syria. Several months later they were living in a tiny rented room with no source of income, and no means of escape.

'We can't go back to Iran,' Nashmi said. 'My husband could face the death penalty there. But we haven't got the money to go any further. We can't even buy clothes for the children.'

Nashmi insisted that she was a political refugee, but it can be a hard point to prove. Others would see her family as part of a wave of economic migrants heading remorselessly westward through Turkey and, in one way or another, the problem is bound to get worse as long as inequality in the global economy is so striking. When images of Western affluence are fed by television into huts and shanties across the world, who can blame those who want to take their chances, convinced that the streets really are paved with gold on the other side. Europe can pass new regulations and patrol its borders more effectively, but it can't plug every hole. For those on the outside looking in, the temptations are too great.

Migrants come in all shapes and sizes, some good, some bad, but all of them united in their search for a better life. I used to get phone calls from a Ugandan refugee in Istanbul called James, a deserter he said from the Ugandan Army. Could I get him a passport, he wondered, or have a quiet word with the local United Nations office? They might help him if they knew that he knew the BBC. James used to call once every few weeks until his payphone cut him off. Speaking perfect English, he never asked for money, only for advice, and for help which I couldn't provide. Eventually the calls stopped as suddenly as they had begun. Perhaps he made it to Europe – he said he had family in the Netherlands. Or perhaps he became another victim of the smuggling gangs, who ply their trade in the currency of human hope.

* * *

When you drive through the rock-strewn mountains into the small town of Yüksekova, near Turkey's borders with Iran and Iraq, something strikes you: amid all the grinding poverty in the region, there are pockets of remarkable wealth here. High-performance cars and Jeeps with number plates from Ankara and Istanbul trundle down Main Street. Away from the shanties, there are big houses on the edge of town.

The local mayor is worried that Yüksekova doesn't have a functioning sewage system, and most of his citizens don't have a job. But a few canny individuals have spent serious money on luxury goods, and nearly all of it has come from the drugs trade. As they say in Turkish in these parts: 'Bir kilo tuz, bir otobüs' (one kilo of dust will buy you a bus). It is big business, but not the sort of thing locals want to talk about to strangers, and who can blame them.

'Three countries meet around here,' observed the mayor. 'We call it the Bermuda Triangle. People disappear.'

A stronghold of Kurdish nationalism and a 'forgotten, abandoned place' according to one resident, Yüksekova is a notorious centre for heroin smuggling. Addiction is a growing problem among the massed ranks of the unemployed, but nearly all the heroin which reaches Yüksekova is packed up and sent west.

First stop: Istanbul. When Turkish narcotics officers raided a small sugar cube factory in a suburb of the city in January 2004, after an international surveillance operation lasting for several months, they couldn't quite believe what they found. Hidden in the basement was more than one tonne of heroin, worth at least thirty million euros, about to be transferred abroad. It was described at the time as the biggest heroin bust Europe had ever seen. Five of the gang of suspects taken into custody during the raid were related to one another, and they all came from Yüksekova.

Small town boys, perhaps, but they knew their market. Demand for heroin in Turkey itself remains relatively small, so the smuggling gangs are anxious to shift their supplies on to Europe, where they can sell them for three or four times as much profit. It's the same lucrative story as the people-smuggling trade: Turkey is a major transit route for drugs, which are cultivated in countries like Afghanistan and consumed in countries like Britain, Germany and the Netherlands.

Exact figures are understandably hard to come by, but an estimated eighty per cent of the heroin sold in Europe comes through Turkey. Huge consignments of drugs pass through the hands of various loosely connected groups, as Turkish and Kurdish gangs ferry them across the Continent. Albanians and others are muscling in on the trade as well, but they are dependent on the Turkish connection because of Turkey's pivotal position on the smuggling routes from Afghanistan. When pitched battles broke out on the streets around Green Lanes in north London in November 2002, rival Kurdish gangs were fighting turf wars to maintain their share of a multimillion-dollar business. Trying to stem the flow of illegal drugs is a major issue for many European countries in their bilateral relations with Turkey.

But who's really in control of the smuggling trade? The Turkish authorities have always pointed the finger at the PKK, saying it finances much of its activities with drugs money. Undoubtedly true, but rogue elements within the state have taken their cut as well. In the mid-1990s a motley collection of counter-insurgency troops and village guards known as the Yüksekova Gang conducted a local reign of terror. Kidnapping and extortion were standard fare, and there were claims that military helicopters were used to transport drugs further west. For years the war in the south-east has provided perfect cover for the traffickers. An almost deserted countryside, a porous border and a population ruled by fear – who could dream up a better place from which to run large-scale smuggling operations?

'We have a saying here,' I was told in Yüksekova, 'the wolves like the misty weather.'

For years it wasn't just mist but thick fog, and it helped local hard men from the south-east become international criminals. One of the kingpins of the Turkish drugs world is Hüseyin Baybaşin, from Lice near Diyarbakır, currently serving a long drugs-related prison sentence in the Netherlands. From behind bars, he still seems to be as influential as ever, thanks to a close-knit family network which is still in business, funnelling its more dubious profits into legitimate companies such as a network of holiday resorts on the Mediterranean coast. Baybaşin was in a European prison before – in London in the 1980s – but when he was transferred back to Turkey to complete his sentence he was almost immediately released. Even now, he says he took command of one of the world's biggest drugs syndicates with the support of Turkish politicians, senior police officers and members of the intelligence service, MIT.

European law-enforcement officials say cooperation with the Turkish authorities is getting better. Mutual confidence is improving as intelligence sharing and training programmes bear fruit, and Britain has more drugs liaison officers in Turkey than anywhere else in the world. But if anyone was in any doubt about how deeply the heroin menace has seeped into the system, they should take a long look at the curious tale of Mustafa Bayram, a tribal leader from the eastern province of Van, to whom thousands of armed men are unquestionably loyal. For years he sat as a mega-rich member of parliament, happily claiming parliamentary immunity to frustrate those who wanted to put him on trial for smuggling drugs.

Even after Bayram's political career came to an end, when he was caught trying to fence fake Picassos, he returned to Van untouched by the forces of law and order. He was simply too powerful. When his son, Hamit, was arrested in a sting operation while trying to sell a large haul of heroin, Mustafa and his clansmen were tipped off. So they staged an armed attack on the local police station, and liberated both Hamit and his heroin. Among the attackers was another of Mustafa's sons, Hecer, a local mayor from the AK Party.

So far, so murky. After a general outcry forced the authorities to act, the two sons were eventually tracked down; at the end of 2004 they were awaiting trial. Their father, the mercurial Mustafa, was nowhere to be seen. But when the parliamentary opposition suggested an official inquiry should be held into the links between drugs and politics, another local notable in Van told them to mind their own business. And if they didn't shut up, he added, they'd better watch their backs. This is the Turkey where loyalty to the tribe is more important than anything else. And in many parts of the wild east, smuggling is what the tribe does best.

* * *

Drugs and illegal migrants, weapons and 'dirty bomb' components, radical ideas and terrorism – in the circumstances it would be hard to blame Turkey if it simply sought to seal off its eastern borders and concentrate on its push to the west. For many years, officially at least, that was pretty much what happened: Syria was dismissed as a country which supported the PKK, Iran as a theocracy which wanted to export Islamic revolution. Iraq was ruled by Saddam, and the Middle East in general was part of a past which the Kemalists wanted to forget.

Before the fall of the Soviet Union, in fact, Turkey was convinced that it was encircled by enemies. Adding Communists and Greeks to those troublesome Kurds and Islamists gave them a full house of enemies of the state. You can still find plenty of reminders of the siege mentality – at Turkish border crossings with Iran, for example, where billboard-sized pictures of Atatürk stare across the divide at equally large portraits of the Ayatollah Khomeini. 'Turkey is a Secular State', the message on the Turkish side proclaims, in case anyone misses the point.

But there's been a thaw, especially since the AKP came to power.

Turkey's secular democracy, its application for EU membership and its close relationship with the United States have long been regarded in Tehran, Baghdad and Damascus with intense suspicion. Islamists look at the secular state which buried the caliphate and think 'betrayal'; and Arab nationalists still haven't forgotten that the Turks are their former colonial rulers. But the new Turkish model – trying to mix greater democracy and Islam together – is now the subject of curiosity and not a little envy.

'They're watching what we're doing,' says the Turkish foreign minister, Abdullah Gül. 'We've been told that many times. They want to know what they can learn from us.'

So while Europe remains its overriding obsession, Turkey has begun to reassess relations with its Muslim neighbours in the Middle East. Turkey and Iran have launched joint military offensives against remnants of the PKK, and economic initiatives are beginning to take centre stage as well. High-level meetings with Iran and Syria – including the first ever visit to Turkey by a Syrian president – have led to a dramatic increase in trade. It began (once again) with Turgut Özal, but under the AKP there is more consultation with Arab governments in general, the Turkish Foreign Ministry no longer boasts about how few Arabic speakers it has, and in 2004, after considerable lobbying, a Turk became the Secretary-General of the Organization of Islamic Countries.

There are plenty of unresolved issues to the east, of course. Iran still has links with radical Islamic groups who seek to do Turkey some harm, and the general staff is worried about Iran's nuclear programme. As for Syria, a glance at official maps in Damascus reveals that it hasn't yet given up its claim to the Turkish province of Hatay, awarded to Ankara after a referendum when the French pulled out in the 1930s. The Syrians also harbour a continuing grudge about the flow of water in the Euphrates river. But worst of all is what's happening across the most difficult border of all: relations with Iraq have been fraught with constant anxiety for years, and it got much worse after the fall of Saddam Hussein.

It is an article of faith among Turkish policymakers that a weak and fractured Iraq is not in Turkey's interest. They've learnt that the hard way. One of the reasons Turgut Özal backed the first President Bush's Gulf War so enthusiastically in 1991 was that he had his eye on a few oilfields in northern Iraq and he thought Turkey could benefit from a division of the spoils. Except there were no spoils – only a refugee crisis with hundreds of thousands of Kurds fleeing across the mountains towards the Turkish border when Saddam Hussein reasserted control in Iraq; and then more than a decade of international sanctions against the regime in Baghdad which cost the Turkish economy tens of billions of dollars in lost trade.

With a second President Bush in the White House, and another Iraqi war looming, the Americans seemed to assume a little too readily that they could rely on Turkish assistance again. In 2003 Washington wanted to send sixty thousand troops into Iraq across the Turkish border. But nine out of ten Turks were against the war in Iraq; the security estab- lishment was deeply concerned about Kurdish autonomy; and months of negotiations on a package of financial aid worth billions of dollars for Turkey led American newspaper cartoons to caricature the Turks as belly dancers trying to tempt Uncle Sam, or greedy carpet dealers haggling over the price.

None of it went down well in Ankara and at the eleventh hour the Turkish parliament (in a vigorous display of democracy) ignored the pleas of the government and rejected the American request. 'Seventy Million Human Shields!' said one Turkish newspaper headline. There was to be no second front in Iraq. The Americans turned instead to the Iraqi Kurds and a much more limited offensive in the north, but the Turkish sleight wasn't forgotten. When a group of Turkish Special Forces was later caught red-handed by the Americans in northern Iraq – accused of supplying arms to ethnic Iraqi Turkomans for possible use against the Kurds – they were treated like the enemy: blindfolded, tied up and eventually sent home.

In Turkey it was portrayed as a national humiliation, and a new low in relations with Washington. Even when the Turks decided to mend fences, and offered to deploy ten thousand troops to help police the American-led occupation, they were rebuffed. This time it was the Iraqis, in the form of the Governing Council, which said, 'Thanks, but no thanks – we don't want you here.' With Turkey seeing most things in Iraq through the Kurdish prism, the idea of Turkish troops was dismissed as far more trouble than it was worth.

It all gave the Turks little influence over events across the border. The presence of the PKK in northern Iraq has always been a major irritant, but the main diplomatic objective in Ankara is to ensure that the central government in Baghdad keeps control of Kirkuk, the strategic oil city which everyone wants. When the Iraqi Kurds come up with slogans like 'Kirkuk is the Heart of Kurdistan', Turkish policymakers get a little hot under the collar. Their greatest fear is that long-term Kurdish control of Kirkuk's oil wealth could lead to de facto Kurdish independence in Iraq, and encourage further demands for autonomy among their own restless Kurds as well.

It will take years for a settled vision of post-Saddam Iraq to emerge, but Kirkuk could prove to be one of the bitterest disputes of all. Kurds, Arabs and Turkomans all lay claim to a city which Abdullah Gül has compared to Bosnia in terms of its potential for ethnic strife. At one stage Turkish newspapers reported contingency plans for military intervention involving tens of thousands of troops if things were to go badly for Turkey in the region. So a strong central government in Baghdad would suit the Turks just fine – Saddam Hussein, they whisper, wasn't all bad. But when they look at Iraq, they wonder when they will ever see stability again.

None of which is good news for the men waiting in line in the withering heat near the Habur border crossing between Turkey and Iraq. A long queue of stationary trucks stretches as far as the eye can see, before disappearing into the smouldering haze which rises up from the tarmac. The smell of diesel is all-pervasive, and the drivers pass the time sitting forlornly in narrow strips of shade, smoking and sipping tea.

'It's been like this for years,' said a driver called Celal. 'With Saddam or without Saddam, it doesn't matter – getting across this border is a problem, and then once we're across, we have to take our chances. God willing, we will all come back.'

There are an estimated fifty thousand trucks based in south-eastern Turkey, and most of them travel across the border into Iraq whenever they can. Dozens of Turkish truckers have been kidnapped, beheaded and shot in the insurgency which followed the fall of Saddam Hussein. They don't go to Iraq because they like it there; they go because they have no choice. The UN sanctions against Iraq, imposed after the 1991 Gulf War, helped cripple the economy of south-eastern Turkey for a decade. Now the region is desperate to get back to business, and Turkish exporters are keen to fill the trucks up. But it's dangerous work.

'I just wish they could sort things out,' Celal said, as he wandered back to his truck. 'The Americans should leave, and let us get on with things here. How long are we supposed to wait?'

* * *

On the narrow streets next to the Fatih mosque in Istanbul the images on the poster jumped out from the wall. They looked out of place next to the small shops selling wool and household appliances. Graphic photographs of civilian victims of the US military assault on Falluja were interspersed with menacing shots of American tanks. 'Falluja is Istanbul', proclaimed the poster. Beneath it was another message scrawled in red – BOYCOTT AMERICAN PRODUCTS, DON'T HELP THE OPPRESSOR.

It may not always be expressed in such stark terms, but it is one of the few issues which reach across Turkey's notoriously bumpy political divides. Whether you're a nationalist, an Islamist or a liberal in Turkey, you probably don't like what the United States has done in the Middle East in the last few years. A close partnership stretching back fifty years has never felt more fragile. In particular, American-led military operations across the border in Iraq have been greeted with howls of popular and political protest, and one senior AKP politician described the US occupation as genocide.

Perhaps it's a passing phase; after all, the US military still has plenty of bases in Turkey, helping supply troops in Iraq, and many young Turks remain obsessed with American popular culture. But there's no doubt that anti-Americanism among ordinary Turks rose sharply in the aftermath of the US-led invasion. When the BBC commissioned a poll from more than twenty countries around the world about attitudes towards George W. Bush and the United States, in the wake of the president's second election victory, there was more negative comment in Turkey than anywhere else. As Bush began his second term, one of the most popular books in Turkey was a novel called *Metal Storm* which describes the Turkish response (they nuke Washington) to an American military attack.

Opposition to American policy in the Middle East has also helped feed opposition to Israel. Turkey has been Israel's most important Muslim ally for more than a decade, but after the AKP came to power criticism of Israeli actions in the West Bank and Gaza began to flow thick

and fast. On several occasions Tayyip Erdoğan accused Israel of practising 'state terrorism' against the Palestinians, and he grew noticeably
cool to the overtures of senior Israeli officials. It made political sense
because it mirrored the opinion of many ordinary people who resented
the fact that ties with Israel had been a strategic project imposed by the
men in uniform.

In the 1990s when Turkey wanted to curry favour with Washington,
and put the frighteners on Syria and Iran, the military led the way in
forging close relations with Israel. A flurry of defence agreements
followed – Israeli planes flew practice runs over Turkish territory (there
is, after all, rather more of it) and joint naval exercises took place in the
Mediterranean with the Americans offering a helping hand. Security and
intelligence cooperation followed, and commercial deals began to
multiply as well, amid talk of a strategic relationship between the two
Middle Eastern democracies.

But the popular mood turned sour. Israeli links with the Iraqi Kurds
haven't helped matters, but the occupation of the West Bank and Gaza
is the most emotional issue of all. Fed by graphic images of violence on
local television channels, popular sympathy for the Palestinians in
Turkey is strong – especially among the conservative folk whose votes
put Erdoğan into the prime minister's office in the first place. For better
or worse, the government has started to better reflect the feelings of
most of its people.

Unfortunately, there is a sinister side to all this as well. There's been
a flurry of open anti-Semitism in parts of the Turkish media, translations
of Adolf Hitler's book *Mein Kampf* made an unlikely appearance on the
bestseller list, and there was of course the reaction of the violent fringe:
the suicide bomb attacks on Istanbul synagogues in November 2003.
Turkey's Jewish community is worried, while the Israelis are dismayed
and looking for a change of heart. Business deals are still being signed,
Tayyip Erdoğan finally visited Israel in May 2005, and plenty of Israeli
tourists come to Turkish holiday resorts to get away from the stresses
and strains back home. But the big picture has shifted a little.

So the Israelis, desperate not to lose their only friend in a hostile
region, are pinning their hopes on another strategic link – water. Turkey
has it in relative abundance, but everyone else in the Middle East is in
desperate need.

'Where's the waterfall?' I asked the waiter, expecting a vision of a Mediterranean Niagara to appear round the next corner at any moment. He gestured through the trees at the Manavgat river which was tumbling half-heartedly over a few rocks.

'That's it?' I said, and he nodded and handed me a menu.

'It's very popular,' he replied. 'It's the best waterfall we've got.'

I didn't want to be rude but it didn't look desperately impressive, even if the tea gardens lining the banks were a pleasant enough place to while away a few hours. So I was a bit disappointed with Manavgat until I got to the figures: five billion cubic metres of fresh water flowing into the sea every year or, to put it another way, five billion cubic metres going to waste.

Just downstream from the waterfall, round the next bend in the river, was the business end of the operation: a new water treatment and storage plant, and a tanker terminal, waiting for its first customers. Turkey is determined to turn its fresh water into a profitable strategic asset.

'Everything's ready to go,' said Mustafa Altundal, the manager of the water plant, as he gave me a guided tour of the state-of-the-art control room. 'Local people only need a fraction of the water in this river. The rest we can send elsewhere.'

It is an intriguing prospect. Parts of Turkey stand to benefit from the water project: Istanbul, for example, and tourist resorts on the Mediterranean, which have to cope with an influx of millions of visitors every summer. But in their more fanciful moments the Turks say the Manavgat project could play a role in bringing peace to the Middle East.

After years of tortuous negotiations, Israel signed an agreement with Turkey in March 2004 to buy fifty million cubic metres of Manavgat water every year for twenty years. Ariel Sharon, the Israeli prime minister, acknowledged that it wasn't necessarily the cheapest way to supply his country's water needs. Instead, he argued, it was a diplomatic necessity – a deal to help protect the relationship with Turkey. When the project will actually begin is shrouded in mystery, and it could still fall victim to political interference. But the long-term plan is for converted supertankers to transport water across the Mediterranean, not just to Israel but to Malta, Cyprus, Libya and other countries as well.

The Turks have been experimenting with water deliveries for some time. The first idea was to use massive water-filled balloons pulled by tugs along the surface of the sea. For a trial period in 1998, water was sent to Turkish-controlled northern Cyprus in these huge plastic sacks which looked more like giant jellyfish than a major diplomatic break-through. I watched the first consignment of ten thousand cubic metres arrive in northern Cyprus, and at the time it felt rather revolutionary. But the project eventually proved to be too unreliable, because the bal-loons had an unfortunate tendency to sink.

Undeterred by delays and false starts, Turkish geopolitical experts are still convinced that they have an ace up their sleeve.

'In the twenty-first century there will be nothing more important in the Middle East than water,' Hüseyin Bağcı of Ankara's Middle East Technical University told me. 'And that means Turkey will be in a vital strategic position. Water can no longer be considered a gift of the Gods.'

Can Turkey really trade on its water supply, either for financial or strategic advantage? It's certainly going to try, partly because it knows how it feels to be without something so important. Turkey lacks the great natural resources of the industrial age – oil and gas – and it has to import nearly all its energy supplies. But its proximity to Azerbaijan, the Caspian and Central Asia, as well as to the Middle East, has allowed it to cultivate a new strategic role: the 'missing link' in a chain connecting these new producers of vast mineral resources with the consumer soci-eties in Europe, America and beyond.

*　*　*

As we approached Istanbul from the Sea of Marmara, on the bridge of the oil tanker *Nilos*, the minarets and towers of the old metropolis appeared suddenly through the gathering gloom. We passed the con-tainer port, Topkapı Palace and the mouth of the Golden Horn, before moving into the narrow channel which cuts through the heart of the city. It's beautiful, the Bosphorus, but deceptive. With twelve changes of course, tight bends and four separate strong currents, it's one of the most hazardous waterways in the world.

I'd climbed on board the *Nilos* a few minutes earlier with its pilot, Saim Oğuzülgen, who had guided ships along the Bosphorus for many years. With his eyes glued to the radar screen, he argued that a critical point had been reached.

'Many of the ships which pass through here now carry dangerous cargoes,' he said. 'It only takes one mistake to put a city of more than ten million people under threat.'

Fifty thousand ships sail down the Bosphorus every year, most of them come from Russia, and many of them don't have a pilot. The Russians point to the complex rules governing navigation, first set out in the Montreux Convention in 1936, which guarantee free passage during peacetime for vessels of any nation carrying any type of cargo. Residents of Istanbul don't care much for the fine print. They're worried that as the tanker traffic increases, a terrible accident will happen sooner rather than later.

Halfway down the channel, waterside villas and restaurants sit just a few metres away from huge ocean-going vessels. Having lunch by the Bosphorus can be an unnerving experience when a passing tanker suddenly blocks out the light. Every year, ships lose power, run aground or fail to take account of the treacherous currents. Collisions are all too frequent, and there have been some genuine disasters. In 1979 a fully loaded Romanian tanker, the *Independenta*, caught fire just outside the southern entrance to the Bosphorus after colliding with another vessel. Forty-three people were killed in a huge explosion: windows in nearby buildings were shattered, the sky turned red, and residents of the city thought they had been hit by an earthquake.

In 1994 tragedy struck again when two vessels collided in the middle of the channel. Twenty-nine seamen were killed in the flames, and oil fires raged across the surface of the water for four days. Now, many Istanbullus live in fear of something much worse. One study suggests that if a fully laden natural-gas tanker exploded in the Bosphorus the force of the blast would be more powerful than the atomic bomb dropped on Hiroshima. And local officials believe the threat of a catastrophic accident, or even an act of terrorism, is increasing.

'Unlimited free passage was agreed before the era of supertankers and nuclear-powered ships,' said Saim Oğuzülgen, as the *Nilos* slipped quietly past the castle at Rumeli Hisarı and under the bridge named after Mehmet the Conquerer. 'Times have changed,' he concluded.

That's why Turkey has gradually introduced tougher navigation rules over the past decade, ignoring protests from countries which depend on the Bosphorus, like Russia and Ukraine. Since 2002 the Turks have banned night-time transit for ships longer than two hundred metres. During winter months bad weather causes further delays, and tankers sometimes have to wait in a queue for more than two weeks. The Russians aren't happy, and nor are refineries in Europe, but the congestion is likely to get worse. Even though new oil and gas pipelines are coming on stream, the number of tankers steaming down the Bosphorus will continue to rise for several years.

The current volume of traffic is already taking its toll on the environment, increasing pollution and threatening more than fifty local marine species. The navigable passage is less than two hundred metres wide in each direction, and big ships have to share the water with small fishing boats and commuter ferries which carry more than a million people across the Bosphorus every day.

'The Straits are dying biologically,' Bayram Öztürk of the Marine Research Foundation observed, 'and the people of Istanbul are under threat. We don't feel safe here as human beings.'

Unfortunately, the safety concerns of millions of citizens have become entangled in a complex web of geopolitical intrigue. The Turkish authorities can regulate the traffic, but they can't stop it. They have warned repeatedly that they will not allow the Bosphorus to be used as just another oil pipeline, but Moscow guards its right of navigation jealously. For centuries czars and commissars coveted Istanbul and its strategic location because it controls access to and from the Black Sea, and Russia's main link with the world's oceans runs straight through the middle of the city.

During the cold war, it was a military argument; now it's all about commerce. As vast new oil and gas fields around the land-locked Caspian Sea come on stream, Russia has been sending the first exports through old Soviet-era pipelines to its Black Sea port of Novorossiysk. From there Caspian oil is transported by tanker through the Bosphorus to the Mediterranean and hungry world markets beyond.

But pipeline politics are just getting interesting. The main new pipeline built to handle the export of Caspian oil, backed by the United States and running through Turkey, ignores Russia altogether. The Russians are furious, and some of them mutter darkly that delays on the Bosphorus are deliberate, part of a plot to force supplies onto the new route. There may be a grain of truth in that because billions of dollars of future revenue are at stake. Turkey doesn't make any money from the ships which pass through the middle of Istanbul every day. But transfer all that oil and gas into pipelines and the government in Ankara could earn a fortune in transit fees.

*   *   *

BTC snakes unspectacularly in a small trench for more than a thousand miles across three countries; when the oil begins to flow it will be protected by anti-terrorist troops and sophisticated surveillance systems; James Bond has already saved it from evil on the big screen, but critics have called it an environmental time bomb: welcome to the world of the Baku–Tbilisi–Ceyhan pipeline.

Turkey is already criss-crossed by pipelines. There are natural-gas pipelines from Iran and – running under the Black Sea – from Russia; there's an oil pipeline from Iraq, hamstrung for years by UN sanctions and now regularly sabotaged by insurgents on the other side of the border. But the most significant, most expensive and most controversial of all is the new pipeline running from Baku in Azerbaijan through Georgia to the nondescript port of Ceyhan on Turkey's Mediterranean coast.

For years Baku–Ceyhan seemed little more than a dream – an idea on the drawing board which was too expensive for anyone to build. But there were pressing geopolitical imperatives at work. Influential players in the United States saw the chance to get huge oil and gas reserves to world markets without sending them through Russia or Iran. The Americans leant on the oil companies, who worried aloud about the pipeline's commercial viability. Successive Turkish governments lobbied furiously to get the project going, and agreed a generous subsidy. It was always regarded as a price worth paying: the answer to a looming disaster in the Bosphorus, and a guaranteed way to increase Turkey's influence in Washington, and among the Turkic republics in central Asia.

There were delays, disputes and damaging accusations. The route of the pipeline runs through difficult terrain in Azerbaijan, Georgia and Turkey – through territory vulnerable to earthquakes, ethnic conflicts and political instability. The lawless Pankisi Gorge – beloved of Chechen separatists and Islamic extremists everywhere – is within striking distance. But the nay-sayers have been confounded: the pipeline was opened in May 2005 in the presence of the US Energy Secretary and the first tankers will be loading up in Ceyhan, carrying Caspian oil to world markets. From 2008, BTC is expected to be exporting a million barrels of oil a day.

A stunning success? Not quite – the jury is still out. Despite the positive impact it will have on Istanbul and the Bosphorus, environmental and human rights groups in the West have been bitter opponents of the pipeline from the beginning. They worry about an ecological disaster caused by a catastrophic leak, and in 2003 Amnesty International warned that agreements signed between the Turkish government and the pipeline consortium could mean 'little right of redress for thirty thousand people' who had to give up their land rights to make way for the construction.

Ferhat Kaya knows exactly what that means. A young political activist from the town of Ardahan, near the Georgian border, he tried to help local villagers affected by the pipeline to take their grievances to the European Court of Human Rights. In May 2004 he was detained by the police for more than two weeks, and he says he was beaten and threatened repeatedly while in detention. Four months later a case against eleven policemen accused of subjecting him to torture or ill-treatment was dismissed for lack of evidence, even though medical reports showed he had sustained serious injuries.

The consortium countered negative headlines by spending millions of dollars to launch sustainable development schemes along the pipeline's route: helping to send children in remote parts of the Erzurum district to school for the first time, and starting local forestry and agriculture projects. But it wasn't just environmental activists who criticized the way BTC was being built. At one point a group of experienced engineers and contractors went public with their concerns, criticizing construction methods and saying the Turkish part of the pipeline – subcontracted to the state-run company Botaş – was a complete mess, plagued by shoddy workmanship and technical incompetence.

BTC will remain a source of controversy, but it has been built regardless. Now all it needs is the oil, and that will be another battle which rumbles on for some time. Russia failed to prevent the construction of Baku–Ceyhan, but it won't stop trying to undermine the economic viability of the pipeline by offering alternative export routes for Caspian oil. One project on the drawing board is a pipeline which would run across Turkey from the Black Sea coast to the Aegean – bypassing the Bosphorus but still allowing Russia and its tanker fleet to be part of the transportation process.

At the same time, Turkey is looking further west as well. A natural-gas pipeline to Greece, which could eventually be extended under the Adriatic to Italy, is due to begin operating in 2006; there are also plans for a pipeline from Turkey up through the Balkans into Central Europe. The EU's long-term aim is to establish new routes from the Caspian to secure the delivery of much of Europe's natural-gas demands. Enormous sums of money are involved, and with Russia and the Caucasus on one side, Europe on the other, and the United States pulling strings from afar, the Turks are right at the centre of this new Great Game. Pipeline politics has increased Turkey's strategic importance at the beginning of the twenty-first century.

*   *   *

Dig a little into the Turkish earth, though, and pipelines are only the most recent of the many treasures you will find buried there. On a warm summer's day in 2003 a friend of mine who lives in Cappadocia drove me down a bumpy dirt road for a sneak preview of the lost city of Sobesos. There wasn't much to see. Under a tarpaulin at the edge of a stony field, the corner of a mosaic floor and the remains of a Roman bathhouse had been carefully unearthed. Other parts of this nascent archaeological site were open to the elements. The only defence against looters was an elderly watchman and an even more decrepit-looking dog.

Locals said it had always been common knowledge that there were ruins under the fields, but no one had ever done anything about it. Excavation had begun the previous year after a chance discovery, but it had soon ground to a halt. There was no money around and local archaeologists had failed to persuade the Ministry of Culture to provide any.

'A few people like you come here to take a look,' the watchman said laconically as the dog scratched its ear. 'We just sit under the tree and wait.'

In just about any country in Europe a discovery like this would have been hailed as a great find, an important addition to national cultural history. Somehow, money would have been made available. But in Turkey sites like Sobesos are ten a penny. It's all about being a crossroads again. So many cultures have trampled through Anatolia and left their mark, from the early Stone Age to the Sultans, that it's hard sometimes to know where to start.

It means that much has been lost. Across Turkey, archaeological treasures worth many millions of dollars have been looted from their resting place in the earth in the last few years and smuggled out to private collections around the world. Sobesos, I reflected, already looked ripe for the plucking. Some ancient sites have been forgotten or abandoned; others have been destroyed by modern development projects. Only occasionally does anyone do anything about it, and even then the whole process seems to be fraught with difficulty. One of Turkey's most exciting recent discoveries, the Zeugma mosaics, was a classic example.

Three years before I peered under the tarpaulin at Sobesos, I had watched in amazement as a team of Turkish and French archaeologists dug into the sandy earth on the banks of the Euphrates river, racing against time. In just ten months, in the shadow of the Birecik dam, they unearthed some of the finest Roman mosaics found anywhere in the world. Every day they knew that the waters were rising fast and the river was becoming an artificial lake. Their dig was about to disappear.

'What we've discovered here is quite simply amazing,' said one of the archaeologists, Yusuf Yavaş, as he watched his colleagues preparing to remove another priceless example of ancient art. 'These mosaics compare with the very best.'

Nearly two thousand years ago this isolated river bank was the site of the flourishing Roman garrison town of Zeugma, on the eastern frontier of the empire. Its position on the trade routes along the Euphrates brought great wealth to its inhabitants, who competed with each other to put the most beautiful mosaics on display. Although there had been sporadic excavations at the site since it was identified in the 1970s, the ruins of Zeugma – apparently destroyed by fire, invasion and an earthquake – had lain pretty much undisturbed for centuries.

Digging only began in earnest when the flood waters generated by the GAP project were on their way. There had been hints before of what could be lying in wait for archaeologists, but the scale of what was found was extraordinary. The dry climate in the region had preserved mosaics of stunning complexity, and vivid scenes from Greek mythology began emerging from under piles of rubble. As the dust was wiped away with a damp cloth, the striking colour of mosaics dating back to the third century AD sparkled into life: Poseidon on his chariot with the water deities, Thetis and Oceanus; Perseus saving Andromeda from a sea monster; and intricately designed images of the Trojan Wars.

More than forty mosaics were removed from the lower levels of Zeugma, before the water seeped slowly in. Many more must have been hidden under the soil: treasures of ancient Rome which now lie fifteen metres beneath the surface of a man-made lake. Some mosaics were sealed and reburied, left for future archaeologists to recover once the dam is no longer in use. But perhaps no one will ever know quite what was lost. A few weeks before the site was flooded a unique bronze statue of Mars, the God of War, was found, as well as the largest collection of ceramic Roman seal inscriptions anywhere in the world.

'Every room has a mosaic,' Yusuf Yavaş said, as we strode through the ruins. 'There may be one hundred villas here that we will never have the chance to find.'

Under a blazing sun, the mosaics which had been saved were covered in white fabric and cut into precise pieces between the tiny stones. After being dug carefully from the earth, they were sent to the state museum in the nearby city of Gaziantep. The most recent arrivals were simply stacked in the garden waiting to be pieced back together.

'Of course I'm upset,' the museum's acting director, Hakkı Alkan, said, as we stood and stared at this priceless pile of treasure. 'But this is state policy. Energy issues always take precedence over any cultural considerations.'

And the state had made its decision. Any delay to its massive hydro-electric project would have cost millions of dollars a month. The Birecik dam was another step towards alleviating the electricity shortage, and irrigating new tracts of land to create desperately needed jobs. Little more than a year after the hurried excavation at Zeugma began, the dam was in full production, and the lake it created was in full flood.

The plight of Zeugma, and the beauty of its mosaics, created a torrent of publicity and offers of help began to pour in. One of the biggest charitable foundations in the United States, the Packard Humanities

Institute, offered emergency funding to excavate and save parts of the city which were still above water. More mosaics and artefacts were rescued, and satellite imaging was used to map the site more accurately, allowing archaeologists to concentrate on the most promising locations. Some of the news was good – much of the ancient city, it was decided, was probably buried beneath the surrounding hills, safe from the rising waters.

But Zeugma and its artefacts soon fell victim to modern political intrigue. Archaeologists who'd travelled to Turkey to help excavate the site grew frustrated with the constraints imposed by local bureaucrats, there were disputes about who was responsible for the condition of the mosaics once they had been dug out of the ground, and a long legal battle broke out between local residents and the state about where the mosaics should be put on display. Once again, archaeology became politicized. It was partly a struggle for economic control. Locals feared that if the mosaics were carted off to Istanbul to be shown to the world, they would never return to their rightful home. There was also resentment of outsiders hogging the limelight.

Properly managed, restored and displayed, the Zeugma mosaics will prove to be one of the finest collections in the world. But the heritage business in Turkey always seems to be mired in one controversy or another. Some of the anger is understandable – who can blame the Turks for wanting the return to Pergamon of the magnificent Temple of Zeus which was dug up and transported wholesale to Berlin in the nineteenth century? But for many years there has been more general suspicion of what foreign archaeologists are up to – are they trying, for example, to promote alternative versions of history? God forbid that they might excavate anything Armenian.

The mood is changing and the authorities seem to have realized – however belatedly – the potential of the cultural treasures they have inherited. Although funding for archaeological excavation and protection remains woefully inadequate, the Ministry of Culture has been merged with the Ministry of Tourism to try to take advantage of this extraordinary legacy. There are also moves to devolve more power to local governments to run museums and archaeological sites, and to loosen the unhealthy grip which the centralized state bureaucracy has held for too long.

As more and more layers of Anatolia's past are uncovered, it should come as no surprise to anyone quite how many different ethnic and cultural groups there are all over the country. Turkey's incomparable archaeological riches are helping Turks understand who they are, where they come from, and the extraordinary diversity of cultures which have been born on their lands. Just a quick glance at the map, and at Turkey's position in the world, makes the old nationalist dream of a purely 'Turkish' Turkey patently absurd.

But not to everyone, it seems. In March 2005 the Environment and Forestry Ministry in Ankara proudly announced that it was changing the Latin names of some indigenous animals to eliminate references to Kurdistan and Armenia. A species of red fox known as *Vulpes Vulpes Kurdistanica* will henceforth be plain *Vulpes Vulpes*, while a species of wild sheep called *Ovis Armeniana* has been renamed *Ovis Orientalis Anatolicus*. Foreign scientists, the Ministry noted gravely, had originally named these species with ill intent – giving them names which 'go against our unitary structure'.

It is another small snapshot which puts the reforms of the past few years into context. Many Turks want their country to be run in a different way, and they want a more democratic society, but the level of hostility to more modern ideas of minority rights and freedoms shouldn't be underestimated. Since the formation of the republic, Turkey has grudgingly accepted a narrow definition of non-Muslim religious minorities, but it's never been prepared to accept linguistic or ethnic ones (sorry, all you Kurds). When a report calling for a radical change in mentality was written by an advisory group within the Prime Ministry, there was uproar.

'The citizens the state should fear the least,' argued the discredited report, 'are the ones who have been granted their rights.'

If that means diluting the idea of Turkishness, though, it is still too much for most people in power. The AKP government hastily disowned the recommendations, a senior general growled with displeasure, and a copy of the report was torn up at a news conference which had been called to publicize it. Perhaps they should all pay more heed to the plea for tolerance contained in one of my favourite old Turkish proverbs.

'Every man,' it notes wisely, 'has his own style of eating yogurt.'

10

THE CULTURAL REVOLUTION

A man staggered along the street and slumped against the gate. His face was a picture of misery. Waiting inside the house was a woman whose life was about to be turned upside down.

'Cut!' cried the director. 'The sun's just gone in.'

They were filming the latest episode of *World of Mysteries* in a quiet suburb of Istanbul. Broadcast on Samanyolu TV, a conservative channel bankrolled by Fethullah Gülen, it's a drama series which has become a big ratings hit in the last couple of years. Every week people who have had their fill of raunchy pop videos and quiz shows can watch a morality tale with religious themes, based on the real-life experience of miracles.

Viewers send their stories in from all corners of the country, and the most striking of them are dramatized. Turks are true believers, one of the actresses told me, when I asked why the programme was proving so popular. It was fairly clear that for most of the cast and crew *World of Mysteries* represented the authentic voice of the people.

'Maybe they're fed up with what they see on the other channels,' mused the producer, Mustafa Kartal, as the director waited for the sun to re-emerge. 'We believe Allah is judging us, and that's reflected in everything we do.'

On the set behind us an actor was playing the part of a wretched estate agent from Muğla, who was slowly coming to terms with the error of his ways. He was convinced that he'd been punished by God after tricking a poor family into giving up their home. 'If you do bad things, bad things happen to you,' Mustafa explained.

He paused as the actors began rehearsing another scene.

'But people always have the chance to change,' he whispered, 'and if you do good things, you'll be rewarded.'

Miracles, and the chance to change . . . I have a feeling that Tayyip Erdoğan would have approved, having presided over a political miracle himself in the last few years. I don't think Kemal Atatürk would have been so impressed, though, and therein lies a problem. The founding father despised talk of miracles, and urged his countrymen to take a 'modern' rational view of the world.

'Can a civilized nation tolerate a crowd of people,' he once asked, 'who let themselves be led by the nose by sheiks, dervishes and the like, and who entrust their faith and their lives to fortune-tellers, magicians, witch-doctors and amulet-makers?'

Only the educated minority in modern Turkey would agree with Atatürk that the answer should be a resounding 'no'. Elsewhere folk Islam in one form or another is as influential as it has always been, and now it has reached the mass media as well. From their positions of power Turkey's elite don't like many of the things they see happening around them, but there's not a great deal they can do about it.

'Everything has been getting more religious in the last few years,' one academic in Ankara confided in plaintive tones. 'We can feel it, we can see it on television and it makes us uncomfortable.'

Perhaps they need to relax a bit. It certainly isn't hard to find religion on TV – either as part of the *World of Mysteries* or during feisty debates on political talk shows and round-table discussions involving leading theologians. But there's nothing too radical on offer, and if you don't want to tune in to conservative dramas or Muslim televangelists there are plenty of alternatives. In fact you can watch pretty much anything you like; most of Turkish TV is harmless pap – cheap entertainment for the masses. It's all a matter of choice.

There are endless game shows, sitcoms and soap operas – the regular diet of populist television anywhere in Europe. (The tens of thousands of Turks who visited the small Cappadocian town of Göreme in the last few years weren't attracted by its stunning natural beauty, but because it was the setting for the cult soap, *Asmalı Konak*, one of the most popular programmes ever shown on Turkish TV.) Several twenty-four-hour news channels vie for attention, and even the most unlikely of

press conferences are packed with TV cameras. A variety of music channels – Western and Turkish – entertain punters in cafés across the
country, and sports fans can subscribe to round-the-clock coverage of
football, basketball and motor racing.

Turks also share the Western obsession for reality TV. During the
2001 economic crisis I became a bit of a fan of a hugely popular programme which featured two middle-class couples trying to survive on
the minimum wage. They walked for miles to get to work, they queued
up before dawn to buy cheap stale bread, and they carried water supplies
by hand from the local mosque. In a country where much of the media
is obsessed by celebrity, and the ultra rich, the struggle to survive struck
a chord.

Since then reality TV has taken Turkey by storm in a way which
would be impossible to imagine in any of its neighbours in the Middle
East – people on these programmes are having far too much fun. There's
been the *Big Brother* variant, *Someone Is Watching Us*, and a local version
of *Pop Idol*; on *Famous People's Farm* preening minor celebrities compete
to see who is best at cleaning out the goats; and *Will You Be My Mama?*
allows Turkish mothers to have their televised say on one of their
favourite subjects – who could possibly make a worthy partner for their
beloved sons.

These are the fruits of media liberalization, and Turks who worry
about all sorts of pernicious influences can't turn back the clock. In 1980
the state-run TRT stood in glorious isolation as the only television station in the country. But there are now more than two hundred private
stations competing for attention, ranging from sophisticated national
channels to local outfits which struggle along on shoestring budgets.
There are more than one thousand radio stations as well, and every small
town seems to have a local newspaper publishing against the financial
odds. Taken together this media explosion pours an extraordinary variety of voices into the public domain. Stay within the accepted boundaries
and you can discuss almost anything, and the boundaries are being
pushed back all the time.

There is fairly robust political debate, particularly in the newspapers,
and politicians of all persuasions come in for a regular hammering. The
government of the day is never given carte blanche, although most mainstream papers and TV stations have been willing to give the AKP the

benefit of the doubt since 2002 because of its dramatic progress towards EU membership. The media moguls, who suffered as much as anyone else during the 2001 economic crisis, also know when it makes good business sense to stay on friendly terms with a powerful government. As one observer in Istanbul put it, rather more succinctly: 'Erdoğan has got them by the balls.'

But there are still some well-established restrictions on freedom of expression. Even in 2004, a journalist named Hasan Albayrak was sentenced to fifteen months in prison for violating Law number 5816 regarding 'Crimes Committed against Atatürk' – yes, it really exists. He'd written an article claiming that the founding father had not been buried with proper religious ceremony – offensive to some perhaps and, as he later acknowledged, not true. But worthy of a prison sentence?

Other limits on freedom of expression also survive unscathed in the new penal code. Insulting the government – the representative of the people – is usually allowed; but if you insult the president – the representative of the state – or the flag or even the national anthem you could end up spending several years in jail. The catch-all crime of inciting hatred based on racial, religious or regional differences (a law often used to prosecute Kurdish activists) remains on the books in slightly amended form. Many journalists are worried that they could face new restrictions on press freedom just as they have got rid of some of the old ones, and much will depend on how prosecutors and judges choose to interpret these new laws in the future.

Broadcasters in particular have to know their limits. Television and radio stations can be closed down for days and sometimes months for offending the puritanical guardians at the state-run Broadcasting Council. It's not just channels deemed to be 'too Kurdish' or 'too Islamist' which fall foul of the law. Others have been punished for 'violating national moral values' or for showing imported children's programmes which are 'too violent'. It is a hybrid system – a combination of openness and state control. Television has the power to reach so many people that the authorities will always keep a close eye on it. But different channels tend to endorse different views of the world, and the days of drab uniformity are long gone.

*   *   *

'Turkish identity at the moment is a grey area – neither west nor east – and for me this is a richness. There is so much to explore.'

Derviş Zaim shifted in his seat, as though he was about to get up and go exploring straight away. He's part of a new generation of Turkish film-makers who have brought the Turkish film industry back to life.

'One of the biggest issues we have to tackle is "What is Turkishness?" What kind of mental or spiritual strength can be reflected in cinema, what are the possible black holes in our history or our culture or our spirit? It's a huge subject area, and I'm fascinated by it.'

Turkey's all-conquering television industry may be the great popular obsession, but over the past decade the world of home-grown films has become far more challenging and more critically acclaimed. Turkish cinema was a flourishing business back in the 1960s and 1970s when about three hundred films were produced every year. The vast majority were careful to avoid political controversy, but they were hugely popular. The industry went into steep decline, though, after the 1980 military coup. It was nearly crushed under the weight of financial pressure, competition from Hollywood and sweeping restrictions on freedom of expression. A gradual renaissance began in the early 1990s with the rise of 'white cinema' (films which examine the nature of Muslim identity in Turkey), and it was followed by a series of films which started to tackle many of the country's long-standing taboos.

Among them were Derviş Zaim's *Somersault in a Coffin*, shot in just over three weeks on borrowed equipment and a budget of fifteen thousand dollars, which charts the life of a homeless car thief on the shores of the Bosphorus. There was also a powerful drama called *The Heavy Novel*, which tells the story of Salih, a young man who comes up against the forces of organized crime. Its gritty portrait of back-street life features poverty, prostitution and drug addiction, but what was most notable about *The Heavy Novel* was that its most graphic scene depicts police torture. Salih's father is soaked in water and given repeated electric shocks which trigger uncontrollable spasms in his naked body.

'It's ridiculous to claim there is no torture in Turkey,' the film's director, Mustafa Altıoklar, said at the time. 'The reason why we can't solve our problems is that we are afraid to confront them.'

Inevitably prosecutors launched an investigation into the film for insulting the police but Altıoklar's previous film had taken aim at a rather different target. *Istanbul Beneath my Wings* told the story of a seventeenth-century flight across the Bosphorus by an inventor who made himself an enormous pair of wings. By ridiculing religious fanatics, who thought the invention was the epitome of evil, the film upset conservative Islamists instead.

Serious exploration of a more relaxed attitude towards the Kurds also appeared first on the big screen. In 1997 the two main protagonists in a film called *Let There Be Light* were an army soldier and a member of the PKK. Trapped together in the mountains after an avalanche, the two have several frank exchanges. The idea that there could be legitimate arguments on both sides of the Kurdish conflict was – and still is – unacceptable to many Turks, especially to the military. *Let There Be Light* was never fully explicit, but it did begin to examine issues which had been taboo for years.

Not only were these new films tackling controversial subjects; they were well made, and attracted big audiences to Turkey's cinemas and rave reviews at international film festivals. Turkish film-makers based in Europe also began winning critical acclaim. *Hamam* (The Turkish Bath) explored homosexuality in a traditional social setting and it was nominated for a Golden Globe (though it was roundly condemned by the Turkish Bath Owners' Association as 'disgusting').

By the late 1990s the industry was back on its feet and locally made box-office hits like *The Bandit* began to appear alongside more challenging independent films. In 1999 the new climate of freedom even allowed the classic Turkish film *Yol* (Road) to be shown in a Turkish cinema for the first time, seventeen years after its director Yılmaz Güney won the Palme d'Or in Cannes. *Yol* uses the story of five prisoners on a week's leave to examine some of the acute political and social pressures which ordinary Turks have to face. Once the characters are out of jail, they are still shown as prisoners trapped in everyday life. When *Yol* was made, its radical politics were deemed to be nothing short of revolutionary.

The revival of Turkish cinema has continued to gather pace in the new century with a series of films reflecting rapid social change, and confronting awkward issues. *Mrs Salkim's Necklace* sparked a huge debate about the punitive wealth tax which was imposed on religious minorities – the Greeks, Armenians and Jews – during the Second World War in an effort to 'Turkify' the country. Derviş Zaim's film *Mud* was a joint Turkish–Greek production looking at past atrocities in the Cyprus conflict and the search for a cure.

'Many of these films have been seen by hundreds of thousands of people in Turkey,' Zaim told me. 'Sometimes the message is explicit; sometimes you have to read between the lines. But it's about reconciliation – we need to show people they can live together and discuss the past.'

Confronting the Kurdish issue has now become commonplace in films like *Journey to the Sun*, *Photograph* and *Big Man, Small Love* which charts the relationship between a retired Turkish judge and a five-year-old Kurdish girl who comes into his care after her family is killed in an operation against terrorist sympathizers. It is an extended metaphor for Turkey's relations with the Kurdish community, and it uses Kurdish dialogue for the first time in a mainstream Turkish-produced film. It was banned in 2002 five months after its release because the security forces complained that it showed them in a bad light (shooting an unarmed woman at point-blank range, for example). The ban was later overturned in the courts, but it was a reminder that the censor was still lurking in the background.

Even the biggest box-office hits now explore controversial subjects. In 2004 a black comedy called *Vizontele Tuuba*, which ends with tragic scenes from the 1980 military coup, was a massive success. With a cast of well-known Turkish TV stars, *Vizontele Tuuba* began to examine another taboo subject for the first time and it made more money than any other home-grown film in the history of Turkish cinema. Set in a small south-eastern town in the months leading up to the coup, against a background of mounting political upheaval, it tells the story of a disgraced librarian sent to a town with no library and an obsession with television.

The town simpleton soon falls for the librarian's beautiful disabled daughter as communists and fascists threaten to run riot. The film is careful – some critics say too careful – not to offend the powerful. But more than four million people saw it, and for a generation which has grown up in the years since the military coup, it was a rare chance to confront honest images of a bitter period in modern Turkish history. Little by little, cinema is helping the idea of democratization to spread.

And Turkey is producing a vibrant new wave of films which can compete with the very best, such as the extraordinary work of Nuri Bilge Ceylan. He casts his friends and family in beautiful lyrical films which explore ordinary lives, the effects of economic crises and the phenomenon of migration from the countryside to the cities. *Uzak* (Distant) won the Grand Prize at Cannes in 2003, and its two stars (one of whom died in a car crash shortly after the film was finished) shared the Best Actor award.

Artists like Nuri Bilge Ceylan and Derviş Zaim are just as much a part of Turkey's quiet revolution as the people who are setting a new course in politics or business or the law. European (and of course American) culture has been imported into Turkey for many years. Now in film, in music and in literature, an increasingly confident Turkish culture is being exported to the rest of Europe, just as it was in the distant Ottoman past.

* * *

'If you had to name one person,' I said, 'who is trying to explain Turkey and Turkish identity to the outside world, most people say it would have to be Orhan Pamuk.'

'Oh my God,' Pamuk grunted, 'how dreadful.'

Modesty aside, he knows it's true. Turkey's leading novelist has been criticized at home by political Islamists for portraying Islamic militants as killers; he's been criticized by Kemalists for writing about human rights abuses committed by the army and the police; and most of all, he's been accused by the left of selling out to Europe and the West, of being more in tune with Western literature than real Turkish life. But he continues to write books of haunting power.

'I see myself as a humble servant of the grand art of the novel,' Pamuk told me. 'I am a European author in that sense. On the other hand I look through my Turkish window, and I try to breathe everything in from my Turkish window. And that's what goes into my novels.'

We were sitting in a café on one of the Princes' Islands off the coast of Istanbul. It was early morning on a grey day and the place was nearly deserted. A flock of seagulls had landed next to the pier and a man with a hammer was doing some noisy repairs on the roof of the restaurant next door. This is where Pamuk comes to write when he loses inspiration in his book-lined office in the city.

'I grew up in a Westernized secular family,' he admitted, 'but most of the rest of the country was very different. We were part of something that has been going on for two hundred years. As a society we're still living through the same dilemmas about our identity.'

Wherever you look in Pamuk's novels, these are the dilemmas which he reflects. *The White Castle* is about a seventeenth-century Venetian aristocrat-turned-slave and his Muslim master who swap identities. *The New Life* is a voyage of discovery on a weird bus ride through provincial Anatolia, inspired by a magical book. *My Name Is Red* is both a murder mystery set in sixteenth-century Istanbul and a sweeping allegorical exploration of Turkey's east–west divide, as three-dimensional Renaissance painting, individuality and new ideas intrude into the traditional stylized world of Ottoman miniaturists.

The success of these books, and a torrent of critical praise, has given Orhan Pamuk superstar status. Apart from Yaşar Kemal, who wrote the epic *Memed, My Hawk* in the 1950s and followed it with a series of other books rooted in rural Anatolia, Pamuk is the only Turkish novelist with a worldwide reputation. In Turkey itself he is a best-seller and a new Pamuk novel is a big and very public literary event. When *The New Life* appeared in 1994 the novel's first line was transformed into a billboard advertising slogan: 'I Read a Book One Day and My Whole Life Was Changed'.

A decade later the English translation of Pamuk's only overtly political novel *Snow* ('I had to get the politics off my chest,' he sighed) was published to further critical acclaim. Set in 1992, its main protagonist is Ka, a poet and political exile, who travels to the dilapidated northeastern city of Kars as a journalist to write about a spate of suicides among young girls. Most of the action takes place during three days when Kars is covered in a blanket of heavy snow – '*kar*' in Turkish – which cuts it off from the outside world. Amid the ghosts of the city's Russian and Armenian past, Turkey's modern political conundrums are laid bare: there's a flurry of Islamic extremism, a newspaper which prints the news before it happens, and a bloody military coup.

'I turned Kars into a microcosm of Turkey,' Pamuk explained, 'with Turkish nationalists, Kurdish nationalists, political Islamists, militant secularists and minorities all thrown in together. It was the Turkey of the early 1990s – Kurdish guerrillas waging a war against the army and the political Islamists rapidly on the move, while the secularists and the modern sections of Turkey were all scared for the future. Are we heading towards full-scale civil war, will we end up like Iran? It didn't happen, perhaps because the possibility of joining Europe was like a light at the end of the tunnel.'

The political sensitivities of *Snow* were enough to worry Pamuk's Turkish publisher who consulted lawyers and hid most of the first print run in the corner of a warehouse in case the book was banned. But there was never any question of that happening. *Snow* was widely discussed, and through the novel the country discussed itself. Few sections of society are spared from criticism in the book, including Westernized intellectuals like Pamuk himself and his central character, Ka. In the aftermath of the short-lived coup, the head of a military special operations team, Z Demirkol, castigates Ka and those who think like him:

> Intellectuals like you, you never have the faintest idea, and that makes me sick. You say you want democracy, and then you enter into alliances with Islamic fundamentalists. You say you want human rights, and then you make deals with terrorist murderers . . . You say Europe is the answer, but you go around buttering up Islamists who hate everything Europe stands for . . . You say feminism, and then you help these men wrap their women's heads in scarves. You don't follow your own conscience; you just guess what a European would do in the same situation and act accordingly. But you can't even be a proper European.

It goes back to those big questions about identity again. Who are we? Where do we belong? As *Snow* examines the nature of modern Turkey, and reflects on religion, love and more besides, it captures the tumultuous debate the country is living through. Everyone is given a voice – the headscarf girls, the militants, the believers and the non-believers. The radical Islamist, Blue, tells Ka that Turkey 'has forgotten its own stories' because it has fallen under the spell of the West. Orhan Pamuk's novels try to tell some of those stories but they never suggest it is an easy task.

'If you write a book set in Kars and put me in it,' a young man named Fazıl warns the narrator in the last few paragraphs of *Snow*, 'I'd like to tell your readers not to believe anything you say about me, anything you say about any of us. No one could understand us from so far away.'

Literature is still perceived as an elite pursuit in Turkey, but there are also signs that the habit of reading books is beginning to catch on more widely. Hundreds of novels are published every year, and a collection of essays by the popular writer Ahmet Altan sold nearly a million copies in six months in 2004. It was priced cheaply and sold from small kiosks on every street corner, but it was a phenomenal publishing success. *A Place Inside Us* examined complex human feelings like jealousy, hatred, love and loneliness and it attracted readers from every social class.

A leading diplomat was even moved to argue that such huge sales of a collection of essays were proof that Turkey was ready to join Europe. When I visited Ahmet Altan in his apartment in Istanbul he took up the theme with enthusiasm.

'When you look at us from Europe we're barbarians, we're ignorant, and maybe it's true,' Altan said, with a twinkle in his eye. 'But this is a way to tell Europe that you cannot easily know us. Don't jump to conclusions too readily – we may be ignorant but we can buy a million books!'

Alongside his growing success as a novelist and essayist Altan is well known for his radical politics, in particular a famous newspaper column written in the mid-90s entitled 'Atakurd'. What if, he asked, there were a country called Kurdey, where minority Turks were suppressed and brutalized? How would people feel if it were asserted that there were no Turks in Kurdey, and that those who thought of themselves as Turks were really 'Ocean Kurds'? What if the slogan 'What Happiness to Say I'm a Kurd!' was plastered across Istanbul? The column caused an uproar and Altan was fired by his newspaper, fined by the courts, and given a suspended jail sentence.

He is by no means the only prominent Turkish writer to have fallen foul of the law – for most of Turkey's modern history it has been an occupational hazard. A campaign to restore the citizenship of the country's most famous poet, the communist Nazım Hikmet, on the centenary of his birth in 2002, was thwarted by right-wing politicians in the government. It didn't seem to matter that Hikmet was also a patriot who had a deep attachment to Turkey and its people.

'I love my country . . .' one of his poems runs, 'I swung in its lofty trees; I lay in its prisons. Nothing relieves my depression like the songs and tobacco of my country.'

Nazım Hikmet died in exile in Moscow in 1963. His poems, which often sided with the dispossessed and the politically exploited, have been translated into more than fifty languages, and they are proudly published by the Ministry of Culture in Ankara. But the opposition in parliament is still campaigning unsuccessfully for his remains to be brought home and buried – in accordance with his wishes – in an Anatolian village; and the decree which stripped him of his citizenship in the last years of his life has never been repealed.

'This is still a strange country,' Ahmet Altan agreed, 'so full of contradictions, but it has changed a lot in the last few years.'

I was about to ask another question, but he pressed on.

'We still have chaos here, and you need chaos to create something. There's no chaos in Europe and you've lost your innovation. We have it, it's dangerous but it's very hopeful. We need your wisdom, your discipline and will-power, and you need our chaos and our energy, our emotions and our ambition.'

He paused, and looked at me reproachfully.

'More tea?' he said.

* * *

There really is a quote from Atatürk about everything, carefully preserved for future generations. So here are his thoughts on music.

'The capacity of a country to change,' he said in 1925, 'is demonstrated by its ability to change its music.'

And for Atatürk that meant mixing some of the traditional Turkish sounds he loved with the music of the West. Western classical music – which had already appropriated Ottoman cymbals and drums to help form its great orchestras – was to be taught in schools. A state conservatoire was quickly established to be followed later by the state opera and the state ballet. Guests invited to banquets at the presidential palace had to learn to waltz solemnly around the dance floor in white tie and tails.

It wasn't a complete break with the past. Western music had first been introduced into the Ottoman Court in the early nineteenth century, and Atatürk's vision was part of a longer process of looking to the West for cultural justification. But he didn't like the Turkish classical music which the Sultans favoured – there were too many Arabic and Persian influences. In the early years of the republic young musicians were sent to study abroad in Europe and America instead, so they could reproduce traditional Turkish folk songs in the Western classical style.

It all went according to plan for a while but – of course – it couldn't last. Serious Turkish classical music with all its Eastern influences is popular again, and since the 1960s arabesque pop has taken Turkey by storm. This is the music of the migrants from the countryside to the cities; it's the music of the *dolmuş* minibuses which take millions of people to work every day; this is the realm in which the remarkable voice of Ibrahim Tatlıses – the poor boy from Urfa made good – is king. Arabesque is all about love and suffering and unbearable despair. It preaches fatalism, and the punters love it.

In the 1980s the government tried to suppress arabesque altogether: it was just too melancholy for the nation's good. It was banned from state TV and radio, and a milder official version was launched, but predictably it made no difference. The arabesque phenomenon continued to grow and it remains enormously popular. Tatlıses is, without exaggeration, perhaps the most famous man in Turkey. The music which brought him great riches had its roots in Turkish cover versions of old Egyptian hits, but it now takes Arabic, Turkish and Western sounds and mixes them together in a long mournful cry.

The same sense of fusion has emerged in all kinds of modern music. Mercan Dede – an accomplished Sufi musician and cult DJ – mixes Eastern rhythms, flutes and clarinets with hard-core house and techno beats to mesmerizing effect. In mainstream pop, when Sertab Erener won the Eurovision Song Contest in 2003, she did it with another classic mix of East and West. Go to a party in metropolitan Turkey and more than likely people will stand around tapping their feet as Western music booms out from the speakers. But put on some Turkish pop to break the ice – Tarkan, or Sertab or Aynur – and the whole crowd will suddenly hit the dance floor.

Tarkan was the first Turkish pop star to build an international following: in Russia, many parts of Europe and the Middle East. When he first appeared on the scene in Turkey in the 1990s, the effect was likened to Elvis or the Beatles. Tarkan-mania was in full swing for years, accompanied by all the dubious trappings of Western celebrity, including teenage hysteria and a steady stream of tabloid revelations about his private life. Atatürk was right – music was indeed reflecting Turkey's enormous capacity to change.

Away from the headlines, older forms of music are also being rediscovered. By the side of the road which leads up from the Golden Horn to Istanbul's Roman aqueduct, just before the underpass where thousands of bicycles are sold at knock-down prices, there is what looks like a run-down shopping centre. It is, in fact, the focal point of Turkey's music business, a small concrete plaza where the offices of publishers, record companies, specialist shops and singers are all crammed together in the same place. During the summer, when the doors are flung open, it is a riot of sound.

The man I'd come to see has an office on the top floor with an old HMV record player in one corner and a piano in the other. Standing on top of the piano is a photograph advertising a 'Grand Concert Oriental' in 1930. Hasan Saltık has probably done more for Turkish music in the last fifteen years than anyone else alive. After founding Kalan Music in 1991 with six hundred dollars to his name, he has unearthed and published forgotten songs from across the country, fighting his way through the courts at every step of the way.

'Our aim has always been to reveal Turkey's true cultural wealth,' Hasan said. 'In the past only the extreme nationalists have been presented as patriots, but for me this is totally wrong. What we're doing is real patriotism.'

Hasan Saltık publishes minority music – folk songs from every corner of Anatolia in Turkish, Kurdish, Aramaic, Laz, Armenian and Greek. After the military coup in 1980 music in any local language apart from Turkish was banned, but a decade later Kalan began testing the limits of the law and recreating sounds which hadn't been widely heard in public for decades. Hundreds of albums have now been released under the Kalan label, and ethnic music is not its only product. Hasan was once saved from jail because the country's most powerful prosecutor was a big fan of his new recordings of old Turkish classical music.

It was, he admits, a lucky break: the authorities have had a bit of a problem with musicians since Ottoman times. (Local singers who travelled from town to town were always an alternative source of information and they were considered a threat.) Until quite recently, Hasan was hauled before the courts several times a year to defend another new rendition of an old song, but when I met him he hadn't been summoned for three years. It is another example of a real change in mentality, and when the Culture Ministry tried to revert to the old ways and cancel his licence, so many people complained that the decision was hastily reversed.

'In the past governors and other officials would come and say, "Hasan, please don't do this. The country isn't ready for it." Now they hand out our CDs when they travel abroad.'

Hasan shrugged his shoulders, lit another cigarette and put on a CD called *Kardeş Türküler* (Songs of Fraternity), which he had produced with a collection of musicians dedicated to preserving Turkey's musical heritage. They play a range of rare folk songs and remixes in their original languages and dialects – songs which for years could only be performed in secret.

'People tried to suppress all this through nationalism,' Hasan said. 'It was never going to work.'

'But they say this kind of thing is dangerous – a threat to Atatürk's vision.'

'They're crazy. Turks will always love Atatürk because of his revolutionary character, and what he did to create this country, but there is such a thing as overkill. They put him on too high a pedestal.'

We listened to a Syriac song from Hakkari with a mournful female vocal, a Turkish folk song from Tokat and a Pontus Greek song – more than a hundred years old – from Artvin, near the Black Sea coast. There was Kurdish drumming, Armenian chanting and – always reappearing in the background – the distinctive sound of the saz. As the music died away it mixed imperceptibly into a multitude of other sounds coming through the window from outside: the deep rumble of the rush-hour traffic as millions of Istanbullus began heading for home, and a cacophony of chants from minarets across the city calling the faithful to the evening prayer.

* * *

On the other side of the Golden Horn, just across the Galata Bridge in the old port area of Karaköy, a huge converted customs warehouse on the seafront has been transformed into Turkey's first dedicated museum of modern art. It's not just a museum, of course; it's a political statement as well. After a frantic renovation schedule, Istanbul Modern opened its doors to the public in December 2004 just a few days before the European summit in Brussels invited Turkey to start talks on EU membership.

The timing wasn't coincidental. The prime minister, Tayyip Erdoğan, had arranged for the warehouse to be given to the private foundation running the museum on one condition – it had to be up and running before the summit took place. With mission accomplished, the prime minister attended the opening ceremony himself and even persuaded a few of his friends to send personal messages of support – a Mr Blair from London, a Herr Schröder from Berlin, and a Monsieur Chirac from Paris. Look how modern Turkey is, they all said.

'This museum is part of making Istanbul a world city again,' said one of the curators, Fulya Erdemci, as we wandered down a sculpted stairway made of chains and bullet-shattered glass. 'People want to know about their modern past, and we want to make art more accessible to the public.'

There is a cinema, a library, a host of educational projects and an impressive array of exhibition spaces. They contain a permanent display of Turkish art since 1900, from the late Ottoman period to the present day, and temporary displays of photographs, sculptures and video art. My personal favourite among the opening exhibits was a short film entitled *Road to Tate Modern*, featuring two Kurds from Diyarbakır playing the roles of Don Quixote and his faithful servant, Sancho. For forty days and nights they trek through the south-eastern mountains on a horse and a donkey, dressed in suits and ties, looking for the road to modernity.

'It's about a Utopia in the age of nothingness,' Fulya explained confidently.

'Sounds about right for the European Union,' I replied, nodding sagely.

We looked on as the two characters asked a local peasant for directions. Tate Modern, he told them, is high up in the mountains, and very far away. All the characters spoke in Kurdish and the only subtitles on the screen were in English.

'They miss out the Turkish language completely,' Fulya said. 'Now *that* is modern.'

The new museum has quickly established itself as a success, but Turkey is still wrestling with modernity and what it means. Huge strides have been taken in the last few years towards Atatürk's vision of anchoring the country he created in the West. For many people the European Union remains the glittering prize, and the remarkable torrent of reforms unleashed since the turn of the century wouldn't have happened without it. But while Atatürk associated modernity and contemporary civilization with Europe, some of his most ardent disciples – the 'hyper-secularists' – are beginning to wonder whether it is all worth while.

That's because their version of 'being modern' is no longer the only one on offer. In fact, their version suddenly seems rather tired. The Turkish economy is going global all around them, there is a thirst for broader knowledge, more personal freedom and better education, and when the outside world looks at Turkey it sees hopeful signs of modern Islam at work: a Muslim country with a secular democracy, run by a reforming government with strong popular support. If it can work in Turkey, goes the argument, there's no reason why it can't catch on elsewhere.

So a lot of influential people feel they have a stake in what happens in Turkey, but they know that plenty of things could still go wrong. Unpredictable events in Cyprus or northern Iraq could damage Turkey's international image and destabilize its politics. Reforms passed on paper need time to filter down through the system. Europe could turn inward and push Turkey away, or offer it second-class membership; on the other hand the EU could change so much in the coming years, that it is no longer the club the Turks thought they wanted to join.

But Turkey now has a chance to fulfil its potential and make a real impression on the twenty-first century. It has already changed in dramatic ways during the last decade – as much as any country in the world – and the next ten years will be equally eventful. The journey towards Europe, and all the irritating scrutiny it entails, will be just as important as the final destination. Whether Turkey ends up joining the EU or not, the process of reform it has inspired is an end in itself.

All the while, Turkey's internal debates will rage on. I've always thought the Turks looked at Europe in two very different ways – there's a craving for acceptance, but there's also a healthy dose of arrogance fuelled by their imperial past. It is for the Turks themselves to decide how European they want to be, and they are well aware that in a globalized world, being modern doesn't have to mean being Western. If the Chinese or the Indians can do it, so can the Turks. The people will decide what they want.

Predicting the future is always a hazardous business but there are few better places to think about it than the terrace of Istanbul Modern, overlooking the point where the Golden Horn meets the Bosphorus, and the currents swirl in all directions. Tugs strain at their mooring ropes on the dockside below, and the silhouetted rooftops of Topkapı Palace rising from the opposite shore look like cardboard cut-outs against a blue evening sky. Istanbul Traditional and Istanbul Modern stare at each other across the water.

'For a long time you weren't allowed to see the view from here,' Fulya said. 'This was all state land, and no one could get in.'

The lights were coming on in the distance and the sound of a horn from a passing ferry echoed throatily through the air.

'It's been reclaimed for the people,' she said.

Not a bad motto, I thought to myself, for the new Turkey.

EPILOGUE

Shortly before this book was sent to the printers there were reminders aplenty – if any were needed – of the precarious nature of Turkey's bid to join the European Union.

Referendums in France and the Netherlands delivered thumping popular rejections of the new European constitution, throwing the EU into disarray and raising fundamental questions about further plans for enlargement. The constitution itself makes no reference to Turkey's potential membership, but both the French and the Dutch 'no' campaigns gained support by playing on fears of Turkey joining the Union in the future.

The constitutional crisis didn't stop Turkey's membership application in its tracks. But it did reveal the extent of public hostility to the idea in Europe, much of it based on ignorance of the full facts. Senior EU politicians began to talk of much tougher conditions for future candidates, and there were calls for a frank discussion of Turkey's membership aspirations. For the statement made at the end of a European summit in June 2005, held just after the French and Dutch votes, a conscious decision was made to avoid mentioning Turkey by name. Things can change rather quickly in six months.

Other political developments could also go against Turkey as the electoral pendulum swings. A prolonged period of centre-right rule in Germany, for example, where the Christian Democrats are openly hostile to full Turkish membership, would add to the sense that many Europeans want to keep the Turks at arm's length. The men who held the highest offices of state across the continent when this new century dawned – Blair, Chirac, Schröder and Berlusconi – were among Turkey's main cheerleaders in Europe. Their successors may not be quite so keen.

All of this is likely to add fuel to the fire of a nationalist revival in Turkey itself. The EU's decision in December 2004 to invite Turkey to begin membership talks was followed – perhaps inevitably – by a nationalist reaction reaching into the heart of the AKP government. Celebrations were short-lived and 'concessions' to Europe – on Cyprus, on attitudes to minorities, on judicial reform – became a focus of renewed political discontent. The government's commitment to its chosen European path seemed to waver, at least for a while.

Further complications were generated by a ruling from the European Court of Human Rights that the trial of Abdullah Öcalan had fallen short of European legal standards in several respects. Another upsurge in fighting between remnants of the PKK and the Turkish armed forces in the south-east of the country added to the gloom.

None of these reactions are terribly surprising. But the success of Turkey's internal reforms, and the future of its relationship with Europe, should be judged over the course of several years, not on the evidence of a few dramatic months.

If the EU has indeed now reached the high-water mark of integration it could be good news for Turkey. A more loosely structured EU in the future – perhaps even a two-tier Union – could be the perfect solution. It would be much easier to accommodate Turkey in an outer rim of EU nations which could include heavyweights like Britain, and much easier for Turkey to join what would amount to a glorified free trade zone in which ambitious talk of political union was a thing of the past.

In all of this debate it should not be forgotten that Turkey won't be considered for EU membership until 2015 at the earliest. Much of the alarmist rhetoric during the French and Dutch referendum campaigns – xenophobic would be the politest description – seemed to suggest that the Turks would join tomorrow.

They won't. This is a long-term process. And if Turkey can continue on the path of reform, at a time when the prospect of future EU membership has become more uncertain, it will win more friends and admirers abroad. During a difficult summer I remain rather optimistic about Turkey's long-term future, whether inside the EU or not.

FURTHER READING, VIEWING AND LISTENING

This is not – nor does it aspire to be – anything approaching a comprehensive bibliography: many excellent books go unmentioned here. But for readers in English who want to know more about Turkey, a few suggestions follow.

Books

There are plenty of books that chart the history of the Ottoman Empire. The most entertaining and accessible is *Lords of the Horizons* by Jason Goodwin. Historical accounts of the Ottoman period available in English include *The Turkish Embassy Letters* by Lady Mary Wortley Montagu, and the translation of Ogier de Busbecq's *Turkish Letters*. The best book on the fall of the Ottoman Empire at the end of the First World War, and a must-read for anyone interested in the modern Middle East, is *A Peace to End All Peace* by David Fromkin.

Andrew Mango's *Atatürk* is a comprehensive and approving biography of the founding father. Mango has also recently published *The Turks Today*, which takes up the story after Atatürk's death. *Turkey: A Modern History* by Erik Zurcher is also recommended.

Several books have been published over the past decade by journalists who have reported from Turkey, notably *Turkey Unveiled* by Hugh and Nicole Pope, and *Crescent and Star* by Stephen Kinzer. More offbeat accounts by visiting writers in the past few years include *A Fez of the Heart* by Jeremy Seal, and *Dervish* by Tim Kelsey.

For more information on the Kurds see *A Modern History of the Kurds* by David McDowall. *Atatürk's Children: Turkey and the Kurds*, complete with striking photography, was produced by Jonathan Rugman and Roger Hutchings at the height of the conflict in the south-east. David Shankland's *Islam and Society in Turkey* provides a comprehensive study of the role of religion in modern Turkey.

Many authors have published books about the history of Istanbul – the best of them, in my opinion, are *Constantinople: City of the World's Desire, 1453–1924* by Philip Mansel, and *Istanbul: The Imperial City* by John Freely.

The biggest names in modern Turkish literature are widely available in translation. Orhan Pamuk's best-selling novels, most recently *My Name is Red* and *Snow*, have now been followed by his own contribution to the Istanbul genre. Published in English in 2005, the personal memoir *Istanbul: Memories of a City* is an absolute joy, helped along by a beautiful translation by Maureen Freely.

The novels of Yaşar Kemal, most famously *Memed, My Hawk*, are well worth reading, and the haunting *Poems of Nazım Hikmet* have been sensitively translated from Turkish by Randy Blasing and Mutlu Konak, and published as an anthology.

For more information about fine arts and travel in Turkey see *Cornucopia* magazine, published four times a year. And for more information about carpets see *Halı Rug Guide to Istanbul*.

Films

A growing number of Turkish films are now available on DVD with English subtitles. *Uzak* and previous films by Nuri Bilge Ceylan are recommended, as is the 1980s classic *Yol*. More recent hits like the science-fiction spoof *G.O.R.A.* and *Vizontele Tuuba* are also available on DVD, with subtitles that try (with varying degrees of success) to translate the Turkish humour.

The Istanbul-based company Imaj has produced a series of subtitled films that reflect the best of recent Turkish cinema. Other award-winning films directed by Turks living abroad include *Head On* by Fatih Akın, and *Hamam* by Ferzan Özpetek.

Music

Turkish pop music is rapidly going global. Tarkan is a big star in Europe and Latin America as well as in Turkey. His albums include *Dudu* and the compilation *Tarkan*. Sertab Erener – who won the Eurovision Song Contest with 'Every Way That I Can' – and Sezen Aksu are also well-established stars.

Kalan music in Istanbul publishes an extraordinary variety of Turkish classical music as well as traditional folk music from across Anatolia. A good introduction to the many different strains of folk music from around the country can be found on the *Kardeş Türküler* (Songs of Fraternity) CDs by the Boğaziçi Performing Arts Ensemble.

For arabesque, look for anything by Orhan Gencebay, or – if you can deal with his erratic reputation when it comes to the treatment of women – Ibrahim Tatlıses. Recent albums by Tatlıses include *Imperator* and *Aramam*.

Rising star Mercan Dede – the 'dervish for the modern world' – combines Turkish Sufism with western electronic music. Albums like *Su* and *Sufi Traveller* have won him a growing audience around the world. Under the guise of DJ Arkin Allen he has also produced the album *Fusion Monster*.

Websites

There is a huge Turkish presence on the internet. More information on how to get hold of any of the above, and a whole manner of other things Turkish, can be found via any search engine.

For the official line on Turkish issues, go to the Turkish Foreign Ministry website at *www.mfa.gov.tr* or the Information Department at *www.byegm.gov.tr*

Finally, to keep up with the day-to-day news from Turkey in English try *www.turkishdailynews.com*, *www.turkishpress.com*, *www.zaman.com* or, for an alternative view, *www.bianet.org*

INDEX